A Boy, His Bibi And A Bari

Dear Ayana,

Congratulations on being a winner on Klarque's radio show.

I hope you enjoy my book as much as I have had the pleasure of writing it.

Shah Alam
Dec 4th '12

A Boy, His Bibi
And a Bari

S R Alam

Matador
9 Priory Business Park,
Wistow Road, Kibworth Beauchamp,
Leicestershire. LE8 0RX
Tel: (+44) 116 279 2299
Fax: (+44) 116 279 2277
Email: books@troubador.co.uk
Web: www.troubador.co.uk/matador

ISBN 978 1780884 257

British Library Cataloguing in Publication Data.
A catalogue record for this book is available from the British Library.

Typeset in 11pt Book Antiqua by Troubador Publishing Ltd, Leicester, UK
Printed and bound in the UK by TJ International, Padstow, Cornwall

Matador is an imprint of Troubador Publishing Ltd

To my father and mother,
without their love and support
I would not have got this far

Contents

No Going Back

There I was, sitting in my seat by the window being accompanied by my uncle – my dad's cousin – to Bangladesh. It was December 1979 and my dad was sending me 'home', as he called it, to become more cultured in the ways of Bangladeshi life. To me, home was England and this cultural trip was a big adventure. I didn't know how long I was going for or whether my parents would join me. Being the eldest son it was seen by my dad that I had to grow up quickly and therefore needed this indoctrination in the ways of Bengali life and culture before I became too westernised. There was no plan as to how this would be achieved but I would be living with my grandmother, whom my siblings and I lovingly called Bibi and who would supposedly oversee my cultural education. However, I knew it would be a different experience. How different or what the experience would be like I did not know, but if I recall Bibi from my days as a toddler the education would be extremely relaxed. I was her first grandson so her love for me would get in the way of any stern education.

Even though I was sitting there in my seat waiting for the plane to take-off, dressed to the nines like a page boy at a wedding, I felt scared and alone. I was leaving my parents, two younger brothers and sister, travelling for the first time on my own and then to live without them for an undetermined period of time. I wasn't sure when I would see them next. Uncle Naz was doing a grand job, continuously talking to me, ensuring I was okay, but within me a sense of apprehension was stirring.

I said to myself, "Hey, here I am on a plane going on an adventure that took me away from school and all other responsibilities. I will be with my Bibi and I will be living carefree without being told what to do, what can be better than this?"

The decision to send me to Bangladesh for schooling in the ways of Bengali life was decided two months ago when Uncle Naz visited our home in the East End, as he ritually did once a week on his day off from running his Indian restaurant in the leafy suburbs of north Kent. It was early evening and my mum was sitting at her Japanese industrial sewing machine making jacket linings, as an outworker for one of the local clothing manufacturers. My dad was working on the second machine, having arrived from his supervisor's job at a paper mill in the docklands of London. The constant buzzing of the machines created a womb-like environment in our basement, which was always the warmest room in our house, where all friends and relatives congregated when they visited.

The basement room also acted as our dining room. Our own family sweatshop was not too dissimilar to many of the other Bengali families on the street. Even at the young age of ten, I was becoming highly proficient at operating an industrial sewing machine. On many Saturday afternoons I would miss out on playing with my friends, sometimes by choice, to help my mum catch up on her work to meet her delivery deadlines.

That day I had come back from school and I was sitting on the sofa with my sister who was four, playing games to keep her amused in between reading my favourite *Dandy* and *Beano* comics. Uncle Naz was sitting at the dining table drinking tea. He was in his twenties, with a thinning scalp and receding hairline. He was a kind and generous man and I would say one of my favourite uncles. He would always bring sweets for us

2

when he visited and during the summer holidays I would spend a week or two with him in north Kent, spending mornings at his restaurant and evenings at his shared home with his business partner's wife and kids.

My brother Alom was upstairs in the front living room watching TV, whilst my youngest brother Gulz was asleep in his cot amidst the rhythmic sounds of the machines. I wasn't paying any attention to what the adults were talking about. Their conversation was interspersed with the buzzing of the machines, as each of my parents pressed the foot lever to operate the needle that sewed the lining pieces together. So what one heard was buzz, followed by conversation, then another buzz and another few words, and that's how the multi-tasking of chat and work played out in our house.

"Bhaisab, I am off to Desh next year," Uncle Naz announced, addressing my dad respectfully as brother. All Bengalis referred to Bangladesh as *Desh*; it was a more loving name evoking greater emotion than just stating Bangladesh. All natives of Sylhet referred to themselves as Bangladeshi and not Bengali. The latter term was used to refer to people from the rest of the country and people from West Bengal in India. This in turn created a huge division with a 'them and us' status quo that to this day exists amongst one racially and culturally similar people. For me, it did not matter and I used Bengali and Bangladeshi interchangeably for all contexts.

"Really?" my dad declared in a surprised tone.

"Okay bhaisab, you are going to get married then I suppose?" my mum teased Naz.

"Bhabi, I am only going to visit my parents who I haven't seen in a few years, I am too young to get married," Naz retorted.

This game of tit-for-tat was a common theme in Bengali culture, where the bhabi would torment her brother and sister-in-laws about marriage and finding a suitable wife or husband. Even though the unmarried party would repel any suggestions of marriage, deep down they were all yearning for their rajah or rani to steal their hearts.

"So, how long are you going for?" my dad asked.

"Only a few months," Naz replied.

"Well, you might as well take Sabu with you?" suggests my dad, totally out of the blue.

Hearing this, my ears prick up and I begin to pay attention to what was being said.

"What do you say beta? Do you want to come to Desh with me? Your bibi will be happy to see you," Uncle Naz asks referring to me as son.

Up until now I had been sitting with my sister, flicking through the pages of my comics. Hearing Uncle Naz suggesting that I join him and go to Bangladesh, I looked up and blurted, "Okay Uncle I'll come," opening my mouth first and thinking later, not exactly knowing what I was letting myself in for or what the consequences would be of my affirmative response.

"Okay nephew that's a done deal then, you're coming with me," continued Naz, letting out a bellow of a laugh and slapping his hands together in a joyous clap.

I looked at my parents, wondering what they were going to say, whether it was a joke or serious. My dad appeared to take my consent as agreement that I would go, however mum turned towards Uncle Naz and questioned with a frown on her face.

"Yes, and who's going to look after him?"

"He can stay at my place," Uncle Naz replied.

Mum brushed it off as a joke and continued with her sewing. Uncle Naz stayed for a couple more hours chatting in general about 'Desh' and how his parents were. These chats were sprinkled with more cups of tea prepared by my mum and plenty of *shupari*; betel nut that people from parts of the Indian subcontinent chewed on after their meals or drinking tea. However, during the remainder of Naz's stay the atmosphere in the room got a bit tense. There was no further mention of me accompanying Naz, the two male adults in the room knew better and did not talk about it. I could also sense that my mum was angry and that this matter was not over yet. I remained quiet, finding it very difficult to contain both my excitement and apprehension.

After Uncle Naz had gone and later in the evening when we were all sat at the dining table having our evening meal of rice and various curry dishes, Dad brought up the subject of me going to Bangladesh. He was being pretty serious about sending me and started talking about how important it was for me being the eldest son that I learn the ways of Bengali life and not forget my roots.

"Sabu is the eldest son and I want to make sure that he is able to read and write in Bengali," Dad stated, to justify his decision.

"You and I have been teaching him and he is pretty good at it, we don't need to send him away from us to ensure he can *read and write* in Bengali," Mum snapped back.

Dad wasn't listening. Whilst Alom and I ate our food we did not look up at our parents as they argued.

"Plus, I don't want him to grow up without any cultural values, respect for his elders and most importantly, not forget his *dharma*," dad replied, his voice having risen an octave when referring to the Islamic religion.

The funny thing about Dad's conviction that I was going to become a wayward son never materialised. Throughout my years growing up in the East End, year-upon-year stories would go back to Bibi and other relatives alike, that my dad was raising three exceptional sons. The stories would then fly back to London and reach my parents ears, making them beam with smiles like that of a Cheshire cat. The tales went like this:

"Those boys are so well mannered…"

"What wonderful boys, they make their dad so proud…"

"Mr Ali is lucky to have such sons…"

And so it went on for a good two decades, until I would not conform to society and settle down and marry a nice Bengali girl, but that's another story.

In order to further convince my mum to come round to his way of thinking in agreeing to let me go with Uncle Naz, Dad also brought up how his mother was aging, that she was lonely and how good it would be for her to see me. It had only been a little over four years since I left the Bangladesh to come to the UK, so in my world the duration was a lifetime, but in the adult world was it longer? I guessed it must have been, as Dad used this as another reason to bring Mum round to his way of thinking.

Mum probably thought Dad was joking earlier on and she couldn't believe what she was hearing. She argued about how he could send a ten year old boy away from his parents and siblings to a country where he may have been born, but had little knowledge of. She continued by highlighting the fact that the country was still unstable from its independence, it suffered annually from floods, disease was rife and there were poor medical facilities, as well as non-existent schooling.

She argued against me going to Bangladesh and said that on no account was I to be sent. However, my dad had made his mind up and in the typical Bengali male 'I am the man of the house attitude', had the final say and stated I was to go. I was going to be pulled out of my school in the East End, namely Harry Gosling Junior School, which I had only joined earlier in the year having moved from the West Midlands city of Worcester. I had only made one good friend and here I was being shipped off to the country of my birth. As I was still in a transition stage and hadn't really put down any roots in my new school, I was quite happy to go along with this interruption in my life. My school was not told about my departure until after I had gone, my dad saying that he would take care of it.

Dinner ended without me enjoying the mutton curry and dhal that Mum had prepared. I hated seeing my parents argue, especially when I was the focal point of their disagreement. That night I went to bed with a lump in my stomach and uncertainty dancing like an imp in the recesses of my mind. My brother asked me where I was going and why and when I would come back. I gave him a straightforward "I don't know," as at that moment in time I wasn't sure what was going to happen.

Over the ensuing weeks leading to my departure an out of sight war of words was being fought. My parents continued to argue about sending me to Bangladesh, which meant that there were instances of silence and uneasiness, especially during the evening meal. My younger brother was oblivious to it all and my baby sister and brother kept me busy with nappy changes when mum was tied up in the kitchen or on the sewing machines.

One weekend we had a visitor drop by, going by the name Montaz Ali, who had just returned from Bangladesh. When the bell rang on our front door I raced up the stairs from the warmth of our basement room and opened to a sight that was straight out of a Bollywood movie. Towering over me was a man wearing black flared trousers, black shoes with a maroon three quarter length leather jacket, underneath which he wore a shirt with the top two buttons undone. He had a thick black moustache and a tan that made him look like a villain from an Amitabh Bhachchan movie.

"Salaam alaikum, who are you looking for?" I asked with the respect due to a stranger.

"Alaikum salaam, are your parents in? I am a grandfather of yours," he replied.

He was about the same age as my dad, therefore I was a bit sceptical about his claim. I yelled down the hallway towards the basement, "Mum! Dad! There's a relative here."

"Stop yelling," Dad shouted back as he walked up the stairs.

"Salaam alaikum Mamu," Dad addressed Montaz Ali as Uncle.

Oh! I thought he must be a grandfather upon hearing Dad's salutation.

"Alaikum salaam," he responded to Dad.

"Come in, come in," Dad gestured as they walked downstairs with me following upon closing the door.

Downstairs, Mum said her salaam to Montaz Ali and introduced my siblings and me to him.

"Is that you Sabu? You really have grown since Bangladesh," he remarked.

I just smiled as I could not recall any knowledge of him or ever coming across him during my early years in Bangladesh. Montaz Ali was the brother-in-law of Bibi's second brother.

Mum got up and went into the kitchen to make tea, whilst Dad began asking Montaz Ali what brought him this way.

"Well, I've just come back from Bangladesh," he answered.

"I didn't know you had gone, when did you go?" Dad quizzed Montaz Ali.

"It's a long story," he began. "I did not fly the conventional way and it took me a little longer than usual," he said smiling.

"What do you mean it took longer?" Dad asked quizzically, as Mum returned with three cups of tea and biscuits.

"Mamu, did I hear you say that you've just come from Desh?"

"Yes, I have."

"So, how is everyone back home?" Mum questioned.

"They're all fine and they all send their salaams and well wishes."

"So what is the story Mamu?" Dad returned Montaz Ali to his story.

"I drove to Bangladesh in a car," he stated, as if it was something everyone did.

"What are you saying Mamu?" my mum exclaimed in shock, "You drove to Bangladesh, how is that possible?"

"That's right, how did you manage to do that?" Dad also joined in.

This tweaked my interest and got me sitting upright in my seat as I listened attentively to Montaz Ali.

"I wasn't on my own, there were two of us and we had a Toyota Liteace which we jam packed with household goods and drove fifteen days all the way home," he elaborated.

"Yah Dada, that is so amazing, were you not scared?" I asked.

"No, Grandson, we had some situations that were not so nice but we managed fine."

"So, there was no trouble at all on the journey then?" Dad probed further.

"Well! We had to pay bribes all the way from Bulgaria and even entering Bangladesh we could not avoid paying the baksheesh."

"Those bloody infidels, they will never become civilised the way they carry on," Dad swore more at the Bangladeshi authorities than anyone else.

My dad is and always has been a man of strong principles. I've never known him to gossip or get involved in other's affairs, he very rarely loans money or borrows from friends or family. He can sit with my mum in the living room and probably say one or two words every hour. I guess Mum got used to it, but she more than makes up for his strong, silent demeanour. Most of all though my dad despises bribery, corruption, nepotism and all those other crimes and vices man can easily succumb to if the opportunity is there. He avoids village and mosque politics that are endemic in Bengali life. He has declined many offers to be secretary of this committee and chair of that group. His friends he can probably count on one hand, which has meant that he is quite a solitary figure but always there for his family. Thus, he has enjoyed a very hassle free life without drama and commotion that many people seem to attract and enjoy.

"Also, when we were driving through Afghanistan we had a few Phatans wave their machine guns at us, and whilst we drove away having paid a bribe of cigarettes they fired the guns in to the air," Montaz Ali elaborated. "That was scary, but being Muslim, the journey from Turkey onwards was pretty straightforward, if you took away the bribe element," he finished off and took a sip of tea and a bite of a biscuit that he had dunked into the hot liquid.

"Well! At least you are safe, but what did you do with the car?" Mum asked.

"I sold it along with some of the goods and I have purchased a plot of land in Sylhet city. I am saving up to build an apartment."

I then made a statement that would resonate through my formative years and into adulthood. "Dada, I want to make the same trip as you and drive to Bangladesh."

Montaz Ali laughed in amusement at my declaration of

intention. "Sure Grandson, when you are older and can drive a car."

My parents did not say anything but looked at each other, both battling in their own hearts and minds about sending me off to Bangladesh soon. Little did I know that statement would remain with me for a quarter of a century until in 2005, when a good friend of mine and I made a similar trip from London to Sylhet. That is another story for another day.

Montaz Ali stayed for a while and explained his main intention for visiting us that day. He was looking for a temporary place to stay until he was able to rent a flat of his own. My parents welcomed him with open arms and he lodged with us for six months or so. This *mi casa es su casa* was to become a common theme in our home. Many relatives arriving newly to London from other parts of the UK or Bangladesh and even in their hour of need were welcomed by my parents into our house. They stayed as long as they needed to sort themselves out. Even to this day my parents' generosity is as much as they are able to accommodate and has been instilled in all my siblings and myself.

As the days came and went and my departure loomed ever and ever closer, Mum battled long and hard to stop me from being sent. Her final remark to Dad was, "Well, he's your son not mine, therefore do what you will."

So there I was on a plane jetting off to Bangladesh. It was the end of 1979 and winter was in full swing in London and I wasn't sure what I was expected to do when I got to Bangladesh, well actually Sylhet, in the north-east of the country. It is funny but Sylhetis never want to be considered as part of greater Bangladesh, they tend to incline towards being that bit different from the rest of the country. A country with a land area three square miles short of 57,000, compared to the UK's 94,060 has just as many dialects as England, Scotland,

Wales and Northern Ireland. If I were to listen to someone from Dhaka I would have to strain very hard to understand and in some instances I would be completely lost, whilst they would also have a similar experience with me.

Strangely enough, the vast majority of the Bangladeshi immigrants in the UK were from the district of Sylhet. Why did Sylheti men mass migrate to the UK? I am not sure. One reason maybe because during the colonial era many of the men from this region worked in the British merchant navy as Laskars and hence visited places like Tilbury Docks, Liverpool, Portsmouth and the docks on the Isle of Dogs. The term Laskar was of Persian origin and adopted into Bengali, meaning sailor or militiaman from the Indian subcontinent. Laskars were employed on European ships from the sixteenth century starting with the Portuguese, with the British having the highest number of Laskars, mainly from Bengal, Assam and Gujarat.

By the 1950's and 60's many seamen from Sylhet started settling in England and subsequently brought their families over. My grandfather worked in the British merchant navy out of Calcutta and my dad was stationed out of Portsmouth. I am the first generation not to go to sea. Well! I would have suffered badly as my sea-legs are not that stable. Even today I struggle on the cross-channel ferries if the vessels do not have their stabilisers extended.

The journey from London to Dhaka was pretty uneventful, Bangladesh Biman's Boeing 707 did a great job carrying its cargo of passengers and their overweight suitcases tied a trillion times with nylon rope and labelled with their destination addresses. The half an hour flight to Sylhet was a different story, the old Fokker was shaky and noisy to say the least. As old Bengali folks would say, with the grace of Allah it got us there. However, once we landed at Sylhet airport, the reality of being away from my family started to sink in, as I was thrown into the maelstrom of life in the tropics.

As I got off the plane at Sylhet Airport and walked down the stairs onto the tarmac, the first thing to hit me was the heat and the blinding light of day. Even though this was the dry season and it was cool compared to the monsoon temperatures, the heat was so thick it felt like wading through warm pea soup and swallowing globules of near solid air. Compared to the grey hues of London, the bright sunshine here gave every colour an extra brightness. Green was the most pronounced. Having only snippets of memory from the first five and half years of my life here I could not recall the many hues and brightness of the colour green. The hills that surrounded the airport were abundant with coconut and betel palms and a myriad of other vegetation that dazzled the eye with their emerald greens to pale limes.

We walked the short distance from the plane into the terminal building and waited for the luggage to be brought in. The airport terminal was a tin-roofed shack of a building. You could see through the whole building from the ramp side to the car park where beggars, relatives of passengers and taxi drivers jostled to see who was arriving. Faces with bright eyes and teeth set against chocolate coloured skin and raven hair, all expecting the wealth of the Londonis, as those who had migrated to the UK were called, to rub off onto them. Whether the émigrés lived in London, Birmingham or Manchester, or any other UK city for that matter, they were referred to as Londonis.

The other colour to hit me was the many shades of brown faces around me. Having spent the last three years in Worcester and then a year in London during the late seventies when there were very few South Asian families, most of the friends that I made had been white. I was taken aback to see so many faces that were my colour, darker and in some cases lighter. Plus, almost all I could see were men and boys, the only women around were amongst the beggars waiting outside the terminal building. Everyone was also so thin to the point of being skeletal.

The terminal building had no baggage carousel and the bags were being dumped inside the building for the passengers to claim. So, my uncle and I and all the other passengers were waiting for the eventual arrival of our luggage. The saving grace of the building was shelter from the sun and sweltering heat, which wasn't helped by the fact that my dad had dressed me in a blazer, trousers, shirt and tie.

I was extremely worn out and jet-lagged by the duration of the journey of almost fourteen hours and here I was, inside a building whose ceiling fans were too high and ineffective to make any impact on the sluggish, tepid air. I left my uncle waiting for our luggage and went to the toilets, which were not exactly private as they were located in a corner of the terminal room, where anyone and everyone can see you entering and exiting after doing your business. I walked into one of two cubicles and when I saw the splatters on the toilet bowl and the nauseating stench hit my nostrils, I walked right back out and held my bladder, trying my hardest not to vomit.

What on earth was I doing here? This was not home. I left Bangladesh what seemed like ages ago so I didn't have that many memories, this Bangladesh that I have come back to was too alien and chaotic. The country was less than a decade from having gained its independence from Pakistan and was still going through a period of serious turmoil. This became further apparent when my uncle had to pay the obligatory bribe to the customs officer in order to stop him from opening our luggage and either charging tax on goods in our possession or confiscating them. The first pang of home sickness arose in my belly, however I put on a brave face and did not meet my uncle's gaze when he said, "Come on nephew, let's go to our *Bari*," referring to our homestead in Purushpal.

My Bibi

We walked out into the sun-baked car park where the noise and the smell hit me like a tidal wave. It was like an alien landscape and I thought this is what Han Solo must have experienced when he first landed on Tatooine. There were many dialects of Bengali being yelled, uttered and spoken, half of which I didn't understand and other dialects, especially from the beggars, that could have been another language all together. Many vendors walked around with bananas, mangoes, berries and a variety of other fruits which I would get to know over the coming months in straw baskets on their heads. The smell from the overripe fruit caused me to blow air out of my nose and breathe through my mouth.

Uncle Naz and I were met by his father Ali, who was a stick insect of a man with a complexion of dark chocolate with the obligatory beard on his chin and prayer *topi*, a cap, on his scalp. He arrived with a Toyota Liteace people carrier which was the mandatory white colour, as no other colour would do in Bangladesh. He ushered us towards the vehicle, which meant jostling through the mass of people surrounding the terminal exit.

The police hanging around looked lethargic and bored. I suppose the heat squeezed every ounce of energy and vim out of their personas. They did nothing to disperse the crowds so it was left to the arriving passengers and their greeters to make their own way out. We gave our luggage to the driver of the

Liteace and Grandpa Ali. I walked behind Naz as we snaked our way through the crowd, whilst several children in muddy brown shorts, matted hair but full of life and energy made a dash towards me.

"Bhaisab, please help me," one begged, calling me brother.

Another stuck his hand out and started stroking my arm. "Oh! Please bhaisab can I have some money, I am hungry and want to buy some food," pleaded the stroker.

I was so shocked by this because even before going to England I had never experienced this level of poverty. I was embarrassed for not being able to do something and the sadness and despair in the faces struck home so hard, as the kids could not have been much older than me. I was instructed by Uncle Naz to ignore them as he turned around and barked, "Hey, kids, get away from here."

The children stepped back but returned again to claw at me. Uncle Naz, his father and the driver had to contend with their own groups of beggars, let alone keep the ones pestering me at bay. This scene was being repeated with all the passengers as they left the airport building. The second time round I just could not bear the sad looking faces and I delved into my pockets, extracted whatever British coins I had and distributed them among the children. The look on their faces was one of total glee as if they had found their own El Dorado. Boy! What a mistake that was. As soon as the other beggars realised that some foreign coins had been distributed I had another horde of kids make a beeline for me. The scene was chaotic, raucous and very scary. At one point I was almost drowning in a sea of hands, with Uncle Naz and his father getting further away from me.

"Uncle!" I yelled. He looked back and yelled out a profanity in Bengali and all the kids scarpered to the four winds.

"Come on son, let's not hang around," he ordered with a

mild annoyance in his voice as he guided me towards the waiting vehicle.

I could sense he was getting tired with the whole journey and the hassle with just getting out of the airport. We eventually got to our hired people carrier, the luggage was stowed away by the driver and I took my seat in the middle of the vehicle alongside Uncle Naz. With no air conditioning the windows were wide open to keep the vehicle interior cool. The next two plus hours were my first experience of a bone-jarring journey along roads that were no more than dirt tracks, dry river beds and open fields. Thankfully, this wasn't going to be repeated until I came back to the airport on my return journey.

The city of Sylhet sits in the Surma River valley and is renowned for its hilly geography and tea estates. Our journey took us through the centre of the city and it was the most chaotic place I had ever seen in my life so far. The roads, if they could be called roads, were overflowing with mainly rickshaws, *telagharis*, a two-wheeled flat wooden cargo carrier powered by men with sinewy muscles, and baby-taxis, otherwise known as tuk-tuks in Southeast Asia, followed by people and then animals. There was no traffic system operating, man, machine and animal made a dash for any new gap in the traffic, thus causing another bottleneck. This subsequently led to horns being beeped, shouting, cursing and rickshaw bells ringing furiously.

We slowly meandered through the traffic and approached the steel bridge built by the British Raj over the Surma River. It was called the Keane Bridge, named after Sir Michael Keane, who was the governor of Assam and had the bridge constructed in 1936. The bridge was built to provide improved infrastructure for Sylhet as the importance and prominence of the city grew.

Beggars stuck their hands through the windows asking for

money, this time there were kids and adults, men and women, all with a look of total hopelessness in their eyes. This was compounded by the stench rising from the open sewers alongside the roads, which was made worse as grown men would squat down and urinate in the channels.

Once over the Surma River we got pretty much a clear run as we headed east. Even though I was dead tired I could not shut my eyes for a nap, the landscape and scenery once we had left the town of Sylhet was beautiful and mesmerising. Our bari was thirty miles or so east in Purushpal, a village that was less than ten miles from the border with India and the state of Assam.

The layout of the land as we left Sylhet was one of paddy fields on either side of the road and then every so often we would arrive at a local bazaar, with its assortments of vendors selling everything from fish and meat to betel nut and paan. The glaringly obvious lack was of any *bideshi,* foreign goods. I could not see any shops selling Golden Wonder crisps or Cadbury's chocolate bars, not even Coca Cola. This sent alarm bells ringing in my head, what on earth was I going to eat if they didn't sell these sweets and drinks? Would any of the Bangladeshi stuff be good? I knew I should have stuffed more sweets in my luggage. I resigned, slumping back in my seat thinking that I would have to make the sweets I have with me last just that bit longer.

Midway we stopped at a fairly large bazaar where Naz, his father, the driver and I stepped out of the vehicle in front of a tea shop.

"Son, what do you want to eat?" Naz enquired.

"Nothing uncle," I replied shyly, not wanting to sound like a demanding kid.

"Come on son, we've got a long way to go, what do you want a drink?"

"I don't mind, you can get anything."

This kind of response from me was drilled into me by my parents. I was always told not be demanding or if offered things to refuse, not so much out of rudeness, but more out of respect and restraint.

I stood outside the vehicle with the driver while Naz and his father went and got some tea and some savoury samosas. Surprisingly, I was given a bottle of Fanta orange, which was ice cold with a straw. I wolfed down the samosa and guzzled the sweet fizzy drink, not realising how hungry and thirsty I was. It was also an opportunity for me to relieve myself, stretch my legs and attempt to dry the sweat from my trousers and shirt by tugging on them furiously in the vain hope that the circulating air would dry my clothes.

Having rested and refuelled ourselves we all hopped back into the Liteace and continued on our journey. The landscape did not change much with it being the dry season and every so often I could see kids playing in the fields, flying kites or kicking a ball around. There were herds of cattle grazing on the dry stumps of rice stalks, being watched over by a solo man sporting a conical bamboo hat and a stick in hand. In the distance the emerald green of trees indicated a village, which provided an unchanging backdrop to the brown fields we rushed past. The fields on either side were roughly five feet lower than the road and without any crash barriers. If the unfortunate were to happen, there was nothing to stop a vehicle flying off onto the hard ground below, like a scene out of a car chase from *The Streets of San Francisco* TV show.

We arrived into Beani Bazaar during mid-afternoon, pulling into the centre of the town and then turning right onto College Road. Beani Bazaar was the main government administrative centre for the *Thana* of the same name. A Thana was a police station and areas were administered according to the station's jurisdiction. So Beani Bazaar police station controlled the locality of the same name which measures just over ninety seven square miles. Within the Thana were all the villages and some of them were big and important enough to have post offices designated to them. The smaller villages would use the postal designation of their larger brethren to have letters sent from overseas. Beani Bazaar, even to this day, has one of the largest diaspora of Sylhetis in the UK, Middle East, USA, Canada and nowadays Southeast Asia and Australia. The other Thanas that share this claim to fame are Golapganj which borders Beani Bazaar, Chattak, Balagang, Biswanath and Jaganathpur which are northwest and southwest of Sylhet city respectively. The latter three Thanas were named after the three children of a Hindu ruler, whose kids were called Bala, a daughter, whilst Biswanath and Jaganath were his two sons.

The name Beani Bazaar literally means 'morning market', originating from yonder days when tigers used to roam the hills, valleys and jungles in the area. The locals could only hold their market in the morning before making a hasty retreat back to their villages in fear of being attacked by the famous royal Bengal tiger. The town also has a college, a football field and direct transport access to the city of Sylhet. It meant that on market day it was buzzing with activity, however today appeared quiet, according to Grandpa Ali, but to me it looked crazy with activity akin to an ant colony. It never ceased to amaze me how busy people were in this part of the world. Activity of all sorts was always being carried out and even the stray cats and dogs seemed busy foraging for scraps of food or battling with each other to take the largest share of a find.

Many people called out to Grandpa Ali and Naz in recognition and a hail of greetings was directed towards us as our vehicle wound its way slowly through College Road. We did not stop but continued onwards to our village. We then came across the dry river bed of the Lula River. Without a bridge we drove down into and out the other side, followed by several more bazaars. We finally stopped outside a bari in the village of Mathiura. With the road being extremely narrow for even one vehicle we could not travel any further without risking falling into a river on our right. The whole length of the river was dry as a bone with only a sliver of water sitting stagnantly along the bottom, covered by water hyacinths.

Uncle Naz and his father hailed a couple of rickshaws that had begun following us from a bazaar not far back, and I could see a crowd gathering as news got around that some Londonis had arrived, who were a rare commodity in those days. Our luggage was unloaded and then loaded onto the rickshaws by the rickshaw-wallas, whilst Grandpa Ali and Naz paid the Liteace driver.

Having got off the bone shaking ride of the Liteace I thought "Ah! At last, a smooth ride," how wrong was I. The rickshaw ride was worse as the stick insect like man strained and pedalled with all his might to get me and my luggage over the potholed road. As he strained to pedal the rickshaw, rivulets of sweat trickled down his neck to be soaked up by the collar of his grimy, yellow, sweat stained vest. His exposed arms were glistening like a well-oiled gladiator. This man's battle was with the potholed road and Tropic of Cancer heat rather than another warrior in the Rome Coliseum.

We finally arrived at the edge of Purushpal, where Uncle Naz and I parted.

"Sabu, I will see you later, your Bibi and everyone is coming over there to pick you up," said Uncle Naz.

"OK Uncle, I will see you later," I replied, as his rickshaw trundled away.

I sat there, thinking there goes my last connection back to England, my family and home. His rickshaw took the main dirt road through the village which snaked left and disappeared into the thick green dense foliage of trees and bushes. The right fork of the road headed into paddy fields as far as I could see and then disappeared into the paddy fields completely. As I sat in the rickshaw, I looked straight ahead and I could see a group of people coming across the dry dusty fields. I sat there for what seemed like ages, the sun beating down on me and sweat dripping from my forehead, as slowly the crowd got closer and closer. Ahead of the group a dark boy of my age came up and said,

"Is that Sabu? Come, I will get the rickshaw-walla to take the suitcases, you go down and walk to your Bibi over there."

"Who are you?" I asked.

"Your Uncle Iqbal," he replied as he starting directing the rickshaw driver towards the village.

I got off the rickshaw and cautiously slid down the drop from the road onto the field and started walking towards the crowd and Bibi. As I neared them I could clearly make out Bibi, my paternal grandmother. She rushed out from the front of the crowd and embraced me saying, "Aarey! My Sabu, how big you have grown," with tears streaking down her face.

She was a short lady, about five foot three in height, dark complexion but very sharp features. She was wearing a dark green cotton sari with a white border, which I would get to know as her trademark attire. Her black curly hair draped her shoulders and I could smell the faint fragrance of pumpkin oil that made her locks glisten in the afternoon sun. Dad and my brother Alom had inherited her curly hair, whereas I had gotten the straight hair gene.

My siblings and I called our grandmother Bibi; it was our own loving name for her. Officially, it was her surname, but to me it was my name for my gran. So it was from the day I could utter any words that I have called her Bibi. Everyone else addressed her according to whatever relationship she held with them, be it auntie, gran, sister or mother.

I looked at her and smiled, but even though she was my grandmother who I was extremely fond of I just could not allay my fears of loneliness. The remainder of the crowd gathered round, they recognising me rather than me knowing who they were. I could feel a swell of emotions bubbling in the depth of my belly and I fought hard to resist any tears or a quiver of my lips showing externally.

Homesick

I walked across the fields with Bibi by my side and the whole crowd tagging along. Each one of them introduced themselves as an aunt or an uncle. However, none of them seemed more than a year or two older than me; this anomaly in relationship was an oddity in my family.

The village where I was born was the home of my paternal grandmother. My grandfather was an only child and he was given up for adoption to Bibi's family. Bibi's parents treated my grandfather like a son and gave him equal share in the family land and wealth. When the time came Bibi was married to my grandfather, I suppose it was a strategic move to keep the wealth within the family. My grandfather worked in the British Merchant Navy, travelling to Liverpool and the docklands in London on his many voyages. During his leave he would also farm the land that he shared with my grandmother's three brothers. Subsequently, my grandparents had my dad, again an only child.

During one of his visits home from the Merchant Navy, my grandfather was out in the fields with a day labourer. It was the monsoon season and they were trying to get the work in the fields finished before the impending storm that was looming on the horizon caught up with them. Unfortunately, it wasn't meant to be and whilst they made their way back to the bari my grandfather was struck by lightning and killed instantly. The labourer ran back to the bari to tell everyone the news. Upon blurting out an incoherent message he collapsed in shock and needed reviving, whilst Bibi and her brothers rushed out to the fields.

The sight that met them was cemented into Bibi's mind forever. She told me many years later that the lightning bolt entered through his right collarbone and exited via his left groin. The heat had seared and sealed the wound that they could see right through my grandfather. Bibi collapsed there and then in shock and grief. Her brothers carried my grandfather's body and half carried Bibi back to the bari in the pouring rain.

Now that Bibi was widowed she needed to be married off again. So, after the grieving period suitors were sought. The search continued for a good length of time as a widowed woman was not desired at all in those days of social taboo. Even today a widowed or divorced woman is avoided when parents seek wives for their young unmarried sons. Eventually, Bibi was married to a man close to Sylhet city. However, Dad stayed with his maternal grandmother, uncles and aunts. Even though Dad was in his late terrible twos I can only imagine the stress and heartache both mother and son went through to be separated at such a tender age, when the bonding process was still in its early stages. So Bibi and Dad would ferry back and forth between the two villages that took a day to travel on foot, ensuring the mother and son love did not wither away. I can attest to my dad's undying love for Bibi; with no father she was his world.

Bibi had a daughter with her new husband, giving Dad a half-sister. But disaster was to strike again. Whilst my half-aunt was a toddler, her father passed away. Again Bibi was widowed, this time though her brothers decided she would come back to her home village and remain with her kith and kin. If another husband came about then they would marry her off, otherwise they would not rush to get her married. So, it was that no suitors came forward and Bibi remained unmarried for the rest of her life. Alas! Bibi's daughter did not accompany her back to her home village, so another heart rending set of years ensued with mother and daughter being separated and the travel on foot continued until my half-aunt was a teenager.

My dad was a year older than Bibi's youngest brother and came into the world before any of his cousins were even a twinkle in their parent's eyes; subsequently I was older than some of my uncles and aunts. This meant that I was the first grandchild for all my dad's uncles and aunts, thus I was doted upon ever since my birth.

Once inside our bari, Bibi escorted me to her house which she shared with her mother, who I called Old Auntie. We entered the bari through the 'backyard', walking along the banks of the huge pond, which was the size of a full length football pitch and shared by all the families of the bari. A bari was a collection of families, usually blood related, who owned a plot of land which was divided equally in most cases, with each family having their house on their plot. Our bari had four families, one of which was my grandmother's to which my dad belonged and thus had a quarter share of all the land, both in the bari and out in the fields. Due to my strange ancestry we had no contact with my dad's paternal family, some of them lived about five miles away and others were scattered throughout the country. For me, therefore, my extended family were here in my grandmother's room, the people who looked so strange but were so close.

Old Auntie came and sat next to me along with a few grandparents and a dozen uncles and aunts whom I would get to know pretty shortly. There was Bibi's eldest brother, his wife and their two adult and one toddler son, as well as two teenage and two toddler daughters. Bibi's second brother's wife with her one adult son and three sons around my age and younger were there. There were also her two teenage and two younger daughters about half my age all gathered around me, staring at me as if I was from another planet. On top of all the people who were part of the extended family, there were also the people from the rest of the bari peering through whatever gap they could find amongst the throng who had amassed around the doorway and windows. It was as if a human eclipse had appeared out of nowhere, blocking out natural sunlight and plunging the room into semi-darkness.

"Hey! Give him some space, my grandson is going to suffocate because of the heat," Bibi barked at everyone.

I sat there with Bibi next to me, waving a *panka*, a hand held bamboo fan, cooling me down. Electricity still had not reached this part of the world and would not do so for another two decades or so. However, within the building the air was surprisingly cool, the ground underfoot was of clay and the roof of corrugated tin with a bamboo ceiling, which acted as storage, as well as containing the heat from the metal roof.

Sitting there I had a barrage of questions fired at me by Bibi and all the other grandparents and relatives surrounding me.

"So, how's your mum and dad?" someone asked.

"How is London?" enquired another.

It was almost twenty four hours since I began my journey in London and I was feeling very tired and all these questions, though making me feel like a mini celebrity, were going in one ear and coming out the other. I answered most of the questions as best as I could, without appearing rude or inconsiderate. The most unnerving thing I found was how close people sat next to me and the stroking of my hair by the various grandparents, even Bibi. I tried my best not to appear to recoil from their touch, which I managed mainly because I was too tired to move or flinch. My fifteen minutes on stage that afternoon seemed to go on for ever, but eventually most of the elders left to get on with their daily chores.

Bibi finally shooed all the stragglers and kids away, leaving me to change my clothes and then take a warm shower at the back of the house in the open air. As there were no private bathrooms, all of the bari's inhabitants bathed in the pond at the back of the bari. Eventually, I would do the same, but for the first few days Bibi would boil water and cool it down and then I would shower using a jug. Boy! Did that shower feel good washing away all the dirt, grime and sweat accumulated travelling on a plane, automobile and rickshaw.

That evening my suitcase was unloaded and half the contents which were gifts for people were distributed by Bibi to those owners who had arrived for the evening to see me. Most of the gifts consisted of Vick's Vaporub or Vaseline petroleum jelly or even a muscle rub, basic over-the-counter medicines which you could not get in the rural towns and villages of Bangladesh. The items were cherished by the recipients and the look in their eyes could not hide their gratitude that they felt. There were also many letters with money and messages for loved ones that Bibi distributed. Telephone was non-existent and urgent messages were sent by telegram. There was no guarantee if letters were posted that they would arrive safely in the villages of Sylhet.

As night drew in the kerosene lanterns were lit one by one across the whole bari. The bari faced west and our building housed four family homes, one being my dad's and the other three being his uncles'. Our household was at the northern end of the bari, the second from last that joined onto the paddy fields stretching north. Standing at this end and looking north, I could see lights way in the distance, but at an elevated height.

My favourite grandfather, Boro Dada, Bibi's eldest brother,

came up to me and asked, "What are you doing Grandson?"

"Nothing Dada, what are those lights up there in the distance?" I replied.

"Those are the hills of Meghalaya in India and the lights from Shillong, the main town of that state," he smiled.

"Have you ever been there?" I asked.

"I have, but mainly for buying cattle or agricultural products."

I continued to look over at the lights and wondered what it was like over there, my curiosity of what's over that hill, or what's round the next bend in the road was beginning and would become a permanent fixture in my life.

"Let's go Grandson, the mosquitoes will eat you alive here in the dark," he suggested, as we walked towards the porch of our house. He left me and went off to say the evening prayers.

On the porch I sat on a bamboo stool called a *mura*, I was wearing shorts and a t-shirt with a pair of flip flops and I could already feel the tingling sensation from the pinprick mosquito bites. I started a behaviour that would be part of my life for the next eleven months in Bangladesh. The act was performed by everyone on exposed skin, which was brushing away the buzzing mosquitoes from legs, feet, arms and face. Sitting there, I watched the women and children going about placing the lanterns on porches or hooks along the walls of the houses. To me the whole scene was magical, as the warm orange lights gave out a beautiful glow that would be welcoming and homely to anyone who saw it.

Even though I sat there enjoying my first night of village life wearing only shorts and t-shirt, everyone went about their duties wearing shawls and scarves and I was wondering what was the matter with them, it wasn't exactly that cold. I guessed for people accustomed to thirty degrees Celsius or more, the winter high teens temperature was pretty cool.

As my eyes adjusted to the low light I was amazed by how dark things were; I looked up at the clear night sky and could see stars twinkling away up in the lofty heavens. Even though the scene was picture perfect, the darkness was a shock to my system and it would be a while before I got accustomed to the lack of lights at night. Standing there I began to ponder what my brothers and sister were doing, I didn't even know how many hours behind they were in England. A pang of loneliness welled up in my stomach which I tried to contain, hoping nobody would notice my quivering bottom lip and the big fat droplets of tears welling in my eyes. I wiped my eyes dry as quickly as the waters welled up. Fortunately everybody was too busy putting the chickens and ducks away, tethering the cattle in the barn and generally tidying up to notice my emotional turmoil.

Having said her evening prayers Bibi came out and joined me. "What are you up to Sabu?" she asked.

"Not much Bibi, I was with Boro Dada out over there looking over the fields," I responded.

"So what did he show you?" she continued.

"Oh! He was telling me about the lights of Shillong in the hills."

"Are you hungry by the way?" she asked, to which I nodded positively, trying to ensure that she did not catch my tears.

"Let's go Sabu, let's go and eat," she stated as we walked to the kitchen.

I made sure my eyes were dry as she escorted me with a lantern in her hand across the courtyard to the rickety old house that was the kitchen, which also had an extra bedroom. It was in that rickety old house that I was born in the winter of 1969. Even to this day the house and room had not changed an iota in décor, construction or furniture arrangements.

We walked through the bedroom and into the kitchen, where log fires were burning in the hearths and a straw mat was placed on the floor with tin dining plates. I took my place next to Bibi, as Boro Dada sat opposite us. Even though he was the eldest of Bibi's three brothers, he was younger than her.

"How are you finding things Grandson?" asked Dada.

"Good for now, slightly dark though which feels very odd," I replied.

"You'll get used to it, just be a bit careful as you go about," he advised. However, he stopped mid-track, looked at me a bit more quizzically and asked, "Why are your eyes red Sabu?"

"Where? My eyes aren't red are they?" I questioned.

"Yes, your eyes are really red," he restated.

"No, I'm just tired," I replied.

"OK, as long as you are alright," he ended.

I don't think he believed me, but he did not pursue the matter any further. I took extra care not to look up too often and meet anyone's gaze just in case they asked about my tear-reddened eyes.

Boro Dada was a short, dark man with sinewy muscles from the years of toiling in the fields. He started working the family land shortly after the death of his father – after whose death my grandfather also passed away – whilst he was still pretty much my age. This meant that Old Auntie and Bibi had to take over the running of the family estate, with no adult men around. This was at a time when British India was being broken up into India, East and West Pakistan, and when a matriarchal family wasn't the norm in a predominantly Muslim region of British India. Yet the two ladies managed to keep other greedy men off their property and hold the family together. They raised three sons plus my dad, as well as Bibi's three sisters. They found appropriate marriage partners for them all and even though the family had its ups and downs, it was amazing what the two women had achieved, which has not been matched by any of the descendants from the brood.

Having finished off our meals of fish bhajee and rice I went back to the room that Bibi, Old Auntie and I shared. I was fast asleep before anybody else could come and ask to talk to me about how it was being a Londoner. I drifted off as Old Auntie, who sat beside me, ground the betel nut, paan and tobacco leaves in a short bamboo canister with an iron pestle. With no teeth and no dentures she was restricted to what she could eat and any betel nut she had to grind to almost a powder to be able to enjoy its addictive juices. I became quite partial to her ground betel nut and paan leaves. I would hang around her when she was grinding the mixture and solicit some off her whenever I could. The odd times she would shoo me away were more in a loving manner than to reprimand me. I was her first great grandchild and her love for me was too strong not to concede to my requests.

The next day my nana and nani, maternal grandfather and grandmother, as well as my Uncle Babul arrived from their village of Sreedhara to visit. Nana and Nani were quite elderly and Nana, who was a slim man, was particularly frail. He was wearing a lunghi and shalwar top, a sarong like garment and a collarless shirt, along with the obligatory white topi. Nani was slightly heavier and I guessed she looked how my mum would appear at her age. Both Nana and Nani were fair skinned which my mum had inherited, whereas my Uncle Babul was slightly darker with a heavier frame and he looked almost bearish to me. They arrived with sweets, biscuits and cakes and were delighted to see me. I hadn't seen them since leaving for London back in 1975 and I didn't have a strong enough memory of them as I did of Bibi, but I was still happy to see them. All three sat on the edge of the bed in my room and asked me questions about how mum was and how dad and my three siblings were doing. I happily answered their questions and reassured their fears, in particular Nana and Nani's, especially about mum being so far away from them where they only heard how she was once a month or so via a letter.

The three of them stayed for lunch, with Nani spending the day chatting away with Bibi and her two sister-in-laws, whilst Nana went to the mosque for noon prayers with Boro Dada. Uncle Babul, my mum's younger brother, was telling me stories about how he would carry me on his shoulders from Purushpal all the way to their bari, which was a good three or four miles away. He eventually went off to hang out with a couple of older uncles who were in their early late teens and a lot closer to his age for company.

Come late afternoon they headed back to Sreedhara, and as they left they asked for Bibi and I to visit and stay over. Bibi said once I have acclimatised to the weather then she would take me to stay over, even though I heard a slight reluctance in Bibi's voice. There is this certain possessiveness of grandkids in Bengali society. The children of sons are revered and obsessively protected by the paternal grandparents, especially sons who are the scions of the family and are there to continue the family line.

Over the next eleven months I would witness an unseen battle of tug-o-war with me over my visitation rights to my maternal grandparents place. Even to this day I see this with my own brothers and sister's kids and other families too. As my parents have become grandparents they are doing precisely what their parents did with my siblings and me.

The following days entailed me getting familiarised with the lay of the land and getting to know all the uncles and aunts. There were seven aunts and seven uncles from the two brothers of Bibi who were still in the country. Her youngest brother had migrated to England at around the same time as my dad in the 1960's. Again, as I got to know the lay of the homestead and village, the striking feature was the lush green flora and fauna everywhere. Even though it was winter and many fruit trees were out of season, there was an abundance of mango, guava, various berries, coconuts, betel nuts and numerous other fruit trees and my senses were feeling overloaded at this profusion, because I knew once the monsoon arrived there would be lots of fruits to savour and eat.

Eventually I was signed up to the local school which was in the middle of the village, alongside the canal that ran through it. It was at the south end of our bari and it only took about five minutes to walk there. I was also signed up for the morning Arabic classes at the village mosque that was situated next to Uncle Naz's bari, just behind the school. Even though I did not like the idea of going to either I went along anyway with other children of various ages from the village.

To get to the school I would walk out of the west entrance of the bari and turn south, then hit the main village thoroughfare that cut through the village east to west and ran alongside the canal. The main road, well not a road, more a path, turned east and directly on the opposite side was the school. The school was one building of just a single floor. It had exposed brickwork, no windows nor shutters and no doors. The pupils would bring their own pencils and books if they could afford it, whereas the majority of them would arrive with slates the size of small notebooks and chalk to write with.

At school there were only three classrooms and most of the pupils were bundled into similar age groups. Everybody called my teacher the Guti Master, because he had very bad pockmarks on his face from childhood chicken pox or measles. He was a kind and patient teacher and he took an immediate fondness to me, ensuring that I didn't feel left out or picked on by any of the kids. The latter didn't happen at all and lunchtimes at school were filled with playing Kabadi in the school yard. I was treated with special regard as I was the 'Londoni's son', plus all the kids in the village knew each other and bullying was unheard of in this part of the world. Of course I saw disagreements and arguments between kids, but I cannot remember a single incident of bullying or fighting.

I became a dab hand at playing Kabadi and during my brief interlude at Bengali school I was always in the thick of it at lunch break. Kabadi is a game of two teams in a tennis court sized field with a halfway marker on the pitch. The teams stick to their own sides of the pitch and the aim is one by one a member of the team is to take a deep breath and say "Chal, dag, dag, dag…" continuously, then go into the opposing team's side and try and tag someone out. To succeed they must tag a member of the opposite team and run back into their half. The opposing team can, however, hold the raiding opponent and grapple him to the floor until he runs out of breath, in which case he is out. This continues until the winning team has tagged out the opposing team members and has at least one remaining member on the field. Being very much a rough and tumble game, it was only played by the boys, with the girls either watching or playing their own games. By the end of each game all the players were covered in dust and mud and in desperate need for a wash. On many days I looked like I was dragged through a mud bath and dried out in the sun. This was accompanied with cuts, grazes and bruises, to name just some of the injuries, but I loved it and even today if the chance arose I'd give it a go.

The school routine was one of four lessons, namely Bengali, maths, science and geography. Being taught in Bengali was proving quite tricky, as I had spent the last four years learning in English. Luckily, both Guti Master and my clan of aunts and uncles were on hand to help me and soon enough the learning for me became quite comfortable.

Whilst I was fitting into life in the village I saw Uncle Naz only occasionally, which was sad as he was my only contact to the world I left behind in England, especially in those days when there were no telephones to call my parents. The only way I had any contact was through letter writing and in emergencies, a telegram. I guess he was busy trying to find a bride for himself and being a young man from London with money he was busy having fun with his peers.

Going to the mosque in the morning was a bit of a chore which I did not relish, having to wake up almost at the crack of dawn and don my topi to learn Arabic. The lessons were only for an hour and consisted mainly of learning the basics in the Qaeda and verses from the Sifara. The funny thing was we, the pupils at the mosque, were never taught to understand the Arabic language but just to regurgitate the teachings without having a clue what they meant. This parrot fashion learning of the Koranic verses were being conducted throughout the whole country by kids like me. This would add another generation of Bengali Muslims who will not know what the words mean. I was quite glad to finish the morning lessons and get to school.

The Arabic lessons were conducted strictly by the Imam, with any indiscretions on the pupil's part being punished with a whip on the palm of your hand from a bamboo stick that was razor thin. Boy, did I get it sometime, mainly for the odd chat here and there. Even though I did not cry it would bring a tear to my eye. On those days I got a whipping I would walk away with bright pink welts on my palms.

Some days after school I would pop over to Uncle Naz's bari and say hello to him and his parents and then rush back to my bari. However, that was easier said than done; a visit to anyone's bari meant tea, biscuits or anything else that they could muster up. No visitor to any bari in Bangladesh is spared the hospitality of the hosts. Even if you turn up unannounced, you cannot depart until you have taken tea and biscuits as a minimum, or a full meal if you were unfortunate to turn up during brunch, lunch or dinner. Uncle Naz, when he saw me, would beam ear to ear. Again, akin to others I was his favourite nephew, even at my tender age he treated me like an adult and often asked me for my thoughts on subjects that required adult answers and solutions. He would also fondly refer to me as the son of a worker lady. In Bengali culture the wife of an elder brother or male cousin, who is called a bhabi, is usually the confidante and best friend to the younger siblings in the family. They therefore would crack jokes and make fun of her, but come to her for advice when serious matters were at hand. Thus, my mum, being the first bhabi in my dad's extended family, meant that she was everyone's favourite and respected the most. As Naz was a weekly regular in our house back in London he would always laugh and joke with mum and thus I was used to being called the son of a worker lady. I knew it was harmless fun, and being greeted as such by Naz was more a loving gesture than anything else. So, when I visited Naz or he came round he would sit and talk to me asking how I was and if I was missing my parents and siblings. I would tell him the partial truth as I did not want him to think that I was a mummy's boy, whereas within me a tropical storm would brew when I thought about my family.

Uncle Naz had a younger brother who was older than me and had Down's syndrome. Even though he had the ability to dress and walk and to a degree talk, he needed watching and caring for. We all called him Feer; I never knew what his real name was. However, out of all the kids I was his favourite, whenever I visited Naz I would also see him. The first thing he would do is grasp me in a bear hug so strong, almost squeezing the last breath out of me and shout "Sabu is here" followed by "How are you?" He would then proceed to make room for me to sit and usher the workers in the house to get me something to drink. Whilst I sat there I would converse in simple, basic sentences with him and he would stroke my hair like a little pet. Even to this day, whenever I visit Bangladesh and I go to see Feer, he will grasp me, except that I am taller and bigger than him and I tend hug him more than he can hug me.

Back at my bari my school chums were Aman, Amad and his brother Iqbal, and after the day's learning was done we usually headed back to the bari and jumped into the *furki*, the large communal pond at the back of the bari. We would swim and play in the pond until the tips of our fingers and toes were wrinkled and our eyes were red. The whole bari was full of kids around my age, some a few years younger and others a few years older, which meant I was never lonely.

Aman was my best sidekick and one afternoon after school he took me and his younger brother Amad down to the fields at the north end of the bari. The fields were covered in well-trodden rice stalks after the rice harvest. Far in the distance I could see shepherds walking with a bamboo stick in their hands, tending their cattle.

"Uncle, let's go further out to the fields, I am going to show you something," said Aman, in the obligatory respectful 'uncle' address.

The age between us was minimal and I would have been fine if he called me by my name, culturally he was obliged to show respect. Yet, I would always call him by his name.

"Why, what's going on?" I quizzed.

"I am going to give you a treat that you're going to enjoy," he smiled.

Amad, who was a couple of years younger, yelled. "Yes, Uncle, it's going to be fun and tasty."

So the three of us walked out of the bari and onto dry paddy fields. We walked for about a quarter of a mile into the fields and with nothing in every direction except rice stalks I was beginning to wonder what they meant about a treat in the fields. Then, all of a sudden, Aman stopped dead in his tracks and he said, "Right, we're here, this place is perfect."

I looked at him quizzically and said, "What?"

Aman knelt down and he started to clear with his hands some of the dried rice stalks, and he asked me to do the same.

"Why?" I questioned.

"Well, if you want to enjoy the treat then clear a line in the ground up in that direction, and get Amad to help you," he replied.

After we had cleared a line roughly twenty feet in length Aman handed me a box of matches and said, "Do as I do over there," and pointed to one end of the cleared line.

I walked over to the location and I looked over and saw him light the match and then kneel down on the ground and set the dry rice stalks at his feet on fire, I then did the same. The three of us stood back and watched the fire spread and burn itself forwards of the line. As the fired burnt I could hear popping sounds, initially I thought it was the dry stalks popping away, but the popping was fast and furious, so I looked over at Aman and asked, "What is that sound?"

"You'll see," he replied, with a Cheshire cat grin on his face.

The fire picked up and was moving quite fast away from us, at which point Aman worriedly said, "The fire's getting too big, I hope it stops."

"Looks like it's not going to do that, the way it is burning," was my anxious reply.

We glanced over our shoulders and back at the bari to see if anyone was coming out onto the fields and scouted the general horizon, luckily no one was around. Aman bolted toward the left flank of the fire trying to get to the front, I did the same and Amad with his little legs scampered after us, trying to keep up.

"What are we going to do?" I yelled at Aman as we ran.

"Let's see once we get to the front of the fire," he panted.

Having arrived at the front of the fire we realised that we had hit the end of that plot of paddy field, which was marked by a ridge of earth about six inches high. At this realisation Aman looked at me with a smile indicating everything was fine. "The fire won't go beyond this ridge, so we'll be fine," he assured me.

By this time Amad had come running up and joined us. We stepped over the ridge and sat on the ground, waiting for the fire to reach the ridge and die down. As the fire hit the ridge it slowly died away, leaving charred and smoking blackened earth behind it. We got up and walked back towards the start of the fire and Aman began walking atop the ash. The ash felt warm underfoot and in some instances we would hop up and down as the heat was strong enough to cause a mild pain.

As he went along he picked up snow white, puffed rice and said, "Here you go, this is the treat, try it."

I munched on the rice puffs that he was giving me and I also began to pick the rice puffs for myself, which looked and tasted exactly like Kellogg's Rice Krispies, only that these tasted better and less salty. We spent the remainder of the late afternoon stuffing our pockets with rice puffs and then stuffing our faces as we sat in the fields and watched the herdsmen bringing their cattle home for the night.

To this day those rice puffs were the best I had ever tasted and I never repeated that trick again with Aman or anyone else. I guessed in that decade when in the villages of Bangladesh sweets, crisps and snacks were non-existent in shops, this is what the children resorted to for snacks. At least the snacks back home consisted of five penny packs of Golden Wonder Cheese and Onion crisps and Bazooka Joe bubble gum, therefore such ingenuity was not called upon, rather getting my parents to part with their cash. Apart from my arson induced snack the only other treat was an orange flavoured boiled sweet called Bolaka that I would buy every so often from the village shop.

Even though it was fun hanging out with kids my age and pretty much doing things that I would never dream of doing back home in London, I still missed my siblings and parents, not to mention the other comforts of a country that had electricity, TV, shops and a whole host of other amenities. So, as we headed back to the bari I felt the twinge of missing my family and being back in England.

There was many a day in the first four to six weeks that I would come home from school and a pang of homesickness would hit me. I would walk out to the back of our house where it was quieter and I would let the tears of homesickness roll down my cheeks. On one such day an aunt walked by, caught a glimpse of me crying and asked what was going on. I hurriedly wiped my tears on my t-shirt and smiled as best as I could, saying that nothing was wrong and I was fine. She came up to me and took a closer look.

"Have you been crying?" she asked.

"No, something fell into my eyes," I lied.

"Then why are you out here in the back on your own?" she continued.

"I just went down to the pond to wash my eyes out," the lie growing bigger.

"Well, come on up front, everybody else is there," she said putting her arms around my shoulders.

Walking back with her I knew that she did not buy that story and she would mention it to Bibi. However, I never heard anything from Bibi or anyone else about the matter and eventually, as the days rolled into weeks and weeks into months, the feeling of missing my family and home passed away. However, on the odd occasion I would recall my brothers and sister I'd wish I was back in London with them and my parents.

Nana's Place

As promised, one day Bibi and I, accompanied by Boro Dada, headed off to my Nana's village. This was my first visit and my maternal grandparents were making a big effort to welcome their eldest grandson's arrival from London. As public transport was non-existent and private baby-taxis were life threatening and expensive, most of my travels would be on foot. Our journey began that day with us walking the distance to Eid Ghah Bazaar. From there we caught a rickshaw, Boro Dada joking that my Londoni legs would get tired too quickly for me to walk all the way to Nana's bari. By the time we reached Eid Ghah my legs were tired, but more importantly I was soaked to the skin with sweat. Once on the rickshaw the wind gently dried the short sleeved shirt I had on, providing much needed relief. The rickshaw ambled its way along the windy main road, going past Mathiura Bazaar and then through open fields up to the Lula River. The road was hard baked earth and our rickshaw would pull aside when the odd baby-taxi buzzed past us tooting its horns. On more than one occasion I thought the whole rickshaw would tumble over the side and into the fields.

When we arrived at the Lula River we got off the rickshaw and walked north along the western bank of the Lula River towards Sreedhara, which was about a mile or so away. The fields to our left were empty bar the odd herd of cattle chomping on the dried golden rice stalks. On our right the riverbed was dry and dusty where the occasional wooden boat was chained to a post, and half buried in the dried mud. The boats looked to the skies for rain to free them from their mud encased prison. Alas! They would have to wait until the monsoons arrived to unleash the heavens and their cargo of rain from the Bay of Bengal.

We eventually arrived into Thri-Muki Bazaar, which literally means 'three mouths', being attributed to the three tributaries that intersected the Lula River at the bazaar. The market was quiet, where only some of the shops were open, with the shopkeepers watching us as we walked into the main square.

"I'll get something from one of the shops," said Dada as he walked up to one of the shops selling cakes, biscuits and other dried foodstuffs.

It was Bengali tradition that you never went to another person's bari without some gift, as it was considered rude. So no matter who you visit, even your own siblings, one would always take biscuits, cakes, Bengali sweets or seasonal fruits. Dada having purchased several items of sweets and savouries from the shop, we continued following the road out of the bazaar and into the village. Nana's bari was only a ten minute walk if that from the bazaar, we took several twists and turns in the road to get to his place. His bari was on the road that ran north through Sreedhara and was about 600 feet from the banks of the Lula River. The bari had a small pond that edged the road, the pond was rarely used and the steps down to it were flanked by two beautiful and majestic coconut palms.

We walked into the bari along the northern bank of the pond. Nana's house was on our left as we walked into the small courtyard. Opposite Nana's house was another building and on the northern end of the bari there were two more houses facing each other, with a path being the divider between the two ends.

The other houses belonged to nephews of Nana; one had emigrated to England during the 1960's and had lived near us in Worcester, where he still remained. He had two wives: his first wife was still in Bangladesh with one of his two sons, whilst he had taken his eldest son from his first wife along with his second wife to the UK during the 1980's. The nephew living opposite to Nana was in the Middle East, whose wife and two sons were still in Bangladesh. The third nephew had moved to Sylhet town with his family during the early 1970's, having built a comfortable living as a construction contractor following the post-war rebuilding that mushroomed in the city.

We walked into the courtyard with Dada in the lead, followed by Bibi and then me.

"Ohh! Is anybody in the bari?" Dada let out joyfully, upon which out popped my Elder Mami from Nana's house – Mami being the Bengali word for aunt who was the wife of a maternal uncle – with a child on her hip.

"Amma, Sabu's here?" she called back to Nani and came out to hug me. Both Nana and Nani followed her out.

"Salaam alaikum bhaisab, salaam alaikum buwai," they addressed Dada and Bibi as brother and sister respectively.

"Alaikum salaam," Bibi and Dada replied.

I also said my greeting as Nani came over to me and smothered me in hugs and nose kisses, which I wasn't too fond of. Dada handed over the newspaper wrapped packets of gifts to Mami.

"How are you Sabu?" Nana asked.

"I am good," I replied.

Nani took my hand and led me in through the small enclosed porch into the main bedroom-cum-living room. I sat at the edge of the wooden bed with her beside me, as she stroked my face and head. Bibi also sat on the bed with Dada as both tried to cool themselves with a bamboo fan each.

"Can you get some water for my grandson, bhaisab and buwai?" Nana asked Elder Mami.

Nani was still holding on to me and stroking my hair lovingly, however to me it just seemed too clingy. In my household such touchy feely display of affection wasn't the norm, my mum and dad rarely displayed such affection – not to say that they didn't love my siblings and me, so this care and affection from Nani was a bit too overbearing.

Nana's house was one of modest construction, it was timber framed with a tin roof and half tin walls, with the lower half of the building being of brick construction. With all these metal walls and roof it felt like being in an oven, so Nani had a fan cooling me as sweat dripped from my nose. The house had three bedrooms, the main one which we were sitting in acting also as the living room. The kitchen with a low ceiling was attached to the main room's southern flank. The kitchen led out to the backyard and the outdoor latrine.

My mum had been born in this house and grew up in this bari before her marriage to my dad a year before my birth. Mum had an elder brother, Nurul, and a sister, both of whom were at least ten years older than her. Her younger brother Babul was only a year or so junior and the two of them had more in common than with their elder siblings.

Uncle Nurul was working abroad in Pakistan, and as far as I knew he was always overseas. Prior to Bangladesh gaining independence from Pakistan, he worked in Karachi and Lahore. He eventually married a Pakistani lady in Karachi and had two kids. However, due to fear of admonishment from Nana he left his wife and two kids back in Pakistan, even though she desperately wanted to come back with him to Bangladesh. So, somewhere in Pakistan I have two cousins and their offspring, who may or may not know that they have a family some 1000 miles or more to their east.

Upon his return he married Elder Mami and had two children, a daughter called Mithun – who Mami carried on her hips when greeting me – and a one year old son, Samad, sleeping happily behind us on the bed. Mum's elder sister lived in a village close to Sylhet town, who rarely visited her parents, not because of want but the distance meant a visit was more likely to be a week or more.

Uncle Babul was the only one left at home and he didn't work or do anything else, but pretty much hung around the bari, like most men in their early twenties in Bangladesh. Most of them wanted to leave their lives in the villages for one abroad, whether it was for England, America or Middle East. Nana had huge tracts of arable land in the fields surrounding Sreedhara. Most of it was leased out to share croppers who, for a percentage share of the crop yield, would cultivate and harvest rice and various other produce. Hence, many young men in the villages of Beani Bazaar didn't feel the necessity to work as there was a barn full of rice and vegetables that could see their families through a whole year. However, with no other income Nana and my uncles over the years would sell the land to pay for unexpected expenses and to cover general living costs. This was a story being repeated across the whole of the Sylhet district. Even to this day some of the most fertile land on planet Earth lies fallow, whilst young men dream of a life overseas.

Elder Mami not only brought us glasses of water but she also mustered up some sweet milky vermicelli dessert. She was dressed in a dark sari and had a gaunt look to her, with sunken eyes and a chocolate brown complexion. She also took a seat on a mura next to the kitchen doorway, with Mithun gurgling on her lap.

"Are you enjoying being back in Bangladesh, Sabu?" Mami asked.

"It's OK," I replied.

"Do you miss your mum and dad?" she continued.

"Only a little bit," I replied, without wanting to sound weak and in need of my parents.

"Where is Babul?" Bibi asked Nana.

"He went to the Bazaar, to get some shopping, did you not see him?" he asked.

"No! But we never stayed too long to notice," added Boro Dada.

A lady walked in through the doorway we had entered. With her she had two boys who were about two and three years old. They could have been twins apart from the fact that one had glistening eggplant coloured dark skin and the other was fair skinned like his mother. The lady said her salaam to Bibi and Dada and came and stood by one of the wooden support pillars that rose from the floor and into the roof.

"This is your aunt from across the courtyard and that's her two boys, Sabir and Shakir," Nani introduced.

The new aunt, who I called Gora Auntie because of her very fair skin, was short and a bit plump with a jolly smile on her face and very talkative.

"What Sabu? Are you well?" she enquired.

One of the quirks I noticed of the Bengali language was the use of the word 'what'. It was used liberally to start any discussion, questioning or greeting. Another oddity of the language was the rote response of 'good'. When asked how you were or how someone else was and even how things are going, the answer was *'balo'*. This literally meant 'good'.

"Yes Auntie, I am good."

"How is your mum?"

"She's good," I replied.

"Here are your two cousins," she said pointing to her two sons standing in front of her. The two boys were looking restless and were on the verge of running off in all directions, which they did, and before I could even acknowledge them their mother was calling after them to behave.

Everyone carried on chatting while I excused myself and walked out through the kitchen into the backyard. Elder Mami followed me out, I suppose in a protective way. Outside the kitchen to my surprise was a dog with a litter of puppies. The dog, a black and white mongrel lay on the dusty ground with five puppies whose mouths were attached to her teats with their eyes shut tight. The pups were a mixture of various black and white patterns and were cute as cuddly toys that were begging to be picked up and cuddled.

"Are they yours?" I asked Mami, with a big smile on my face, but fearful enough to keep a distance from the dogs.

"Yes, your uncle Babul got the mother as a guard dog, we'll keep maybe one or two of the pups and give the others away," she explained.

As cute as they looked I was not keen to stroke or hold the pups. I'd never had a pet and since leaving Bangladesh and my exposure to animals was non-existent. Being in a rural environment where animals were all around, it took me a while to even get to the point of helping my uncles tether cattle in the evenings.

I asked her if I could walk around, which she agreed to and said not to go too far. I left her and went to the *ghat*, stone steps leading into the pond and looked out onto the main road and beyond. I then walked around the pond and onto the main road. Looking up and down there was no one to be seen, except a rickshaw lazily meandering its way from the direction of the bazaar. I left the road and walked towards the bank of the Lula River. I looked up and down the dry river bed strewn with half buried boats, like the skeletal remains of cattle seen in those all too familiar images of drought stricken countries. However, the river snaked its way through a land of lush green foliage on either side. Even during the driest of dry seasons the water table in the Ganges and Brahmaputra delta was high enough to maintain a tropical lushness that often belied a drought.

My usual curious self would have had me running down the banks of the river to the other side, but not on this occasion. I didn't get any urge to explore the surroundings here and I was already feeling the need to go back to Purushpal. For one there was no one else who was my age, so no playmates and being a guest just felt awkward, as if I was being watched and I couldn't be free to come, go and do as I pleased. Putting my hands in my pocket and with my head down I walked back to the bari, hoping that Bibi and I were only going to stay for two nights. Any more would mean endlessly boring days under the watchful gaze of Nana and Nani, which was going to kill me.

Heading back to the bari I came across Uncle Babul, who was returning from the bazaar with several paper wrapped packets under his arm.

"Salaam alaikum Uncle," I greeted him, trying not to display my boredom.

"Alaikum salaam Sabu, what are you doing out here on your own?" he asked.

"I was just having a look around," I replied.

"When did you get here? And is your Bibi with you?" he continued.

"We've been here quite a while, both Bibi and Boro Dada are here."

"Well, let's go into the house," he said putting his arm around my shoulder and guiding me into the house.

He handed the shopping to Elder Mami and sat on a mura to find all the elders still seated and deep in conversation. Uncle

Babul greeted Bibi and Boro Dada and joined in on the conversation. I got up and lay back on the bed, listening to their voices as the words drifted over my head, and before I knew it I had dozed off.

I was awakened by Bibi to get up and eat lunch. I went outside to the tube-well adjacent to the kitchen, pumped some cool water to rinse my face and gulped a few handfuls. Tube-wells were the only source of clean water throughout the country and only for those who could afford to have a borehole dug. The very poor relied on drinking water from the open ponds and some even from the rivers. Dysentery, diarrhoea and waterborne illnesses were rife. In the first month or so I had my bouts of stomach aches and passing stool until I felt wafer thin and the front of my belly was inches from my spine. Little did people realise that the supposed clean water from the tube-wells contained arsenic. Decades later it would emerge that people were dying from being poisoned by the metalloid compound that existed in the ground water.

After lunch Boro Dada stayed for a while, long enough to get to his second serving of betel nut and paan, after which he headed back to Purushpal. Bibi was content with helping Nani in the kitchen and chatting about the coming monsoon, crops to plant and general matters that a ten year old had no interest in. I went with Uncle Babul to several other baris throughout the surrounding neighbourhood. I was introduced to numerous uncles, aunts, grandparents and cousins as the Londoni nephew. The ones who were old enough remembered me as a toddler, but to me they were strangers of whom I had no recollection and did not have much in common with. All the introductions went along the line of, "This is Mina's eldest son Sabu," to which everyone replied, "Are you Sabu? My, you've grown."

The greeting was followed by being asked to sit and then

glasses of orange juice or warm cow's milk were offered, the former being made from powdered orange concentrate, the taste of which was overly tangy and left a synthetic plastic sensation in the mouth. By the time we had completed our rounds my bladder was close to bursting and my taste buds were confused like the Spaghetti Junction. My mouth did not know whether to savour the spicy fried rice fritters, the sweet vermicelli, the Nabisco malted biscuits or the fake orange juice.

We headed back to Nana's bari as dusk drew in. Upon arrival Nana asked me if I would like to go with him to the bazaar to buy some fish. I took up on the offer and after Nana had said his evening prayers we headed off. Nana, with a torch in hand lit the way, stopping to say hello to numerous people on the road before we arrived into Thri-Muki Bazaar. What a contrast to earlier in the day. It was as if I had entered another world. The whole bazaar was a hive of activity, there were fishmongers squatted beside their baskets of fresh fish, sprinkling their wares with water to stop them drying out. Fruit and vegetable sellers gathered in their corner of the market. There were buyers arguing and shouting to get a better price. The only illumination was from pinpricks of oil lamps and kerosene lanterns, with the pungent smell of these burning fuels permeating the air. Restaurants were cooking fresh *parathas*, fluffy fried bread, *shingaras,* Bengali samosas and other mouth-watering delights that started a small rumbling in my belly. This was compounded as we walked by street vendors frying spicy *dhal bhora*, small lentil patties which sizzled in the huge woks they were fried in. Mouth-watering and appetising as these fried delights may have been, I could not face any more food after todays forced gluttony tour. The whole market was full of men and boys, with no women or girls present anywhere, which seemed very bizarre, as it wasn't something

I was used to back in England. This was the patriarchal world of Asia and a Muslim one at that.

We did a round of the bazaar, whereby I was introduced to even more people, but luckily they were all busy and we had fish to buy. We walked back to the fishmongers' quarter, some of who had only one type of fish and others had a variety of species to sell. Nana went for the bigger fish, namely the *chandpuri hilsha*, a kind of silvery carp, eels and catfish, all of which were from freshwater rivers. I could literally smell the river, being so far inland meant the locals never received any saltwater fish from the Bay of Bengal. Refrigerated transportation was decades away to allow Sylhetis to savour the tasty rupchanda fish from the Bay.

"Sabu, can you handle a hilsha?" he asked.

The hilsha was the national fish of Bangladesh, its popularity and fabled taste could evoke watery eyed memories and emotions in any person that hailed from this small nation. Its eggs and oil were highly prized. The fish itself, however, is literally saturated with fine, hair-like bones that if caught in the throat can prove troublesome to remove.

"Yes Nana, I can," I replied boldly.

The thing was that I enjoyed eating bony fish, having grown up on herrings and sardines back in England, therefore it wasn't a real worry for me. However, ever since I arrived everyone would try and give me the fillets of boneless fish, and then I would surprise them with my deft handling of a bony fish.

Nana went round looking at the hilsha displayed by several vendors and looked at the gills to check how fresh they were. After having chosen two fish for purchase he approached the vendor.

"So, how much are you selling these two for?" Nana enquired.

"Twenty five taka," the vendor answered, giving the impression that he wasn't interested.

"Get away miah, how much do you really want to sell it for, tell me?" Nana began bartering.

"Bhaisab, I said twenty five taka, no more, no less," the vendor replied raising his voice an octave or two.

"Look, I'll give you fifteen for the two," Nana insisted.

"Bhaisab, give me twenty two taka and you can take them," the vendor said without meeting Nana's gaze.

"If you're going to give them to me give them for eighteen and no more talking," Nana went on.

The vendor muttered under his breath and then without looking at Nana strung the two fish with reed strings through their gills and handed them to Nana who paid the man the money and we walked away without any further exchanges. With no way to store fish overnight or freeze their catch, most vendors were at the mercy of the buyers. The sellers knew they had to dispose of all the fish on the night or end up with stock that would ruin.

"Do you want anything to eat, Sabu?" Nana asked.

"No, nothing for me," I declined his offer, placing a hand on my belly.

"Let's get you some Bolaka sweets," as he headed into a general store.

"No Nana, I won't need any sweets," I resisted.

However it was to no avail, he purchased half a dozen Bolaka boiled sweets. I put them in my pocket as we headed back.

Back at the bari, Bibi, Nani and Mami were in the kitchen preparing the evening meal and when the fish arrived the three of them cleaned and prepared the hilsha in a flash. With no electricity and refrigeration the fish had to be prepared and cooked straight away. In the absence of such modern amenities the spices used to cook any food became the main preservative. As they fried the hilsha cutlets in a spicy marinade the aroma was enough to make everyone's mouth water and tummies rumble.

Dinner consisted of hilsha cutlets, fried eggs from the fish and numerous vegetable dishes, plus plain boiled rustic rice. The rice was not brown but had a reddish vein and a nutty flavour. My favourite was the fish eggs and Nani, clearly seeing that I was enjoying eating them, gave me extra servings.

After dinner everybody gathered round in the main room, except Uncle Babul who had gone out for the evening, where everyone chewed on betel nut with paan and talked about the upcoming pre-monsoon storms, the rice to be planted and other agricultural topics. I stayed in the background, occasionally interjecting where I had an interest or was asked a question. Eventually, the long day had worn me out and I was fast asleep, with the chatter of the conversations humming in the background.

The following day was uneventful except for more visits to other people's baris, this time with Nani and Bibi. I wasn't enjoying the day at all, wanting to be back in Purushpal with my peers where I could be having so much fun. By the end of the day I was like a caged panther, highly strung and dying to get out of my confinement. Bibi realised this and towards the end of the day mentioned to Nana and Nani that we would be leaving the following morning. Upon hearing this, my spirits lifted a bit and I could not wait for the night to be over.

On the morning of the third day I was up bright and early and packed my dirty shorts and tees into a jute bag and was ready to go. Having had breakfast of rice cakes and dhal I began pestering Bibi – out of earshot of Nana and Nani– as to when we were leaving. Bibi told me to be patient and that we would go shortly as Nana would accompany us to the bazaar.

It wasn't until late morning that Nana, Bibi and I left for the bazaar, even though before we left Nana, Nani, Mami and Uncle Babul all tried to make Bibi leave me behind to stay for a few more days. Bibi and especially I resisted vehemently, it was almost like waging a battle of words and tenacity. Such tug-o-war would be waged every time I visited Nana's bari and I hated going through the process. Why couldn't we simply come, stay for a day or so and leave without these battles?

I was therefore glad that we were on our way and at the bazaar we said farewell to Nana and began our journey back to Purushpal along the banks of the Lula River. However, the return journey did not include a rickshaw ride, as once we hit the intersection with the main road to Purushpal there were no bazaars nearby to hail a rickshaw. So Bibi and I walked back to Purushpal. The walk was fantastic as the journey was silent, devoid of any noise from cars, trucks or rickshaws. The silence of the countryside was beautiful, yet eerie. We walked through bazaars that showed no sign of life or noise and then under the bamboo groves that lined the edges of baris, the silence being broken only by the rustling of leaves in the wind. Eventually, after what seemed like ages we sighted our village.

Back in our own bari I let out a sigh of relief, and as Aman and the others returned from school I joined them and jumped into the pond for a rejoicing and refreshing swim.

My future visits to Nana's place were never longer than a day, I only stayed if Bibi stayed and that was usually only one night at a time. I dreaded visiting Nana's place and it wasn't until my mum arrived that I stayed for a longer period of time. Goodness knows why but I was never comfortable at Nana's bari and even to this day I do not like staying more than is necessary.

My Beautiful Bari

Even though I was starting to settle down into a life of going to school, mosque and carefree living with kids of my own age, there was more unsettling changes coming my way. My dad owned his own bari about four miles east of Purushpal on the outskirts of Beani Bazaar. He, like many other Bangladeshi men who went to England in the 1960's, believed that once they had made enough money and built themselves a nice big house in a bari of their own they would return to Bangladesh. The big dream of my dad, akin to many others, was that he would build a house for each one of his three sons and they would come and live here and be upstanding Bangladeshi citizens. Little did he and many of his generation realise that their dreams were to be shattered by the Western European influences on their children, and the fact that many of the offspring were more British than Bengali. It would also transpire that his generation did not want to spend all of their time in Bangladesh, let alone their children, who most probably would never return.

Bibi was asked by my dad to move into the property instead of leaving it vacant, to prevent any chance of squatters moving in. When I arrived the bari was being looked after by some tenants who Boro Dada had put in to ensure some human presence. It was about two months after my arrival that Bibi and I moved to Shupatola. On the day we left Purushpal we were accompanied by Boro Dada. We walked to Eid Ghah bazaar, which was the nearest market en route to Beani Bazaar. From there we caught a baby-taxi to Beani Bazaar, which took almost an interminable length of time as the ride was along the main dirt road to Beani Bazaar, with potholes and hazards primarily from cows, goats and people. Once in Beani Bazaar, Boro Dada hailed us a rickshaw and said he would meet us at our bari, as he went off to do some grocery shopping for us.

The bazaar was teeming with life as people were going about their business. Having been in a village since my arrival where I only saw various shades of green, here my sight was bombarded with colours of the rainbow, from the numerous clothes shops to the fruit and vegetable vendors. Even though the people were of one shade with varying degrees, the lunghis and shirts worn were a profusion of colour. I thought they were all going to a wedding. The striking feature of this market scene was again the absence of women. The women who were there were dressed in black burkas and it was only the girls who were visible with their colourful *shalwar kameez*, loose pants and tunics. The smells were just as exciting, with the aromas of shingaras and dhal bhora tantalising my nose, causing my stomach to grumble. However, this was overridden occasionally by the stench rising from the open sewers running parallel to the road.

The scene at the bazaar was also one of utter chaos. There were cows, goats, sheep, dogs and humans. All of them were trying to navigate the dirt roads and alleys, competing for space with rickshaws, baby-taxis and buses with unnaturally high centres of gravity; it was a miracle they stayed upright. Amongst all this the most prolific mode of transport, the motorcycles, zipped in here and out there. Wealth levels had not reached the stage where people owned cars, so the epitome of Londoni wealth was riding a Honda 125cc motorcycle. Most of these were carrying two passengers as a minimum and in some instances up to four men.

Last but not least you had the cargo carrying telagharis. They moved anything from fruit and vegetables to cement and rocks for construction. The men who pulled these were usually from extremely poor backgrounds and a lot of them from the south east of Bangladesh. The amazing thing was people, animals and vehicles all seem to do a dance around each other, without any major infractions. Of course, there was the odd cursing, shouting and yelling and it was usually the worker or the poorest fellow in the pecking order of things that got it in the neck.

Our rickshaw ride to Shupatola took about twenty minutes. The rickshaw-walla was a very dark, wiry man, his features being distinctly different from the local population, which meant that he was probably from the districts of Noakhali or Comilla. Most of the rickshaw-wallas in the area like the telaghari pullers were poor and lived hand to mouth. They were paid daily, so if they worked and if they got paid then they could eat and feed their family; if not then they went hungry. The disparity in wealth between the Sylhet district and the rest of the country was extremely stark, so much so that the district was sparsely populated. Most people were landowners, whereas in other regions of the country a high proportion of the people were tenanted farmers, squatters or slum dwellers.

As the man rode south out of the bazaar his sweat permeated through his vest soaking his back and the wind blew the smell of his sweat into my nostrils, which wasn't pleasant. Consequently, I turned my head and looked at the scenery giving my eyes a visual satisfaction not afforded to my nose. The country here was markedly different, it was hillier and the earth had a more reddish hue to it. The air was less humid and the flora seemed slightly different from the paddy fields around Purushpal.

After leaving the bazaar we took the first main right turn

into the village of Shupatola and wound our way deeper into it. The ground underneath was one of compacted sand rather than hardened clay, providing a much smoother ride. As we entered the depths of the village the hillocks on either side of the path seemed to be encroaching onto us. With the light blocked out by huge bamboo groves that leant over the path, it felt as if we were entering a dark and foreboding place from where there was no return. I looked around at the bamboo shooting high into the air as the shafts of sunshine that filtered through dappled the path with pools of light. Then all of a sudden from the corner of my eye I caught a movement in the branches of trees behind the bamboo. I looked carefully for any further movements and there it was again, something the size of a small child jumping from one tree top to another.

"What's that in the trees?" I yelled.

"Where?" Bibi looked around frantically.

"That's the local troupe of langurs," answered the rickshaw-walla.

"Really, how many of them are there?" I questioned excitedly.

"Oh! There's so many, nobody knows," replied the rickshaw-walla.

"They're mainly in this village as there are quite a few Hindu baris, and they tend to feed and care for them," added the driver.

I continued to keep an eye out for the monkeys, but did not see anymore. We came upon a small break in the overhanging bamboo and trees where we turned left down a path through which the rickshaw just about managed to squeeze along. The path wasn't very long but had less sunlight filtering through the dense foliage than the one we had just come off. I thought where on earth is our new bari? It seems a bit too far away from anything, especially as I could not see any life signs in the way of people and children. I wondered if my companions and playground were going to be monkeys and the jungle-like environment of this village. We then came out onto another path which intersected us with the new path going left and right and the whole sky opened up. In front of us was our bari.

There were no overhanging trees or bamboo to hide the light and it was a relief to see bright sunshine bouncing off the many shades of greens that I could see in front of me. However, the bari was a dense jungle and I could not make out the other end because of the abundance of trees, palms, creepers and various other plants whose Bengali names I would get to know over the coming months.

We turned right and then sharply left onto another path in between our bari's western perimeter and a neighbouring bari. We came upon the entrance on our left and the rickshaw went straight up into the courtyard. The courtyard was a deep reddish pink colour with earth walls surrounding it on all four sides, except the western and eastern ends that had entrances cut into the walls. Our new home was located along the western earth wall, a mud hut with tin roofing. I looked at it and became despaired at going from London to Purushpal and now this. Yet the excitement of possibly not going to school anymore and exploring the new bari, especially the primate and other wildlife that seemed to populate this part of the world, pushed my gloom into the dark recesses of my young mind.

The tenants, an old lady and her young daughter who were staying in the house, came out to greet us and the lady from our adjacent bari came up the path to see who had arrived. Bibi and I, having alighted from the rickshaw and paid the fare, walked into the house. We walked straight into the kitchen at the far left so we could get a drink of water. As we drank, a group of people gathered at the doorstep, watching us as if we were aliens from another planet, whispering, "This is the Londoni family that owns this place."

There were two further rooms, each with a wooden bed and there was a smaller room at the far northern end of the house where all the provisions and firewood was kept and Bibi's soon to be chicken hut. Bibi and I moved into the one room that wasn't being used and unpacked our belongings. Now that we had arrived, the tenants would leave our bari at the end of the week.

Our bari was unique in the sense that it was completely detached, with public paths encircling it. Most baris adjoined other properties, with many a squabble with the neighbours. West of us were two baris, both owners quite troublesome, the lady who came to visit, who was the friendlier of the two, her husband – Arzomond – was a quack doctor prescribing you something for anything. All the locals who could not afford a visit to the doctor in Beani Bazaar would make a trip to Arzomond, who would look them over and use his stethoscope in a very officious manner and prescribe one of a range of medicines he kept in his cabinet. Arzomond took a fondness to me and even though he was Bibi's age, he would always find time to chat and joke with me.

The other family was another story altogether, with the head of the household being Makoy Haji. They were a bit more notorious, with the man himself in jail for an attempted murder. To the east was a hillock that was empty and adjoining it was the rear of a Hindu bari, where the langurs congregated. South of us was another hill that was also occupied and to the north were the corners of three baris that backed onto the path we had approached through.

Our bari did not have any walls or fences, so the general public had a tendency to take shortcuts through it instead of going around the path. Hence, as I stood on the porch a total stranger walked into our bari, crossed the courtyard and straight on through towards the southern end. He looked at me and raised his hand as acknowledgement and moved swiftly on.

Bibi had gone into the kitchen to see what she could do in terms of fixing up something for dinner tonight. Arzomond's wife joined Bibi; her daughter who was with her was hanging around the kitchen door looking at me as I stood on the porch, taking in the lay of the land. She walked over to me and asked, "Are you from London?"

"Yes," I replied.

"How long are you going to stay here?" she questioned.

"I don't know."

"Is this your bari?" she continued.

"Yes," I answered.

"What's your name?" she continued.

"Sabu, and your name?" I returned.

"My name's Bolai."

Bolai was about my age, with a distinctly fairer complexion than mine and she was dressed akin to me in t-shirt and shorts. Both of us could have been brother and sister, but little did I know at that initial meeting she would become my best friend, accomplice and I guess you could say my second childhood crush. My first crush was at the age of about eight with a girl in my class in Worcester. She had her blond hair always tied in a ponytail and the two of us would be inseparable in class. Then, on the weekends, she would visit our house and my mum would make us sweet and savoury pastries, which she enjoyed just as much as I did. When we moved down to London in 1979 that friendship ended. I guess that is the way of life, old friendships dwindle and new ones begin, even as far flung as this one with Bolai. Bolai and I chatted away, asking each other about school and our siblings. I asked her if she would come visit and play with me, which she agreed to, saying she did not go to school and was free most days, except when doing chores for her mum.

Another person walked up the path into our bari and I recognised the familiar face of Boro Dada. With him he had a jute shopping bag in one hand, with some vegetables sticking out the top, and a hilsha fish with a string through its gills in the other. He walked up and asked, "Where's your Bibi?"

"She's in the kitchen with some people, what did you get Dada?"

"Oh! Some fish, vegetables and spices for you and your Bibi."

Bolai and her mother left shortly afterwards and whilst Bibi prepared the evening meal, Dada took me round the bari to show me what was where. The earth walls that surrounded the courtyard were about four feet high and I think that was one of the heights of the whole bari, maybe higher, because looking at the hills to the east and south I could see how high our bari probably was. The walls had old established jackfruit and lychee trees growing on top. The outside latrine was located at the south-eastern corner of the courtyard next to the lychee tree.

At the northern end of the courtyard was a dense grove of spikey *Jara Lebu*, a variety of lemon, which reminded me of the impenetrable forest of thorns surrounding Sleeping Beauty's castle. The thorns on these citrus bushes were so razor-like that only the fruit growing on the outskirts of the grove could ever be reached. The eastern wall had an opening leading to the rest of the bari, with a path running north to south. The path south led to the bari's pond and north was where a beautiful and majestic Thal palm stood in an opening, with dozens of betel nut and bay leaf trees worshipping around its base. On the eastern fringe of the bari was a grave that contained the previous owner. My dad never disturbed the grave and the deceased man's family visited occasionally to pay their respect.

As Dada showed me the grave and instructed me not to point at it as it was considered rude, the hillock beyond the eastern path was a cacophony of cackles and screams. Looking over we saw the troupe of langurs bounding down from the treetops and onto the clearing at the top of the rise, where they gathered to preen each other by picking nits from one another's bodies.

"Their leader is called Broken-handed: be careful because he can sometimes attack people," Dada informed.

"Do they come onto our bari?" I asked.

"Oh yes! They eat all the fruit that grows here," he said sadly, "Even the jackfruit and there's no stopping them."

Jackfruit was Dada's favourite fruit and our bari had an abundance of them. Behind the house on the western end there was another earth wall with an opening that led onto the main path. The wall had about half a dozen huge mango trees, their dark green leaves and trunks reaching way up into the sky. Looking up at them I could see that the trees were in full bloom with small clusters of white flowers dotted in a field of emerald leaves. At the north-eastern corner of the courtyard stood a coconut palm that had a string of young coconuts in their bright light-green hue. They would be perfect for drinking the milk in several weeks and ripen in a few months. I smiled as Boro Dada educated me about the flora and fauna of the bari. On the southern edge of the house were a couple of papaya trees that were always in fruit, but they were mercilessly raided by the langurs, even if it was to snap the young shoots off. It seemed that the monkeys got some sense of sadistic pleasure from attacking the trees willy-nilly. The trees, though, persisted, for life being about continual change, adaptation and growth meant that new shoots were not far behind and they would soon flower and fruit.

The two of us returned to the house and sat on a mura each on the porch when Bibi called us for our evening meal. It was a bit earlier than normal as Dada had to head back to Purushpal and he was going to walk back instead of going via Beani Bazaar. After the meal we said our goodbyes to Dada, but he was a regular visitor to Beani Bazaar and on each of his visits he would always stop by for lunch, dinner or even stay the night.

As the night drew in I was feeling a bit lonely and bored, having left all my uncles and aunts back in Purushpal. I sat on the porch alongside Bibi while she chatted away to the tenant lady and her teenage daughter. I looked up at the clear night sky where the moon shone brightly, flanked by an army of stars, washing the courtyard with a silvery hue. I sat there thinking about what I was going to do over the coming months; would I have to join a school here? Where I didn't know anybody, who would be my new friends? These and other questions were running through my head, answers to which I didn't know and I didn't want to ask Bibi for the fear of knowing the answers too early.

The next day brought a whole array of different people coming to our bari, having heard that the new owners who were Londonis had moved in. Even in those days, families resident in England were a rarity as it wasn't until the mid to late 1980's that a huge number of people migrated to the UK, when men reunited themselves with their families.

First to visit was Makoy Haji's wife and her son along with another boy, about my age. She arrived with a pumpkin as a gift for us, introducing herself and her son Goni. As Bibi invited her into the kitchen for some betel nut and paan I got to know Goni and his friend Beng. Goni was in his teens but it was hard to tell exactly what his age was and people in those days very rarely noted the birth dates of their children, the implication of this being no one knew how old they actually were and so nobody celebrated birthdays. Worst of all, almost all of my dad's generation and even younger men who went abroad had birth dates that were incorrect. This wasn't intentional, but without any record they had to guess as best as they could. This also applied to wives who subsequently joined these men overseas. For example, my dad's birthday was based on him being born at the start of World War Two. The exact date was not known so an arbitrary year, month and day were picked.

I guessed Goni was older than he appeared; he had a hardened look about him and with his father behind bars he was already working the family land, which didn't help him look any younger. His friend Beng was a funny looking kid, short and scrawny with big eyes and an oversized mouth. I wondered why he was called Beng, because it was the word for frog in Bengali. I could see the features similar to a frog and would be enlightened later by Goni that it was precisely why he was called Beng. Thus, the nickname stuck, I never asked what his real name was and he never offered. They introduced themselves and I also told them my name. I had the funny feeling that Goni was trying to size me up, for what I didn't have a clue.

"So will you go to school?" asked Goni.

"I don't know, my Bibi hasn't said anything yet," I replied.

"Do you two go?" I questioned.

"No!" replied Beng.

"Your bari is a great place to play and hang out," Goni commented.

"Yeah! It looks fun, I haven't had a proper look yet but I've got plenty of time."

"Where's your bari?" I asked Beng.

"It's past the mosque on the western edges of the village."

"You've got to be careful when you walk around your place, 'cos there are so many snakes," Goni added.

"Really? Have you seen any?" I asked, fascinated as well as frightened at the prospect of finding a snake.

"Well, in the bamboo grove there's a cobra, in the pond there's an adder and many others dotted around the bari," he pointed out.

"You've also got to be careful of the tree cobras around these hilly areas, they tend to hide in branches, blending in with the leaves and strike you on your head if you're unlucky," he continued.

"Yes, there are loads of snakes about and now the rains are starting they come out more," added Beng.

I wasn't really expecting this and truthfully, I was a bit scared to hear these stories, but I imagined that Goni was being a bit of a scaremonger. I took what he said with a pinch of salt; I wanted to check the facts out with Bibi first. They didn't stay long, leaving with Goni's mother who I could see had a handful of betel nuts that Bibi had given her. Other ladies popped round to see us throughout the day, each keen to know who these Londonis were and in the process making friends with Bibi. I would say my obligatory hellos and loiter in the background whilst they chewed on betel nut like cattle chewing cud.

That evening at dinner I asked Bibi about the snake stories that Goni told me, which she pretty much confirmed as true. Bibi warned me that during the monsoon I should be extra careful, she also warned me about the leeches. She told me the ones in the water were pretty nasty as they were big, black and very tenacious in their pursuit of drinking blood. Their smaller cousins can be found on land and hiding in blades of grass.

These weren't as bad as they only grew to about the size of a matchstick, but still had a voracious appetite for blood.

That night I had the heebie-jeebies truly in me and had a restless sleep tossing and turning. I had nightmares about snakes swimming with me in the pond and leeches wrapping themselves around my legs and I just could not get away from either of these critters.

The following morning I awoke groggily, feeling tired and not wanting to do much. I didn't tell Bibi about my nightmare and it wasn't until I had the first visit by Bolai before I went about getting to know the bari properly. From this day on Bolai became a permanent fixture in the bari, always alongside me, my accomplice in pursuits good, bad and indifferent.

When she arrived I explained to her about the snake stories Goni had told me, but I held back about the dreams I had as I didn't want to sound like a weakling. She said that there were snakes pretty much everywhere, but if you just stayed on the main paths and clearings it was quite safe. She also added that I should be a bit careful about Goni, which I asked her to explain. She continued saying that he carried a knife and was a bit of a trouble maker. I took note of what she said and the two of us headed off into the bari to explore further.

We went to the northern end of the bari where there was a small clearing, lower in elevation than the rest of the bari. It appeared someone had previously removed earth from here and took it elsewhere. The small clearing was surrounded by bay leaf trees and other generic trees that were used as firewood for cooking purposes. The clearing was slightly wet with small clusters of taro plants protruding from the ground.

"This is where the monkeys gather sometimes to soak up the sun and pick nits from one another," informed Bolai.

"Do they always hang around this bari?" I asked.

"That's because your bari is empty, plus the Hindu bari feed them and look out for them and then you have the hillock over there which is also empty," she explained.

We skirted the bari eastwards and treaded carefully among the high grass and prickly bushes. The abundance of bay leaf trees and betel nut palms gave the impression of the previous owner being a trader in these two cash crops. We turned into the bari towards the Thal palm and as we approached the clearing around it a smell of rotten eggs hit my nostrils.

"Aaaghh! What is that?" I made a vomiting noise.

"That's what a snake's breath smells like," replied Bolai.

I nearly jumped out of my skin, but instead froze on the spot.

"Where's the snake?" I asked darting around looking for any slithering movements in the grass.

"Don't worry about it, it's probably nowhere near us, it may be passed here a while ago," Bolai said trying to allay my fear.

I hurriedly walked into the clearing and sat down on the grass, breathing out a sigh of relief. Bolai laughed at me and fell down next to me. We lay on the grass which was carpet-like only in this clearing, whereas elsewhere the grass was like the quills on a porcupine's back.

"So how old do you think this Thal palm is?" I asked.

"I don't know, but it's been here for ever, and they say *jinns* live in some of them," she replied.

"Have you ever had a jinn get you?" I asked her.

"Not that I can remember, maybe when I was younger," she answered.

Jinn, another word taken from Arabic and brought over by the Muslim conquerors, the Mughals and the Arab traders and proselytisers who came over during their reign. Jinns were evil spirits that were said to occupy certain types of trees, usually the old gnarly ones like the Banyan. They were also found in unclean areas and preyed on the innocence to possess their souls. It was said that some were of the mischievous variety, playing games at night like running across the tin roofs of houses or throwing stones at them. Such stories were passed on through the generations and I had my fair share from my uncles and aunts ever since I had arrived.

The two of us lay there for a while not saying anything, time seemed to stand still. Even though in my current situation I had no concept of time except getting up in the morning, going to bed when tired and the dining times in between.

After a while we got up and the two of us carried on heading towards the pond, before which lay the grave and a ditch on our left. To me the ditch looked pretty big, about thirty feet square and four feet deep, with sloping sides. There was about an inch or so of water at the bottom with taro plants at the edge. The surface of the water was speckled with dry bamboo leaves that the wind had blown in.

"You've got to be careful there Sabu, people have seen snakes in there," she warned.

"Let's not hang about here then," I said quickly as we walked past the grave and to the ghat of the pond.

We skirted the pond's western end and walked towards the southern path, past the bamboo grove on our right.

"Now, there's a dangerous place," Bolai pointed at the bamboo grove. The bamboo looked foreboding and uninviting and I was in no hurry to go venturing in there. "There are several cobras in this bamboo grove," she stated, not appearing too worried about the possibility of coming across one.

I was impressed by Bolai's coolness at all the danger around us and I was glad to have her as my buddy whilst I trekked around my bari. Beyond the bamboo grove there was a four foot drop and another pond which was covered in dark green water hyacinth. The pond looked as if someone had taken a chunk out of the rectangular shape of our bari.

It wasn't until many years later that our family found out how Makoy Haji had forcibly 'stolen' the corner from the previous owners by erecting a fence and then digging the pond and claiming it as his own. The true owners did not bother to argue with Makoy Haji, as to get it back would mean either fighting the man or greasing the palms of the police, the courts and a whole host of other 'middlemen'.

The two of us walked past the pond and onto the southern path, which was really a stream with clear cool water running towards the Lula River. Even in the dry season there was water in the stream, and I guessed there must have been a natural spring somewhere in the surrounding hills that acted as the source. We followed the stream west, walking past Makoy Haji's bari where we saw Goni tethering two cows on a pasture field.

"What are you two doing?" Goni shouted.

We jumped over the small drainage canal onto the field.

"Nothing, we're just walking around seeing things," I replied.

"I'm showing Sabu around his bari and the surroundings," Bolai added.

"What are you up to then?" I asked.

"I'm off to the fields after this, got a lot of work out there to be done," he replied. "Come round sometime, the both of you," he offered. With that he headed towards his bari and we continued on our way back onto the path following the stream.

"Do you go to his bari that much?" I asked Bolai.

"Only with my mum, never on my own," she said in a wary tone.

"I don't think I will go to his place either," I added.

With my second interaction with Goni, my gut instincts told me to stay well clear of the boy and quietly I promised myself that I would avoid any prolonged dealings with him. We walked further west along the path for a while, occasionally seeing farmers carrying their plough on their shoulders, walking behind their bullocks, steering them with a bamboo stick. There was also the odd vendor of fresh vegetables or fish carrying his wares in two baskets attached at either ends of a bamboo pole, which he carried on his shoulders. The men carried the goods with such ease and grace, bouncing up and down under the weight of the load. They made the task of carrying heavy loads look so simple.

The deeper we went in to the village, the darker and more dense the foliage seemed to get. The baris and their houses were barely visible from the paths, the only sign of life was the odd cockerel crowing, the quacking of a duck or the mooing of a cow. Our walk deeper into the village revealed baris that were distinctly poorer, with some buildings only constructed of bamboo and roofs made from dried palm fronds. Where we came across the odd adult they would stand and stare, particularly at me. After a while the two of us decided to turn back and return to my bari. I was surprised how at ease I was with Bolai and the two of us walked and talked, or not, as if we were old friends. She was the first true friend I had and the relationship was easy without any complications or stress.

"Where have you two been all morning?" Bibi questioned worriedly, as we entered the courtyard.

"Nowhere in particular, just here and there," I answered with a smile.

"Your Nana's here and he's been waiting for ages."

With that Bolai scooted off to her bari, saying that she would come by later. I wasn't too keen on seeing my Nana, not that I didn't like him or anything, it's just that he would ask me to go with him to Sreedhara, which I wasn't keen on at all. I sullenly followed Bibi into our bedroom, where on the edge of the bed sat Nana chewing on betel nut.

"Salaam alaikum Nana," I greeted.

"Alaikum salaam Sabu, are you well?" he smiled.

"Yes Nana, I am good, how is Nani?" I asked.

"Ah! She's coping well, she's longing to see you," he added.

I knew what was coming and I avoided adding any further comments to that by taking a biscuit from the plate set for Nana and munching on it. Having realised I wasn't going to offer to visit, Nana continued.

"Have you heard from your mum?"

"No, not lately, I guess they're good," I replied, adding their wellbeing status before being asked.

"Do you long for your brothers and sister?" he asked.

"Yes, a little bit I guess," I did not know what to say, because yes, I was missing them, but I could not do anything about it and I was getting asked the same old questions again and again, not only by Nana, but all and sundry.

I felt like a bit of a lemon hanging around waiting for the inevitable question. The thing was I had a special bond with Bibi, with her being my paternal grandmother it was only natural, but with my maternal grandparents, my memories before going to England are very scant. Then to come back after four years the connections were even weaker than before. I guess from their point of view I will always be the five year old grandson they put on the plane to London all those years ago.

Eventually the question did arise, whereby Nana asked me to go with him to Sreedhara. I looked to Bibi to save me, who turned to me and said.

"Do you want to go?"

"No! I don't feel like it, I'll go another time," I squirmed.

"Come on Grandson, you will be back after two or three days," he requested.

"I'll go with Bibi soon," I replied, because by going with Bibi it usually meant we would be back by evening.

"Bhaisab, I will take him and go in a few days' time," Bibi said, coming to my aid.

I think by this time Nana realised his pleas would be futile so agreed to Bibi's suggestion. I let out a silent sigh of relief as the pressure lifted from my shoulders. Bibi and Nana continued chatting and I dawdled until he left just after midday. Afterwards, Bibi turned around to me and asked, "Why don't you want to go to your Nana's bari?"

"I just don't enjoy it there, it's boring," I replied.

"Well, we're going to have to go in a few days' time," she added as she went off to do some chores around the bari.

The Wedding Jamboree

Uncle Naz, on the other hand, had been busy with his wedding and had found a bride to marry. He stopped by one day to see our new bari and announced his upcoming wedding date. Even though the wedding invitation wasn't needed, the official invitation would however come from his parents to Bibi.

It was another hot, sunny afternoon when he dropped by, bringing with him his signature generosity of fruits and biscuits and some sweets for me. Bibi made him a cup of tea accompanied with some Nabisco glucose biscuits, which he took sitting on a mura on our porch.

"So Sabu, it's been a while since I saw you, how are you?" Naz asked.

"Good Uncle, it's a bit lonely here but it's fun," I replied.

"Have you heard anything from your mum and dad?" he enquired.

"No, not so far," Bibi replied.

"See son, your mum and dad have already forgotten about you," he joked.

"Ha ha! No Uncle, they'd never forget me," I laughed nervously.

"You know son, you're not really your dad's son, we found you as a baby and he decided to bring you up," he jibed.

"Nooo!" I retorted.

This banter was a standing routine between Naz and I. Almost every occasion he saw me after some time he would start the joke. It would not be until I was a teenager that he stopped it. I never minded as I knew it was one of his ways of showing his affection for me. With that he dunked a biscuit into his tea and took a bite.

"Auntie, my wedding has been set in two weeks' time," he told Bibi.

"Maashallah, where is the bride from?" Bibi congratulated.

"She's from Koshba, and her family is of good stock."

It was very important that a potential bride was of good standing and from a good family. Even though there wasn't a distinct caste system, people knew which families to get brides for their sons and marry their daughters into.

"So, Sabu will I see you at the wedding?" he asked me.

"I will definitely go Uncle," I beamed.

Bibi looked over and stated, "You've never been to a wedding, have you Sabu?"

"No Bibi," I replied.

I had never been to a wedding before, let alone one in Bangladesh, so this was going to be fun and interesting to say the least. Uncle Naz stayed a while longer and then after popping a small packet of betel nut and paan into his mouth he left just as suddenly as he had arrived. As he walked down the path I ran across to Bolai's bari. I found her standing on the porch outside her kitchen. I ushered her over and we both ran off into the depths of my bari and then over to the eastern hill.

Two weeks later Bibi and I headed back to Purushpal for the wedding. Our journey on foot was the first of many that Bibi and I would take back and forth between Shupatola and Purushpal. The route took us out through the western end of Shupatola over a bamboo crossing spanning the Lula River. These bamboo bridges, used for centuries on the subcontinent, were a treacherous way to cross a body of water for the uninitiated like me, as well as the experts. The bridges were one or two bamboo poles wide on an x-shaped support of two bamboos set several feet apart across a river. You had to cross by removing your sandals and carrying them on one hand, then using the free hand to hold the bamboo rails running at waist height along the bridge and also manage somehow to carry any other possessions you might have with you. This difficulty was compounded whenever it rained and the bamboo bridge was slippery as an eel. Over the coming months there were times when I slipped and fell into the water before getting a true handle on crossing such bridges. Fortunately, those times that I did fall, I either fell in shallow waters or managed to get back on shore safely.

Once we crossed the bridge we walked along the raised edges of paddy fields until we hit a small, elevated dirt track that ran past a collection of mud huts, surrounded by banana plants and coconut palms. Eventually, the track joined the main road between Purushpal and Beani Bazaar. We continued walking along the main road until we passed Battar Bazaar. There were three bazaars en route to Purushpal: firstly it was Battar Bazaar, followed by the biggest which was Mathiura and then finally, the small Eid Ghah. During the trip Bibi, akin to all womenfolk when out travelling, carried an umbrella that served two purposes. One was to provide protection from the sun but also as soon as they walked into a bazaar, the women would shield themselves from the menfolk by pointing the umbrella in the men's direction. Battar Bazaar was closed today with none of the usual hustle and bustle of trading. Bibi explained that most of the smaller bazaars opened on specific days. Shops would be open selling general goods, but when market days were held then everything was available to purchase, from livestock to farm equipment.

Once past the bazaar, we were joined on our right by the Mathiura River, which ran parallel on our journey and escorted us into the market. Here the market was open every day and today I could see cattle tethered to posts, with vendors and buyers haggling over price. The fishmongers displayed their catch of the day on the bamboo baskets and many fruit and vegetable sellers squatted on mats with their wares on display. The edge of the market which we skirted along was lined with majestic hardwoods, under which other traders sold betel nuts and paan or cigarettes from briefcase size boxes.

There was one noticeable element to these bazaars and this was the lack of beggars compared to Sylhet town and the airport. Walking past the bazaars I could see the odd one or two beggars, but they didn't seem to be pestering anyone. There was one man underneath a tree with legs unnaturally misshapen, sitting on a mat, wearing a lunghi, kameez shirt and a topi with a begging bowl in front of him. The sight of him was disturbing for me as I had not seen such a sight since my arrival at Sylhet airport.

Once past the bazaar we walked towards Pursuhpal with the river still on our right and the baris of Mathiura to our left. We finally walked through the Eid Ghah bazaar, before arriving at the western edge of Mathiura village. Mathiura, in comparison to Purushpal, was a sizeable village approximately five or six times bigger, and as far as I can remember there was a bitter rivalry between the two. The two villages would hold football matches where fights would break out, or bull fights with the victor claiming a win for the village rather than a personal triumph.

In Purushpal we walked through the village and past the school. I consciously walked with Bibi on my left so as to shield myself from the school and the teacher who I thought could easily see me. Even though this fear of being caught by the teacher was unfounded, every time I walked past the school during a school day I would ensure I wasn't recognisable or seen. I just did not want to go back to school, no matter what.

Arriving into the bari was like entering a funfair with numerous relatives who had come early for Naz's wedding. There were Bibi's two sisters, Kutina who had five sons and two daughters, all of whom except two had arrived. Merzaan's children were adults now and would arrive nearer the day, even though she still had a daughter-in-law and a grandchild in tow. There were children everywhere you looked and adults either telling them off, feeding them or sending them on an errand. As Bibi and I walked up the path into the bari, one of my teenage aunts shouted "Sabu's arrived!" and then all of a sudden an army of people came out of the kitchen, calling out to me and Bibi. This announcement of our arrival became a clarion call. Whenever we visited it fell on the first person to see us coming up the path to shout out my name.

The wedding was on a Friday and the groom and his family would make the trip to the bride's village to perform the Muslim marriage rites and formal wedding celebration, as well as bring the bride back. This first trip was known as the Borjatra. The second half of the wedding was the following day, whereby the bride's family would come to the groom's village for another celebration. This wasn't as lavish or as big but still had significance. It was known as the Walima. Both days involved the slaughtering of a cow or two, depending on the number of people, dozens of chickens, cooked with pounds of potatoes and onions, spices and masala to make cauldrons of curries for the guests.

In the Bengali wedding tradition, when a man gets married it is usually his accompanying younger brothers, sisters and cousins who have the most fun. His soon to be wife will become the youngster's bhabi, and more of a friend than a sister-in-law. So they are the ones who carry out pranks, tell jokes and mess about in general at the wedding because it is expected. I, on other hand, being a nephew could not get involved in such revelry and had to watch from the side line or play with kids my age.

When I had put my travel belongings away and changed into my less formal shorts and t-shirt, I was off with Aman and the other boys into the pond for a swim. I had missed swimming and splashing around in the water for hours with the boys. The pond back in Shupatola was not big enough and there weren't that many children to provide the crowd size required for a good swim coupled with fun and games.

When the big day arrived, I woke up with an attitude of a grizzly bear just out of hibernation and I just did not want to be in Purushpal. I didn't feel much like getting dressed up and going off to a wedding. To put it mildly I had a frown and walked around with a scowl and a bad attitude all morning. I really don't know what came over me, but a depression the size Mount Everest was shadowing me.

Most of the people had left the bari and gone to Naz's to get him ready and prepared for the trip to his in-law's village. Bibi was trying to cajole me into getting dressed and going to Naz's place.

"Come on Sabu, get ready, what will your uncle say if you don't go?" Bibi pleaded.

"I just don't feel like it, you go I will be OK," I tried to excuse myself.

"What are you talking about? You have to go," Bibi trying to get angry at me.

However, Bibi loved me too much to get truly angry or to force me to do anything, and I suppose that was the power I had. Hence, I wasn't going to budge from my standpoint of not wanting to go. I felt sorry for Bibi as I was being a manipulative, spoilt brat. I knew that what I was doing was wrong but I could not shake off the melancholy and obstreperous attitude. Bibi was too patient and kind, but she must have thought, *what on earth is the matter with this boy, today of all days?* I guess this was the first time she had seen me like this, therefore did not know how to deal with it.

Eventually she gave up and sent Aman to Naz's bari as a messenger, to say that I wasn't coming to his wedding. This also didn't bother me much as I knew Uncle Naz wouldn't get mad at me either. So Naz turned up in his lunghi and shirt around mid-morning. He was yet to have a bath and get into his outfit for the wedding. I was standing on the porch looking out towards the entrance of the bari, waiting for anyone to come along for a showdown akin to ones held at the OK Corral. When I saw Naz I stood fixed to the spot, determined that I was not going to budge come hell or high water.

"What's the matter Sabu, are you not coming to your uncle's wedding?" he asked, annoyed that here he was on his wedding day, having to cajole a ten year old to come to his wedding.

"No Uncle, I don't feel like going, you go and I'll see you once you're back," I replied impudently.

"What are you talking about? How can I go to my wedding when you will not go, what will I tell your parents? I am supposed to be looking after you just as much as your Bibi," he said in a voice that was rising a decibel or two.

I dug my heel in now and said "No Uncle, I am not going to go," and started walking off out onto the path leaving the bari.

"Listen son, you're going to come to the wedding, I say," Uncle Naz said loudly, almost on the verge of shouting.

By this time my temper had risen and I had reached the end of the bari's path where I turned right at the end and headed off towards the fields. Uncle Naz started following me with Bibi in tow, when I saw him approach I sprinted down the embankment and off into the fields which had been ploughed since I was here last. However, my little legs could only take me so far before Naz, who had given chase, grabbed me by the scruff off my neck brought me to a halt.

"Let me go," I yelled, as I tried to twist free of Naz's grasp. "Leave me alone," I continued. "I don't want to go to no wedding," I shouted at the top of my voice.

"Listen son, don't do this to me, you are such a good kid, what will people say if they heard you did this and it got back to your parents," he warned.

I had calmed down a bit as it was futile trying to break free. I thought about what Naz had said, I wasn't going to school which was bad enough. I suspected my parents were aware of this and would question me about it. So to have this further misbehaviour reported back to them would not help my cause. As Naz continued to plead with me to get back to the bari and get ready for the wedding, I carried on thinking about the consequences of my actions. I could almost hear my grey matter whirring and cranking away upstairs.

"OK Uncle," I grumbled lowly under my breath as I looked at my feet trying not to meet his gaze.

"I will get you some presents and toys when I visit your bari next time," he offered.

The bribe did not really appeal to me but rather my perceived admonishment from my parents pretty much did the trick. I could see Bibi standing at the embankment with a crowd of kids and elders that had gathered to see this unprecedented event. Nobody had ever heard of a groom on his wedding day running out into the paddy fields to coax a ten year old boy to come to his big day.

Naz, with his arms around my shoulders, I guess more to prevent me from running away again rather than affection, steered me back to the bari. At the path he handed me over to

Bibi and dashed back to his bari, where everyone was waiting for him to get ready to depart. Bibi and I went back into the house, where I got ready begrudgingly. Even though Bibi wouldn't accompany the wedding party, she would remain at Uncle Naz's bari along with her sisters.

All I heard from Bibi was, "Did you really have to do this? It is shameful behaviour."

I did not respond to it, after which I never heard any more about the incident. Bibi and I shortly arrived at Uncle Naz's bari where there was a crowd of people surrounding three men in the middle of the courtyard. There was a hubbub of advice and corrections from numerous people to the three men. Bibi left me and walked towards the western end of the courtyard where the women folk were standing on the porch of the kitchen, watching the goings-on.

I looked for Aman, Iqbal and a few other uncles, who were near the centre watching the three men. I wriggled my way into the centre and I took a position beside Iqbal, where I saw two men I didn't recognise dressing Naz in his wedding outfit.

I turned to Iqbal and asked, "Who are they?"

"Oh! They're Naz's friends, it's their job to dress him up," he answered.

Naz was standing on a bamboo mat and at his feet were his light cotton tunic, a three-quarter length Nehru coat and a pair of pants known as a *Punjabi*. There was also a pair of Aladdin slippers with curled ends and a hat with a fan at the front. As he stood there in his lunghi and a white vest, his exposed arms and face had a yellowy orange glow from the Gaye Holud ceremony from the previous night, where younger female cousins and sisters would have daubed him with turmeric paste to give his skin a fresh, golden glow.

One of his friends picked up the tunic and put it over Naz's head, whilst his other friend took the Punjabi and gave it to him to wear. Naz sheepishly pulled the pants under his lunghi without trying not to expose too much of his legs to the onlookers. The remainder of his wedding garb went on painstakingly slowly, then finally the hat went on and a chair was provided for him to sit on. It was coming up to noon and the sun was reaching its zenith. Naz looked like a man being sent to the gallows rather than his wedding. He had a long, distant stare and appeared frightened. He was also sweating profusely from the heat and I guessed his nervousness compounded the perspiration.

Naz's father shouted, "Hey! Someone bring an umbrella over here," as the beads of sweat rolled down Naz's brow, which he continuously dabbed with his handkerchief.

Then came a glass of milk brought over by a young female cousin of Naz. He drank it in a couple of gulps whilst his father Ali hovered in the background, wanting to get on the road to get to Koshba.

Eventually, it was time to go and a general confusion began as to who was going where and who was to walk alongside the groom. Boro Dada was there to lend a hand, he directed Naz to pay his respects to his mother, Bibi, his other aunts and his grandmother. He went over to them sitting on the kitchen porch and touched their feet with his right hand which he then placed on his forehead. He was then led by Boro Dada and his father at the head of the procession, accompanied by his two friends and then the rest of the wedding party. The party comprised mainly of men and some younger female cousins of Naz who were towards the rear of the procession. We walked out of Naz's bari, past the school and over the bridge onto the main thoroughfare, where a decorated rickshaw was waiting for Naz. He got on with his two friends, who squeezed beside him. As the rickshaw trundled away on the uneven, sun-baked dirt road the rest of the party began walking to Mathiura, where several cars and people carriers were waiting. Looking back I could see Naz's mother, Bibi and other womenfolk on the bridge with tears in their eyes as they bid farewell.

In Mathiura people packed into the vehicles beyond their design capacity as villagers from Mathiura came out to look at the commotion at the doorsteps of their baris. Once everyone was in a vehicle the motor cavalcade headed in the direction of Beani Bazaar. I was sardined with Aman, Iqbal and a few other people into one of the cars, and even though the windows were fully open the heat within was unbearable. When we arrived at Beani Bazaar the procession stopped, so that everyone could say Zuhr prayers in the central mosque. All the travellers exhaled a sigh of relief and fanned themselves to cool down once outside the vehicles. Having said their prayers the party jumped back into the people carriers and continued northwards out of the bazaar.

At the bride's bari the vehicles all parked wherever they could, whilst a lookout party of young children alerted everyone that the groom had arrived. At the entrance to the bari the bride's younger brother and other young male relatives had set up a gate and the groom had to pay the gatekeeper to gain access. This was a cultural ritual and was intended to give the youngsters some fun. Naz, having arrived at the gate, had to haggle to get into the bari. This was performed by his two friends who bartered on his behalf to gain access without paying the fee, which was a couple of hundred takas. The haggling and bartering increased in intensity with some of the older men in the groom's party requesting to end it all and let us through. Finally, one of Naz's friends paid half the requested sum and shoved past the gatekeepers.

Once inside the bari we were all directed towards the courtyard, where a tent had been erected and lined with tables in long rows. At one end of the tent was the main stage, where

Naz would sit with his two friends by his side. All the guests began seating themselves, with everyone trying to vie for a position nearer to the stage. There were other guests from the bride's side who also began seating themselves. I could see Boro Dada and Grandpa Ali mingling with the elders as they all sat together, dressed in identikit outfit of lunghi, a white tunic and the topi on their heads. The guests were all greeted by the elder male relatives of the bride with whom they hugged twice, one on each side and said their salaams. I sat down with Iqbal, Aman and several other youngsters, namely brothers and cousins of Naz. There were some young girls seated about with their dads or brothers but not many: this was a male dominated wedding party akin to most Bengali weddings. Most of the women were within the confines of the various houses surrounding the tent. With the elders sat the local Imam, who was given instructions on the wedding vows that uncle Naz had to declare.

When everyone else had sat down and there was a general hum of conversation going on, Boro Dada, the Imam and a few others made their way to the stage. Once there they sat down and the Imam asked everyone to be quiet as the vows were to be read by Naz. The same process was being performed by the bride in a room in one of the houses. As a hush settled across the gathering the Imam began reading the vows in Bengali and asked Naz to repeat after him, which he did, a bit uncomfortably. With the vows over the Imam began the prayer, where everyone joined him with raised hands, cupped at chest level and lowered their gaze in humble reverence of Allah. The Imam began to recite a prayer in Arabic followed by some prayers in Bengali blessing the couple, their families and their future life together.

The prayer was over with everyone saying amen and thus followed a mad, panicked rush as several people – from the bride's side – dashed out of the tent to start serving the food. In came bowls of water to wash hands, dishes of plain rice, meat curries, chicken curries and small plates of lebu and chillies. Others brought in jugs of water and glasses. As soon as the food was placed on the table the guests tucked in voraciously with their hands, wolfing down the food as if there was no tomorrow. The scene was one I had never seen before; it was as if everyone had saved themselves for this meal and that if they didn't eat fast enough the food would go. People ate the rice and curry heartily and devoured every scrap of food they helped themselves to. There were some who had a green chilli in their left hand which they crunched on, they were the ones regularly wiping their brows just in time to stop the sweat dripping onto their plates. Others bit into the lebu wedges and you could see the grimace on their face as the tanginess of the citrus fruit hit their taste buds.

Soon enough the sweet yoghurt desserts arrived, even though some people were still eating their main meal. The whole affair seemed a bit hurried, the hosts bringing everything in at once so as not to give the impression that the guests had to wait for the food.

However, Naz, on the other hand, got a sumptuous dish of several roasted chickens with pilau rice, boiled eggs, several curries and salad. He was timidly nibbling at the chicken bits, sweat dripping down his forehead whilst his two friends ripped away at a drumstick here and wing there. I guess the magnitude of the event and the day itself had taken Uncle Naz's appetite away. He looked distinctly frightened and overwhelmed, I'd never seen him like this ever, nor would I ever again see him so lost.

One by one people finished their meals and tucked into the compulsory betel nut and paan. In those days video cameras were non-existent and there were no professional cameramen in Beani Bazaar, so the recording of this momentous occasion for Naz was left to the amateur photographers from both sides of the wedding. The cameramen were young male relatives from both sides who were dressed in tight, multi-coloured shirts with fly-away collars and slightly flared trousers. They could have been picked straight out of a seventies disco, though I suppose the year being only 1980 it was going to take a few more years before the fashion of the west caught up with them.

For what seemed like an eternity people lingered about doing nothing, strolling here and there, consuming more betel nut and paan. My uncles and I went about running into the houses around the bari and just being riotous in general. Not knowing the next stage in the ceremony, I suddenly glimpsed out of one of the corners of the tent a group of people approaching, huddled around a lady dressed in a red and gold sari. They walked gingerly towards the stage and she was sat next to Naz, his friends having been banished from his sides.

Once the bride was seated by Naz's side a long procession of immediate family and cousins began to take their seats beside the bride and groom to feed them *Gulab Jamun* and *Rasgulla*, extremely sugary sweets made from milk curd and cheese respectively, whilst the would-be David Baileys continued to snap away. By this time I was really getting bored, the fascination of the wedding was over for me and I wanted to get back home. Fortunately, the whole affair was coming to a close as early evening drew in.

Once all the various people had fed sweets to both Uncle Naz and his wife and the photographs were taken, then after much discussion and what seemed to me like pointless toing-and-froing, the word started to spread that we were leaving. Just like the arrival and consumption of the meal, the departure was just as crazy and hectic. There were orders being shouted to get the groom into the car, children being pulled here and there to ensure that none were left behind. With the sun already behind the tops of the palm trees the move to get going was being sped up by Grandpa Ali and Boro Dada.

Uncle Naz slowly started to make his way towards the car, with people chaperoning him. The people carriers outside the bari were started by the drivers in eager anticipation of departure, whilst the bride, as she sobbed and cried, was carried by one of her brothers to Naz's car. She was accompanied by one of her younger sisters and cousins to comfort her during the journey. The bride's mother and father along with other close members of her family stood outside the bari and wept as our procession drove off. Behind us a train of telagharis were carrying all the dowry presents that were being gifted by the bride's family. The dowry contained wooden beds, wardrobes, dressing tables, chairs and a whole host of other furniture items made of fine hardwood. The gold dowry was being worn by the bride, which consisted of an intricately designed necklace, bangles and earrings.

We retraced our route back through Beani Bazaar, where shop keepers lit their oil lanterns as night fell. Once we crossed the Lula River it was pitch black as with no street lighting of any sort the darkness seemed to swallow us whole. The next illumination we came across was at Mathiura Bazaar, which was busy as market goers went about their business. The customary tooting of the horns was used to clear the narrow road. Once we passed Eid Ghah bazaar we had to continue the remainder of the journey by foot. Almost everyone had a torch to light the way; those who didn't stuck close by to the light bearers. I held onto Boro Dada's hand to get an extra surety of where I was treading. This, being the first time I had travelled late at night, was quite exciting, even though a bit treacherous as snakes or other night creatures could be lying across the path. All around us we could hear the croaking of bullfrogs warning us of the upcoming storms before the onset of full monsoon.

The bride, who had boarded a *phalki* – a wedding carriage carried by four men – once we had left the motorised vehicles, determined the speed at which we travelled, which was quite slow. We arrived at Naz's bari where all the womenfolk were waiting with abated breath to see the new daughter-in-law of the house. As the wedding party crowded into the bari the bride was taken to the specially prepared bedstead with flowers and decorations adorning the whole structure in Uncle Naz's room. I, on the other hand, was desperately tired and sought out Bibi, who took me into the kitchen and gave me my evening meal. As I was finishing my meal Iqbal came by.

"Uncle Sabu, come with me and meet your new aunt," he asked. Even though he was a year or so older than me it was perfectly normal for him to call me uncle.

I followed him out of the kitchen and across the courtyard, into the house where Naz's wife was on display for all the relatives, villagers and well-wishers to see. There were so many people in the room, where my new aunt sat on the bed in her full wedding splendour. I could see Aman beside Amin and Kukon, two of Naz's brothers and some of my aunts, who were all joking and chatting with their new bhabi.

"Hey Sabu, go up to your new auntie and give her a slap on her back," Iqbal said mischievously.

"Why Uncle, I'll get into trouble," I questioned.

"Don't worry, everyone's done it, so it's your turn," he egged.

Aman and a few others came over.

"Yes Sabu, it's your turn, come on," they pushed me towards Naz's wife.

So not wanting to feel left out I got onto the bed and crawled nearer to the bride. I sat there pondering what I was about to do and trying to pluck up enough courage to do so. Then someone distracted the bride and she looked away momentarily, so I took the opportunity to slap the bride square on her back. She screamed and turned around to grab me as I scampered away but stopped in mid-reach as aunt Runi, Boro Dada's eldest daughter, said to her.

"That's Sabu, he's your nephew who came over with your husband."

I darted off the bed and out of the room whilst Iqbal, Aman and the others howled with laughter. As I ran off I could hear all the women folk and the girls joining in on the laughter, however I could not see the funny side and was wondering what trouble I had got into now.

I went back out into the courtyard, face flushed with mild embarrassment. I saw Uncle Naz on the kitchen porch in a more relaxed outfit of lunghi, shirt and sandals. He beckoned me over and, as I hoped, nobody came out of the house after me.

"So son, what are you up to, did you enjoy yourself today?" he asked.

"Yes Uncle, it was quite fun," I replied, trying not to look too guilty of the slap I had inflicted on his wife. "When are you going back to London?" I asked.

"Let's see how things go, I'm looking at taking your auntie with me, which could be a while," he replied.

We were joined by some of his friends who he turned his attention to. Bibi then came out of the kitchen and I froze with fear of being reprimanded for my misdemeanour. Either Bibi did not know or she realised that I was tricked into it, but she did not say anything about the slapping.

"Let's go Sabu, your Old Auntie is alone," Bibi started.

"Stay for a while longer," interjected Uncle Naz, hearing of our departure.

"No Naz, we should go, we'll come tomorrow morning," Bibi replied.

"OK, see you tomorrow Sabu," he said, looking towards me.

Boro Dada also accompanied us with his torch and Bibi had an oil lantern too. As we crossed the bridge and turned left onto the path heading towards our bari, coming up on our right we could see the first of the telaghari pullers arriving with the dowry gifts.

It had been a very long day and an interesting introduction to my first ever wedding. Back at our bari Bibi went off to do her ablutions and say her evening prayers, whilst I made my way to bed. I crawled onto the hard wooden beds, which were waist high and softened with a couple of layers of blankets. Even though it was no match for a comfortable mattress bed back in England I was so tired that I could have slept on the hard, earthen floor. Old Auntie was in the adjacent bed saying her prayers and as I drifted off to sleep I could hear Bibi rustling her prayer mat and unfurling it on the floor. Falling asleep, little did I realise that the slapping incident coupled with my shenanigans in the morning would make a mini legend of me in the eyes of young and old alike. It became the highlight of the wedding and would even be retold to Naz's children years later.

Mango Fool

The following day was the Walima, which saw the second half of the wedding party, this time at Naz's bari. Everyone from our bari attended and fortunately I was able to enjoy it a bit more as the surroundings were more familiar and it was home territory.

The Walima was the flip side of the visit we had made on the wedding day. This time the party of people arriving from Uncle Naz's in-laws was smaller and again everyone was dressed in their best clothes. There was another feast of curries and rice and the obligatory sweets and yoghurt desserts. The whole affair was quieter and over quicker. It seemed people were still recovering from the excessive consumption of the previous day, even though a lot of food was still tucked away in as many bellies. Aman and I returned back to our bari pretty much immediately after eating. The day was nice and sunny and we wanted to get some swimming done. We were joined by his brother Amad and it wasn't until Bibi, searching for me, shouted out my name from the back of the house that we emerged from the water.

Bibi and I stayed a few more days. It gave her an opportunity to catch up with her two sisters Kutina and Merzaan. They were both younger and with Merzaan living nearer to Sylhet, Bibi rarely saw her. Kutina lived east of Beani Bazaar, though not too far by distance, they too hardly saw each other. As I was now a visitor there was no need for me to go to school or mosque. Whilst Aman and Iqbal were at school I would wander out onto the fields or play with Amad and some of the younger kids in the bari.

One day after the two uncles had come back from school we were out playing in the northern fields, when we saw a huge commotion to the east of us. There was a group of people making their way slowly towards us and from what we could make out a bull was being escorted by the horde. There seemed to be a tension in the air and it was quite frightening, to say the least.

"What's going on?" I asked of Iqbal.

"Aaah! We're going to have a bull fight," he said with a whooping howl.

He could not finish his sentence as we turned to the west and saw a man running trying to restrain a bull on a leash. He was also followed by a throng of people who were shouting, yelling and making all sorts of noises. The man managed to bring the bull to a slow canter, while the animal let out a war bellow. The western mob rushed past us and headed towards the crowd coming from the east.

"That's the Purushpali bull and the one coming over there is from Mathiura," Aman explained.

We started to run behind the Purushpali crowd, the ploughed earth was not making the sprint easy and frequently someone fell down. Some of them even lost their lunghi, exposing their decency. Nobody cared though as the fight was more important than losing one's clothes.

The bulls were of the Zebu variety and both were black with the signature humps on their shoulders. By now both parties had reached each other and there was no distinguishing who was with which bull. Both creatures bellowed at each other and the supporters of each were poking them with nails on their rump; I presumed to get the animals angry and aggressive, which worked pretty well. Then all of a sudden they were let go and what sounded like rock smashing on rock as the two animals hammered their skulls together. They immediately locked horns as they twisted and turned trying to get an advantage over each other.

This created a dangerous situation where men and boys were close to being trampled underfoot. I stayed well out on the fringes of the melee with Aman, whilst Iqbal was in the thick of it somewhere. I could see steam rising from the bulls' nostrils and clods of earth being kicked up by their hind legs. The men shouted and yelled with the boys joining in.

The battle went on for what seemed like ages, with the bulls locking and unlocking their horns again and again. Each time, the crash of skulls made me cringe, thinking they must be dead or their heads split wide open. Then all of a sudden there was a feeble cry as the Mathiura bull gouged the neck of his opponent. The cut wasn't serious but enough for the Purushpali bull to concede defeat then turn and run west with the owner running after it. The victor let out an almighty bellow and his supporters screaming, shouting and jumping up and down with joy.

Just as quickly as the fight occurred it vanished, leaving no trace but fresh kicked up earth. As the two creatures and their patrons headed in the opposite direction the three of us headed back to our homes with our feet caked in dirt and our whole bodies covered in flecks of mud.

The next day Bibi and I departed Purushpal, taking with us Auntie Rani, one of Boro Dada's daughters. She was a year or so older than me and as chatty and lively as a babbling brook. As we departed, Kutina invited Bibi and I to their bari one day, this invitation went out especially to me. Her four sons, two who were older and two younger than me wanted to take me fishing and boating. Kutina explained how eagerly they anticipated my visit and they wanted to show me their homestead. Bibi accepted the invitation and said as soon as it was convenient we would visit.

We left Purushpal early in the morning of departure day, after a breakfast of rice pancakes accompanied with some vegetable bhajee and dhal. Pre-monsoon storms had also started so the travelling was becoming hazardous. Especially with claps of thunder, streaks of lighting and sudden downpours, the day we left looked like a good day to travel, so we made haste. With no TV or radio there was no chance of learning about the weather. With electricity being non-existent in the rural areas, TV could only be watched if someone had a generator to power one. Most of the weather data was borrowed from India and transmission was sporadic at best. Therefore, weather forecasting was left to farmers and old wives tales.

The three of us headed for Shupatola, walking the same route Bibi and I took when we arrived for the wedding. Throughout the journey Rani and Bibi chatted away about the wedding and Naz's new wife. She mentioned what I had done in the way of slapping my new aunt on the wedding night. Bibi quizzed me asking if I had really done that, scolding me mildly. She went on to caution that being a nephew it was not socially acceptable for me to play pranks and jokes on aunts. However, Bibi's admonishments were rarely strong enough to cause concern. A grandmother I guess could never really pull it off like a parent, Rani however laughed it off. The journey started well, but as our slow walk progressed the air was one of impending storm, the wind was brisk but warm and the clouds were racing overhead. As we crossed the bamboo pole bridge across the Lula River looking back we could see rain falling on the lands we had left behind.

"We better speed up and get to our bari quickly," Bibi hastened.

We picked up our step and headed into Shupatola, where overhead the tree branches were duelling with each other, as the wind roared through their boughs. The wind chased us into our bari and as soon as we stepped into the courtyard the rain started.

For the remainder of the day the storm did not let up and with not much to do I just paced up and down the porch all day. With no TV, no comics, no books, no music and nothing to do, this kind of weather caused boredom on a monumental scale. Fortunately, Bolai saw us coming and joined us shortly afterwards. She ran across the path and onto our courtyard barefoot and wearing a farmers conical bamboo hat.

"What are you up to, Bolai?" I asked, as she jumped onto the porch and put her hat in a corner, and tried to shake herself dry.

"Not much, I thought you weren't coming back for longer?" she replied.

"I wanted to come back even earlier, but my uncle's wedding went on for so long," I replied, extremely happy to see her. "Have you ever been to a wedding?" I asked her.

"No, not yet, I think my sister Leela will be next to get married, but not sure when," she replied and took a mura on the porch beside me.

Bibi and Rani were in the kitchen and I could hear Rani's voice more than Bibi's, accompanied by pots and pans clinking and clanking. I looked out at the bari, the rain falling in sheets and casting a grey hue across the green vegetation, giving it all a dull complexion.

"I was hoping it would be dry so I could wander around the bari and see what fruits had started to ripen," I commented.

"Yes! It's now time for the lychees and *bubi* berries, the green mangoes are gorgeous with a bit of salt and pepper," Bolai said mouth wateringly.

"Have you tried any yet?" I asked.

"In our bari the green mangoes have been falling when the storms have been fierce, my sister's been making chutney with them."

"I will get my Auntie Rani to make me some tomorrow. Do you want to go pole fishing at our pond sometime?" I asked.

"Have you got a *bori*?" she asked, referring to a bamboo pole with a fishing hook.

"No! I can get my Bibi to make one, I suppose."

Rani came out of the kitchen, with a small basket of freshly roasted groundnuts that she had prepared in our kitchen's log fired hearth.

"Who's this?" Rani asked.

"Oh! This is Bolai from the next bari, Bolai, this is my Auntie Rani, she's come to stay a few days," I introduced.

"Here you are, let's eat these, Bolai you have some as well," Rani offered.

Initially Bolai was a bit unsure and shy about sharing the snack with us, but I insisted and she tucked in too. We sat there and listened to the rain drum on the tin roof and drench the world, whilst Rani struck up a conversation with Bolai. As the afternoon drew to a close the rain abated for a while. This gave the three of us the opportunity to jump into our pond for a quick bath. The rain had made the water pretty cool so we didn't stay too long before coming out, with Bolai running back to her bari in her wet shorts and t-shirt, ironically wearing the conical bamboo hat to stop herself getting wet from the raindrops that had started to fall.

"I'll see you later Bolai," I shouted at her as she disappeared across the path and into her bari.

The weather wasn't improving any further as evening drew in. Bibi with the help of Rani prepared the evening meal, as I sat at the mouth of the kitchen door and watched the rain and wind pick up again. By the time we had sat down cross legged on the floor to eat our meal there was a storm raging outside and we had to batten down the hatches like on a ship to ensure water-tightness. Having finished our meal of fish curry, rice and a bhajee, Bibi and Rani cleared up the plates, ladle and cups and I went into the adjacent room where Bibi slept. The two of them eventually joined me and under the glow of the oil lantern Bibi finely cut some betel nut and trimmed several leaves of paan. The three of us sat on the bed chewing on the after dinner digestion aid, with me taking the weakest option of only nut and paan, Rani with nut, paan and some limestone, whereas Bibi went for her usual potent mixture of nut, paan, flavoured tobacco and limestone. I learnt my lesson once by taking the same mixture and shortly afterwards suffering from a constricted throat, dizziness and breaking out in a sweat, symptoms that took a good half hour to pass, after having drunk copious amounts of water and sweet molasses.

"Auntie, how long will you be staying with us?" I turned to Rani and asked.

"Perhaps a week, maybe two, Fufu what do you say?" she asked Bibi, calling her auntie.

"Let's see when your dad comes over in the next few days," Bibi replied.

Suddenly there was a huge bang on the tin roof as if someone had thrown a rock or some other missile. All three of us jumped out of our skins, simultaneously saying, "Oh! Ma goh," a phrase often uttered by people when shocked or surprised, which literally meant "Oh! Dear mother".

As we gathered our wits trying to discern what the noise was, another bang caused us to rush to the door. Bibi opened the front door with the lantern in her hand and walked out onto the porch. Rani and I came following out and didn't see anyone or anything, then there was a third crash on the roof and a small dark object rolled down onto the semi-flooded courtyard.

"Get the umbrella Rani," Bibi ordered Rani.

Bibi, with the umbrella, stepped onto the courtyard and picked up the object and two others which we presumed made the first two noises. She came back onto the porch laughing.

"It's only the storm blowing off the green mangoes from the trees," she smiled.

Bibi gave the mangoes to Rani. I went into the storage room and came back out with two large, woven, bamboo baskets.

"There must be dozens of mangoes littered around the back of the house and on the path, let's go and collect them," Bibi suggested, as she placed the mangoes in one of the baskets.

The three of us stepped into the dark night, Bibi with a lantern, umbrella and one basket, Rani and I with another lantern, basket and umbrella held by Rani. The path was littered with green mangoes and it could be said that it was literally raining these hard, green fruits. It wasn't long before we had filled our basket and we heard Bibi calling us to come back. However, we could not contain our glee and we strayed further along the path and next to Arzomond's earth wall that marked his property.

"Over there in that clump of plants there's quite a few mangoes," Rani shouted.

"Where?" I replied.

Rani led me over to where the mangoes were and while she held the umbrella, which by now was of no use as the two of us were completely soaked, I picked up about half a dozen huge mangoes.

"Yah! These ones are huge," I shouted.

"Hey! Who is out there?" a yell came from Arzomond's bari

and we could tell it was the old man himself.

I put my finger to my lips in a silent 'shhh' to Rani as we stood our ground, hoping he wouldn't hear us, not realising that in this rain and storm he would have to be pretty close to hear our sounds of excitement. We looked up beyond the earth wall and we could see the flickering light from a lantern moving closer. The two of us looked at each other and holding the basket between us ran back to our Bari giggling impishly. Back on the porch Bibi was waiting for us with her basket load as we deposited our one next to hers. The three of us looked at the baskets and were astounded at the number of mangoes we had collected.

Bibi told us that we could check tomorrow for anymore mangoes and ordered us to change clothes and go to sleep before the exposure to rain made us ill. We put the baskets of mangoes away in the store room and changed into dry clothes. By now the three of us were completely exhausted and slowly made our way to our beds. With the rain drumming on the tin roof and storm blowing violently outside, Rani and I excitedly talked about the mango chutney we were going to gorge ourselves on over the coming days. Then, one by one, the three of us drifted off into deep sleep.

The next day was one of bright sunshine with freshness to the air that only came after a heavy thunderstorm. The rain water had drained away in the sandy soil and the green leaves of trees and plants glistened like emerald jewels in the sunshine. The three of us, after a quick breakfast, went around the bari and the path surveying the damage and to search for any more mangoes that would have fallen during the night. We did find some more mangoes albeit only the odd one here and there. However, we concluded that if there was any more they would have been picked off by the farmers who would have travelled through here at daybreak. There were also branches strewn all over the bari and path. We collected all that we could and stripped them of the leaves and laid them out in the sunshine to dry out so that they could be used as firewood.

Bolai came round mid-morning to see if I would come out to play, which was a misnomer because for me there was nothing else but play, with no school and parents it was a life I was really getting used to. The days were spent wandering around our bari and the hilltop on the east side. We rarely went too far as there was so much to explore in the immediate surroundings. Especially with the fruit season in full swing Bolai, Rani and I spent our days looking for that ripe guava or a bush of plump and juicy lychees.

However, today was mango chutney day. The three of us got the key ingredients together, namely green mangoes, roasted garlic, wild spikey coriander, green chillies and a touch of salt. We sat on the porch as Rani mixed the ingredients together. We then took a saucer full each by which time Bibi had joined us, and sat on the porch in the late morning sun savouring the chutney. The coolness of the delicacy combined with the tangy hot taste went down a treat. With Rani staying a week I had another companion alongside Bolai to engage with to go fishing at the pond, playing marbles or just lazing the days away.

One such day after Rani had left, Bolai and I were standing on the wall opposite the house next to the lychee tree, looking for the odd ripe fruit. We were fully aware that if we didn't get in there first the troupe of langurs would plunder the fruits before sunrise. The two of us carefully rummaged through the branches trying to pick out the fruits. We were not only collecting them in our short pockets but also peeling the fruits and popping them into our mouths, I suppose we were doing just what the monkeys would do. The two of us were so engrossed in our fruit-picking that we didn't notice the latrine door opening and out jumped the langur called Broken-hand, howling at us.

Bolai and I yelped "Oh! Ma goh" and leapt back off the wall, however as I was nearest the latrine, Broken-hand took a swipe at me with his good hand. He clawed my right thigh as he jumped onto the trunk of a betel nut tree. The two of us screamed as loudly as possible and headed towards the house stopping mid-way and turning back to look at Broken-hand. The monkey was half way up the tree trunk but staring at us ferociously and barking his defiance at us.

Bibi ran out of the house and yelled, "What's the matter with you two, why are you screaming?"

The two of us, with adrenaline running through us and breathing rapidly, blurted out a jumble of words that must have sounded like the cacophony at the fish bazaar. Bibi told us to calm down and asked me to explain what had happened, before I could do so Bibi looked at my leg and screamed, "Ya! Allah, what's happened to your leg? Look at all the blood."

Even though I felt Broken-hand scratch me as he bounded up the tree I didn't think to take a look at my leg until Bibi noticed the blood. I looked at my right leg where a crimson streak of warm blood was running down to my bare feet. Seeing my own blood did not make me wince, cry or become faint, I just put my hand on it to stem the flow.

Bibi grabbed me and took me onto the porch whilst she told Bolai, "Bolai, go and ask your mother to bring some *fichash* leaves right now."

Bolai sprinted off to her bari, whilst Bibi got a jug of water and rinsed the blood from my leg. I screamed in agony as the water stung my open wound, of which there were two cuts that weren't very deep but hurt like hell. With no first aid kits or any antiseptic products nor any painkillers it meant that I had to have treatment based on Bibi's knowledge of plant medicine.

I explained to Bibi what had happened and she told me that I should have been more careful as the monkey is known to attack children.

Bolai and her mother were nowhere in sight, so Bibi told me to keep rinsing the wound and walked over to the entrance to our Bari and shouted across to Bolai's place, "Hey! Bolai, tell your mother to come over quickly with the *fichash.*"

"We're coming," Bolai's little voice piped back.

Bibi returned and checked if the blood flow had stemmed, which had slowed a bit but not stopped completely. Bolai and her mother emerged from the side of the house with a bunch of some plant leaves in their hands.

"What's the matter with your grandson," asked Bolai's mother.

"Broken-hand has clawed his leg, Bhabi can you go and crush some of the leaves into a paste, the pestle and mortar is near the kitchen door," Bibi requested.

"OK," she replied and went off into the kitchen, leaving some of the leaves with Bibi, who went into the house to look for a strip of cloth.

"Is it hurting much?" Bolai asked with a look of pain on her face, as if she were also experiencing my discomfort.

"It really stings," I answered, with tears of pain welling at the corners of my eyes. It was only now that the pain was intensifying and the discomfort increased, but I gritted my teeth and waited for the herbal medicine to be applied.

Bolai's mother returned with a green mush of the leaves in the mortar bowl, which she gave to Bibi, who took a small amount of the paste and made it into a patty. She then placed the patty on the wound, explaining that it would sting, so I grit my teeth even harder in expectancy of the pain. My! Did it sting and burn, it felt like someone had got a hot needle and stuck it into the wound. I screamed in agony with tears streaking down my face as Bibi placed a couple of the leaves over the patty and then bandaged the whole area with strips of cloth cut from an old sari.

"Aarey! A little monkey has been beaten up by another monkey," joked Bolai's mother.

"Is he your friend or something? I reckon you put Broken-hand up to this," I retorted, with a scowl on my face, being in no mood for jokes.

"Ma! Leave Sabu alone, he's hurting," Bolai came to my defence.

Even though she was making fun of me and I knew it was harmless, right then I just could not see the funny side.

"She is only kidding Sabu," Bibi trying to soothe me.

My young ego had been bruised by a wild creature and now I was being mocked, so I got up then huffed and hobbled off into the bari. I was angry now and I wanted revenge by yelling at Broken-handed or even throw a stone or two.

"Hey, where are you going? Come and sit down and don't move the leg," Bibi called out.

I didn't get far as the pain was quite acute and I returned back to the porch shortly, feeling even more embarrassed. The elders realised my little male ego was bruised and I needed some time to myself. So, Bolai and her mother left, Bolai said she would come by later to see how I was. Bibi, on the other hand, went about some chores of cleaning and tidying around the house. It seemed Bibi was always doing something, even with only her and me being kind of low maintenance, she found something to do. I admired her work ethic and strength. Here she was with a huge property to manage, custody of a boy from England and in a man's world trying to keep it all together in a strange village.

As the three people went about their way I walked into the house and lay on the bed. Eventually I dozed off and was fast asleep. By the time I woke up dusk was settling across the bari, I didn't realise how long I had slept and Bibi said that Bolai had come and gone. I hobbled down to the pond to wash, keeping an ever watchful eye for Broken-hand and his minions.

I had been told stories by Bibi that if I went swimming or bathing in the pond and left any belongings by the steps leading into the pond, the monkeys, if nearby, could run off with them. Fortunately, there was no sign of the primates and I quickly washed my face, hands and feet and rushed back to the house.

That evening Bibi prepared a potion brewed from various leaves and plant extracts to help with any fever or pain that may arise during the night. Luckily, I slept like a baby throughout the night and awoke fully refreshed but with the pain in my leg still present and the wound yet to heal.

The next few days Bibi insisted that I avoid any tumble and fall activities to ensure the wound healed. I couldn't do much anyway as the primitive bandage kept leaking the plant juice with any strenuous movements, so Bolai and I pretty much kept within the confines of the courtyard and played marbles and other sedate games. Otherwise we would sit on the porch and watch the world go by. My confinement was further aided by the rains. When they came the wind would warn us of their arrival, then the rains would fall steadily for hours without a gap. It was as if the skies did not take a breather from pouring water on the land beneath. So there was a permanent dampness permeating the air, nothing dried, everything felt wet, which was further compounded by the humidity.

One day around noon Uncle Naz visited us, as he had promised on his wedding day – even though I had forgotten. He had with him seasonal fruits of Maldoy mangoes, lychees, sweetmeats and several bottles of Fanta. I was with Bibi getting ready for a lunch of dhal, rice and dried fish stew. Both Bibi and I walked out of the kitchen as we heard the ringing bell of a rickshaw and the familiar voice of Naz.

"Oh! Moy, where are you?" he called Bibi.

"Salaam alaikum Uncle," I greeted him.

"What are you up to Sabu, salaam alaikum Auntie," he replied smiling.

"Alaikum salaam," Bibi welcomed Naz.

"Come and join us, we are about to eat," Bibi invited Naz.

"Yes I will, Auntie," accepted Naz, as he paid the rickshaw walla and alighted from the vehicle.

"Sabu, can you go and get a lebu from the bush near the entrance to the bari, I've missed the taste and flavour of those Jara Lebu," Uncle Naz asked.

I ran off into the direction of the bush, narrowly avoiding crashing into the rickshaw as it left the bari. The grove of lebu trees alongside the entrance to the bari was huge, about the size of a kabadi court. It was impenetrable, with thorns as big as my ten year old fingers and limes that grew as big as a de-husked coconut that I needed both hands to hold one. Consequently, neither I nor anyone I knew ever managed to enter the middle of this grove, where some of the biggest fruits would ripen to a golden yellow, fall to the ground and rot. Here I was trying to find the biggest, greenest lebu on the trees, because I wanted Uncle Naz to enjoy the sweet juice and flesh they offered. I didn't have to search for too long before I spotted one that was just the right size, not a monster, but it was a perfect oval shape and had a dazzling green hue to its skin.

Back in the kitchen Naz was just washing his hands and Bibi had the *daa,* a kukri shaped knife on two legs, out to cut the lebu. As she sliced it open the fragrance burst from the skin of the fruit and took over the whole room.

"Wah! How beautiful is that scent?" exclaimed Naz.

"Uncle, our lebu are the juiciest and crunchiest you'll ever taste," I smiled at him.

"Your uncle has got a letter here from your dad," Bibi interjected.

"Really Uncle? Can you read it? What does it say?" I blurted, hardly able to contain my excitement.

"Let's eat first, your uncle's not going anywhere," Bibi added.

Naz and I sat cross-legged on the mat and Bibi squatted with our plates in front of us, Bibi then dished out the rice and dhal. With lebu slices accompanying the meal, Uncle Naz commented on how lovely the food was. Finishing our meal Naz and I went out onto the porch whilst Bibi cleaned up in the kitchen before joining us with the betel nut and paan thali. Sitting on our muras we chewed away on the nut and paan.

"What son? You also chew betel nut? You definitely have become a Deshi boy," Naz joked.

"Come on Uncle, please read the letter," I asked impatiently.

He opened the blue airmail letter and immediately I recognised Dad's big, bold, handwriting in black biro ink. I could almost read the Bengali lettering from the outside as my dad had a tendency to write with a lot of pressure on the nib of the pen. The letter was addressed to Bibi, who could neither read nor write and therefore Uncle Naz read the letter out to her.

"Salaam alaikum Mother, I hope you are well and your grandson is doing well too. Your daughter-in-law sends her salaam, as well as your grandsons and granddaughter. We are all doing fine here in London.

Did you go to Naz's wedding? We heard it went well. Can you ask Naz to write sometimes?

I sent some taka a few weeks ago to Boro Mama, write to me when you have received it and let me know.

110

*Mother, also take care in the new bari. If you have any trouble
or problems let me know straight away.*

God bless"

"That's all for you Auntie," Naz ended the letter, but he
turned over to the other side and a smaller section at the bottom.
"There's also a bit for you Sabu," he continued.

*"Baba Sabu, I hope you are well, we are all doing well here. Your
mum and your brothers and sister miss you and send their love.*

*Are you going to school and mosque? Make sure you go
regularly and don't give your Bibi too much trouble.*

God bless you Son"

That was it, no indication of whether I was going back to
England or if Dad or Mum were coming over to get me. In a
way a sort of disappointment hit me, thinking that I would be
stuck here forever. Yet, I was also glad that he didn't know
about me not going to school nor the trouble I caused at Uncle
Naz's wedding. I had a short lived expectation of my Dad
saying that I could come back home now. I was a bit deflated
after having raised my expectations.

Bibi did not react much to the letter, she enquired with Naz
about the money from Dad. "Did your mama say anything
about the taka?" she asked Naz.

"He did actually, and yes some money has arrived from
Sabu's dad," he replied.

"When I go next I'll pick it up or maybe he'll bring it
round," she mused out loud. "Is there any other news?" Bibi
enquired.

"Well, I've made the application to take your *bahu* to
England with me," he explained about his wife.

"How long does it all take?"

"Several months, so I will stay to complete the whole thing, get her visa and then take her back with me," he replied.

"That means you'll be here for a while then?" Bibi asked.

"Yes, definitely Auntie."

"Good, as you're here you may as well enjoy a long break, I don't know when I'll see you next, once you go back," Bibi replied.

Uncle Naz did not stay long afterwards as he had to walk back to Beani Bazaar before catching a ride on the back of someone's motorcycle to Purushpal. Both Bibi and I walked him to the entrance of our bari and bid him farewell. I always enjoyed visits by Naz and relished the time he spent with Bibi and I. Standing there I looked over at Bolai's bari and told Bibi that I was going to her place.

Walking into Bolai's bari there was a house on the left and right, both of which faced the courtyard and a house on the opposite side of the courtyard, which housed the kitchen. All three houses were of mud and tin roof construction and had a greyish brown hue to them. I could see Bolai squatting on the kitchen porch with her mother, preparing a fish with a *daa*. I walked up to the two of them and leant against one of the bamboo poles that supported the porch.

"What are you doing Bolai? You haven't come round today," I asked.

"I was going to earlier but I saw you had a relative come over," she replied.

"Yeah! That's my uncle who I came with and whose wedding I went to," I explained.

"Well, when are you going back to London, Sabu?" asked Bolai's mother, as Leela, her other daughter, came out of the kitchen and stood by the door.

She was in her teens and slightly chubby, again not being schooled either. Both Bolai and Leela, like thousands of children around the country, were kept out of school due to the cost of schooling, plus the kids were an extra hand around the house to do chores, or even earn an income as hired hands at wealthier family's baris. So even though Bolai, at the earliest opportunity, would run over to my place, some days she just had to stay at home and help, clean the houses, sweep the courtyard, tether the cattle, bring the chickens in to roost and so on.

"I don't know, I got a letter from my dad today but he didn't mention anything about me going back."

"Stay Grandson, as you're here there's no harm in staying," Bolai's mother encouraged.

"Yah! Allah, Sabu's mother and father have forgotten about him, he's not going to go back to London anymore," piped in Leela.

"Don't be silly *beti*, stop this nonsense talk," scolded Bolai's mother, referring to her as a woman.

I was starting to develop a thick skin in terms of these kinds of taunts so I wasn't really upset by Leela, but I just didn't want to be reminded of it.

"Bolai, come round to my bari tomorrow morning, there's some work we've got to do so try and come early," I asked Bolai.

"Why? What is the work?" she queried.

"You'll see tomorrow," I smiled and left the porch, heading back to my bari.

Bolai got up followed me up to her bari's entrance.

"Tell me Sabu, tell me!" she begged.

"No! Just wait till tomorrow," I replied as I crossed the path onto my bari.

She followed me but I was not revealing anything. She tugged at my arms but my lips were sealed. I was enjoying teasing her, but she must have felt that with a concrete friendship like ours I shouldn't be doing so. Consequently she turned around and fled back to her bari in a huff. I looked towards her and gulped, hoping I hadn't made her too mad.

Monkey Business

The following morning before Bolai had come round I had to convince Bibi about a proposition I had thought of. It was a nice sunny day and she was going about the courtyard tending to her various plants and seeds she had sown around the edges. When I approached her, Bibi was at the back of our house tending to a papaya plant which had been attacked by the monkeys early that morning, before we had risen. They tended to go for the tender shoots of the plant or the young fruits of papaya.

"Bibi! Bolai and I want to go the bazaar and sell some of the lebu from our grove," I blurted out, expecting to catch her off guard and get a straightforward no.

"Can the two of you do this?" she replied, looking up at me with a worried looked.

"We can do it Bibi, let us go, we won't do it again just this once," I pleaded, grasping this opportunity of getting a yes from Bibi to carry out this daredevil stunt.

"It's not easy, you know, and there are *chor* and *dacoits* who will con you," she referred to thieves and bandits.

"Let us go Bibi, nothing will happen," I begged.

I didn't know what she was thinking or what her basis of reasoning was but Bibi turned around and said, "Go on then, but don't stay too long and come back by noon." I was so gobsmacked that she agreed to such a crazy idea that I almost jumped with joy.

I did not wait for her to finish the sentence as I dashed off towards Bolai's bari.

"Bolai! Bolai! Where are you?" I yelled running up into her courtyard.

"Hey! Who is it shouting this early?" Arzomond said popping his head out of the house opposite the kitchen.

"It's nothing dada, I'm looking for Bolai," I explained.

Bolai, in the meantime, approached me from the corner of her bari where the pond was.

"What's matter with you? And why are you shouting and screaming?" she stated, looking a bit annoyed. I guessed she was still upset from yesterday and my reluctance to give her a clear answer.

"Come quickly, we've got to go," I said animatedly, as I grabbed her hand and headed back to my bari.

"Wait a while, I need to tell my mum," she halted.

As she went into the kitchen to speak to her mum I was impatiently pacing up and down, wishing for her to hurry up. She came out of the kitchen towards me, with no sense of urgency.

"What's up with you?" she asked with a quizzical look, probably thinking I had gone mad.

"We are going to the bazaar to sell some lebu," I told Bolai.

"Your Bibi will kill you, what lebu and from where and how?" she warned.

"I have asked Bibi already and she said it is fine," I replied, "You have to help me pick some of the fruits to take to the bazaar," with that I literally dragged her to my bari.

Once there I sent Bolai to go and pick the lebu and I headed into the house.

"Bibi, where's the shopping bag?" I yelled.

"It's in the kitchen near the pots and pans," she answered from the back of the house.

I went from the bedroom into the kitchen and grabbing the two jute bags I ran back out to the lebu grove. Bolai had already picked four fruits and the two of us continued to look for the best looking and biggest ones so we could get a better price. We walked around the fringes of the grove and picked two dozen lebu and put them into the bags carefully, so as not to bruise them. The two of us, carrying a bag each, went over to Bibi to show her what we were taking. She gave her seal of approval and I asked her to pop open two of the Fantas that Uncle Naz had brought. Bibi told us to take care as Bolai and I slung the bags over our tiny shoulders with the bottled drinks in one hand and headed off to Beani Bazaar.

The two of us, bare foot and in our trademark shorts and t-shirts, walked the half mile or so to the bazaar. The walk was thirsty work, so much so that we polished off our Fantas before we had reached the southern end of the market. It was at this end of the market where some of the fresh fruit and vegetable sellers displayed their wares and this was where we had to find a spot to sell our lebu. We walked to a point where there were a couple of huge mango trees by the main thoroughfare. We decided to park ourselves next to one of the trees and face the main road to catch the traffic as it went by.

There were a handful of merchants with large bamboo baskets with their huge selection of fruits and vegetables laid out in splendour of greens, yellows, purples, reds and every other rainbow coloured fruit I could think of. Nobody paid any attention to what we were up to and pretty much left us on our own, except for one vendor who sat several feet behind us, who eyed us without looking directly in our direction. We opened our bags and placed the lebu in groups of four known as *'one alee'*, which was a common denominator for selling produce. The bags acted as our display mats on the floor. The two of us sat feeling very proud that here we were, in the grown-ups world doing what they were doing. It was mid-morning by the time we had set up, waiting for our first customer to come by. In terms of pricing the fruit we didn't have a clue, we had failed to ask Bibi and we didn't want to ask anyone in the market in case they tried to rip us off. The two of us came to an agreement that we would sell them at a couple of takas per alee.

Several market goers asked us how much, or picked them up and had a good sniff or nicked the top to release the fragrance, but no one was buying. After what seemed like ages the two of us were losing patience, so I asked Bolai to see if she could go and exchange the two empty Fanta bottles for any money so that we could buy some snacks. She went off into the bazaar looking for a restaurant or a café. Standing there I was looking up and down to see if anyone was showing interest, there was very little vehicle flow, with mainly rickshaws and telagharis moving up and down the bazaar. There were some people about, most of who were going about their business, without much straying. From the south of the bazaar the smell of freshly cut lumber wafted in the air from a saw mill and the noise from the machine fought for airspace with the rickshaw bells, and market vendors haggling over price trying to sell their wares. Out of some shops came the blaring sound of Bollywood movie songs played on a screeching cheap tape player.

Opposite where we were positioned was a row of shops, one selling saris and lunghis, another selling construction hardware. The shopkeepers sat on the bamboo mat covered flooring that was raised a foot of the ground, where they could move up and down the shop whilst the customers sat on chairs or muras at the entrance.

"What son? Are you Sabu Miah?" some strange man blocked my view and snapped me out of my gaze.

"Yes, but I don't recognise you," I quizzed.

"I am an uncle of yours from Purushpal, what are you doing here?" he questioned.

"I am selling these lebu which are from my bari," I explained.

"Does your grandma know about this?" he went on.

"Of course she does, I told her before I came," I answered defiantly.

"How much are you selling them for then?" he wanted to know.

"Two takas per alee," I stated.

"You might as well give me an alee then," he asked.

He opened his shopping bag, I put the lebu in amongst other shopping and he gave me the two taka.

"Acha son, when you go to Purushpal come to my bari," he smiled and went off towards College Road.

I did not have a clue as to who he was and I never saw him again, even in Purushpal, as I didn't know where his bari was or what his name was for that matter. I wasn't too bothered as I had made my first sale and was delighted. I could not wait for Bolai to get back so I could share the good news with her. I looked north towards the College Road junction and I saw Bolai's small figure rushing back towards me.

"So, did you get any money back on the bottles?" I asked.

"No! The men won't give me any money, so I gave them the bottles anyway," she answered.

"That's fine because I've sold one alee, look here's the two taka," I showed her.

I explained to her about the man who bought the lebu. Over the remainder of the morning we sold another two alees but we both were getting tired, thirsty and hungry. But as luck would have it the vendor sitting behind us who had been watching us all morning came over.

"Hey! Boy, these lebu? How much do you want for the last twelve?" he asked.

"Six taka," I replied.

"I'll give you four," he offered.

"No! No!" the two of us blurted out simultaneously.

He was taken aback by our boldness; I guess he didn't expect us to rebut his offer so quickly.

"Acha! I will pay five take then," he countered.

The two of us looked at each other and nodded in agreement before accepting and exchanging the goods for the money. We had eleven takas in our pocket and considered ourselves rich. So we began wandering the bazaar thinking of what to buy, there was so much on display. There was *ghee cham cham, chana chor, hawa mitai* – caramelised sugary sweets, savoury chick peas and candy floss respectively, and other delights on display at the various stalls and shops. With so much choice we wanted to buy everything, we eventually settled on some sweet tamarind, two freshly prepared chana chor and I gave into the temptation of a jackfruit and bought a small one. From the cash we had two taka left which I split with Bolai, which put a huge smile on her face.

We walked backed to our village munching on the spicy chana chor, which was a concoction of chick peas, onions, chillies, spicy flavouring seasoned with coriander and salt. The snack was fairly hot from the chillies and we had to take sharp intakes of breath to cool our mouths. As we walked through the cool, shaded path of the village we recounted the day and how much fun we had. The two of us agreed that it was something we wouldn't repeat, not in the near future anyway, we were too impatient to sit all day in the bazaar selling lebu. We got to our baris and both went our ways saying that we would see each other later.

Bibi heard me talking to Bolai and came out to see me lugging the jackfruit over my shoulder, the sweet tamarind in one hand and making my way up to the house.

"What have you got there?" she asked.

"A jackfruit," I replied.

"Bolai and I sold all the lebu and then we saw this jackfruit and bought it," I explained.

"How much did you sell the lebu for?" Bibi enquired.

"Eleven taka for the six alees," I answered.

"Yah! You could have gotten a bit more for them," she gasped.

"We didn't know what price to sell them at, so we just took a guess," I justified.

"Well, what's done is done and you managed to sell them at least, do you want to go again?"

"No, no, the two of us don't want to do this again," I shook my head.

"Why?"

"Too boring and the time does not pass."

"Well, let's have a look at the jackfruit and see if it is any good," she asked.

I gave her the bag and followed her into the kitchen, where I got a glass of water from the copper water urn. I gulped the water down as Bibi began to split the fruit open. It was a pretty small fruit compared to how big they normally can get, with their spiky exterior and thick, sweet, gooey fruit within. Opening the fruit let out a pungent, thick, sweet aroma that filled the kitchen, Bibi gave me the first try. The fruit pod wasn't as gooey, but quite crunchy, I guess because it was still early in the season they wouldn't be as ripe, but altogether sweet. I removed the oval seed about the same size as my toe and put it on the floor. The seeds would be dried in the sun and when roasted they tasted very much like chestnuts back in England.

"Mmm! It's quite sweet," I commented.

"And crunchy too," Bibi added.

I had a couple more as she extracted about two-thirds of the fruit pods. She placed fruits in equal amounts in two separate tin bowls.

"Here! Take these to Bolai's bari, they'll enjoy them," Bibi asked.

I washed my hands with some water, picked up one of the bowl of jackfruit and headed off to Bolai's. I walked into her bari and straight into the kitchen where she and her family were sitting down for their lunch.

"Is that Sabu?" asked Arzomond.

"Yes! Dada, here's some jackfruit for you," I gave the bowl to Leela.

"Are they from your tree?" Bolai's mother questioned.

"No! Bolai and I bought it from the bazaar this morning," I explained as Bolai looked at me and smiled.

"Oh! You two have been real smugglers today at the bazaar," Arzomond joked.

"Oh! Sabu sit down and join us and eat," his wife offered.

"No, I must go, Bibi is getting our lunch ready too," and with that I headed back to my bari.

Later on in the day Makoy Haji's wife and son Goni visited. Bibi and the old lady had a deal whereby Bibi would give her some of the betel nuts from our trees in exchange for one of her sweet pumpkins that they cultivated out in their fields. The betel nut from our trees was the sweetest in our neighbourhood and Makoy Haji's family cultivated the tastiest pumpkins, so the trade was deemed fair. The two ladies sat on the porch chewing betel nut and talking about their gardening efforts in spite of the monkeys.

Goni and I walked off into our bari towards the pond. Beside the pond there were a couple of guava trees and being this far from the house it was almost impossible to get the fruits as the monkeys beat the humans to it. The two of us looked up at the branches to see if there were any fruits that looked ripe.

There were one or two that had the pale green hue of ripeness. The tree trunk was too fragile for Goni to climb up so he hoisted me up to the lowest branch. I precariously grabbed a couple of guavas and carefully slid back down the smooth tree trunk. We sat by the pond side and relaxed, sitting there in the late afternoon warmth peeling the guava with our teeth. Biting into the fruit revealed the pink flesh inside. The fruits were not fully ripe yet but in a day or two they would have softened up, however by then they would be sitting inside the belly of a monkey.

"Hey Sabu, do you want to do some bird hunting sometime?" Goni suggested.

"With what and where?" I asked.

"Well, I've got a catapult and Beng's got one too, so the three of us could go hunting, and your bari is perfect, it's almost all jungle, which is ideal for birds," he detailed.

"So, when do you want to do it?" I continued.

"Soon, let me speak to Beng and we'll come over one day, you're not going to Purushpal are you?" he queried.

"No, not that I know," I replied.

With that decided we sat there enjoying the fruits until Goni's mother yelled.

"Hey! Goniiiii, where are you?"

Goni jumped of his backside and jetted back towards the house. "We'll be around soon," he shouted as he disappeared up the path.

I got up also and slowly made my way back to the house, where I found Bibi already preparing the pumpkin she traded with Makoy Haji's wife to make a bhajee. That evening the pumpkin bhajee went down a treat, it was absolutely delicious with the sweetness of the pumpkin combined with the spiciness of the *panch puran* – five spices masala.

Over the next few days there was no sign of Goni or Beng

to go bird hunting. With the monsoon season in full swing I was pretty much housebound and my days were spent with Bolai. The heat and humidity began to reach extremes and it was unbearable during the day and impossible at night. At night I kept cool with the aid of Bibi slowly rotating the small hand held bamboo fan. Even when she was fast asleep she could maintain the steady rhythm of rotating the fan, I didn't know how she did it. I on the other hand, worked up more of a sweat trying to stay cool. Unless I was feeling extremely hot I didn't even bother using a fan half the time.

With the rains the river transport system in the country was up and running and my dad had ordered pebbles to be delivered to our bari for the construction of a house. The plan was that Dad would arrive sometime over the coming months to start building a proper house of bricks and mortar and putting up a brick wall around the whole property. The pebbles were piled in two mounds at the northern end of the courtyard. These mounds of pebbles would sit there for many months, even long after I had gone back to England.

A week had gone by and I had completely forgotten about the bird hunting when one morning, after a heavy night of rains, I sat on a mura on the porch. I heard two voices coming up into our bari, I got up off the mura and looked at who it was. It was Goni and Beng. Every time I saw Beng I could only think of a bullfrog with his bulging eyes and a wide mouth which looked poised to flick out a tongue and catch an insect. I liked Beng, but he hardly came round on his own as he lived further into the village and Bibi was not too keen to let me go that far out. With Goni I still kept my guard and avoided getting into anything too deep or committed. He had a dangerous glint in his eyes which gave off a hint of volatility to his character. Yet I wanted to be like him, I suppose being older he had a coolness that I wanted to have.

"Hey! Sabu," Goni called out upon seeing me.

"I thought you two had forgotten about going bird hunting," I quizzed.

"I couldn't come as I had to work out in the fields," Goni explained.

"What's your news, Beng?" I asked teasingly, stating his name.

"Get away man, don't call me that," he frowned.

"Aarey! Miah, we're only joking with you," I replied.

"Let's go you two, we've got birds to hunt," Goni ordered.

"Bibi, I am over at the northern part of the bari," I yelled as we headed towards the pebble mounds.

"Acha!" Bibi replied from the kitchen.

We stuffed our pockets with small pebbles for the two catapults we had. We then headed off towards the Thal palm tree, where numerous betel nut, bay leaf, mango and other species of trees populated that part of the bari. The ground underfoot was moist which helped us tread quietly as we sought out birds to hunt. One bird that was particularly prevalent in this part of the world was the Jackfruit Whistler. It was the unofficial name given to this bird which was very active during the jackfruit season. It had a brown plumage and was known by its mating call.

"Woo-woo, woo-woo!"

The three of us looked up to see one sitting on a low branch of a tree dead ahead of us.

"There! Look," shouted Beng.

The bird heard the noise on the ground below and flew off towards the denser treetops up above.

"Aarey Beng, why did you have to shout?" Goni admonished.

"Hey, keep quiet next time," I joined in.

However, I felt sorry for him afterwards seeing that he was

quite hurt, and as he had one of the catapults which I wanted to have a go at, I didn't want to put him down too much. Walking off further into the trees I nudged him playfully and he beamed a smile back at me.

We didn't have much luck in our bari so we decided to hit the path on the eastern edge of the bari to check the overhanging branches, but also to go onto the empty hill to the east. The path was waterlogged and there was a steady stream of water trickling south. Goni and Beng both made a few attempts with their catapults at killing a bird or two with no joy, for some reason there seemed to be very few birds visible or audible. We continued onto the hill, the top of which had a clearing about the size of a badminton court, with various trees and bushes surrounding it on all four sides. We climbed to the top and sat down, taking a rest as the sun warmed the air and evaporated the excess water into steam from the ground and the leaves of the plants.

The three of us sat there silently on the rise and carefully listened out for any birds chirping in the treetops.

"Listen," whispered Goni.

Towards the bushes, deeper south on the hillock, we could hear several birds chirping ferociously as if they were having an argument of sorts. We quickly moved in the direction of where we thought they were and there in the low branches of a jackfruit tree two birds were singing to their hearts content. They were both a golden yellow in hue and about the size of a sparrow. Goni signalled us not to move as he took a pebble out of his pocket, aimed at one of the birds and let the pebble fly. Suddenly, there was a thud as the pebble hit the bird and it let out a strangled chirruping noise, the poor creature hit the ground in a ball of feathers, whilst its partner flew away in a flash.

We all rushed over to the bird in its death throes, making a last desperate attempt at getting some air as its body quivered and became still. Goni and Beng looked at each other and grinned, whereas I was feeling a mixture of emotions and wasn't sure about the whole hunting experience. On the one hand I was elated that we had hunted a bird and on the other it was a poor, defenceless creature that had done us no harm and we had extinguished its life in seconds. I also smiled, putting on a brave face, trying to be one of the boys. However I had lost my appetite for hunting.

We carried on for the rest of the morning with Goni bagging one more bird and Beng and I not hitting any bird at all. My desire to hunt had gone so I guess I was sabotaging my own aims deliberately and avoiding hitting any birds. We ended our expedition by finishing back up in my bari underneath the Thal palm. The three of us sat there enjoying the midday sun warming us up as we talked about how we nearly got this bird and that bird, the stories getting wilder as we continued.

Goni was sitting with his back to the palm trunk with Beng to his right and I was sitting cross-legged opposite the two of them, when Goni came out with a question that caught me quite off guard.

"Hey, Sabu, have you been circumcised?" he asked.

"Yeah! Why?" I replied quizzically.

"Just asking," he shrugged.

At this point I had a bad feeling about where this conversation was going. He then pulled up his lunghi which he had worn quite high anyway and took hold of his penis. This freaked me out and made the alarm bells in my head start to ring like the Bow Bells of St. Mary-le-Bow church in London when he turned to Beng and asked, "Get your one out too and let's have a look."

Beng didn't even bat an eyelid and unzipping his shorts he got his penis out as well, I knew what was coming when Goni requested the same of me.

"Get lost, I'm not doing that," I refused, then got up and ran back to the house.

I didn't know what that was all about and I had never experienced anything like this before. As far as decency and the values I was brought up on, at this young age boys weren't supposed to show their penis to each other. Back at the house I found Bibi sweeping the porch as I walked past her into the kitchen and got myself a glass of water.

When I came out I saw the Goni and Beng walking into the courtyard and towards me. I avoided eye contact and stood close to Bibi, who looked up as they approached.

"What did you catch then?" she asked.

"We got these two birds," Goni replied.

"Auntie, do you want to keep one," Goni offered.

"You keep them, get your mother to cook them for you," she replied.

"We'll see you around Sabu," the two of them said as they walked away.

From that day on I never went hunting again and I avoided Goni like the plague. Occasionally, I would see Beng walking by my bari and sometimes he would come round and we would play games. During Beng's visits I ensured Bolai was around, he never raised the incident and we never talked about what happened ever again.

The remainder of the day I stayed in my bari, I didn't even venture out to Bolai's place to see if she was up for a swim or a bit of pole fishing in our pond. She didn't visit either, which was good as I would not have been ideal company given the events of the morning. That evening Bibi announced that we would be heading off the Purushpal in a few days' time so she would need me to help her to securely store away our valuables and generally tidy up around the bari before we left. I was glad to hear that we were going away as it would get me away from having to see Goni or Beng.

Over the next few days Bolai helped us to sort things out and get our personal belongings ready. The day before our departure for Purushpal the sun was blazing down, its rays bounced off the courtyard's light sandy earth causing all who dared look out to squint. I was in the storeroom putting away some sweeping brushes and Bibi was somewhere in the kitchen tinkering with pots and pans, when all of a sudden there was a bang. Both Bibi and I rushed out of the house and onto the porch trying to discern what had happened.

"Hey! What is that noise?" Bibi exclaimed.

"I don't know, looks like it came from over that wall," I replied pointing towards the east.

Both of us, scared out of our wits, were wide-eyed and breathing fast, like deer in the crosshairs of a rifle. The two of us walked towards the gap between the earth walls into the interior of the bari, and there on the ground was a jackfruit that had fallen from one of the high branches overhanging the path. The fruit was slightly larger than a football and had split. Fortunately the contents hadn't spilt onto the earth. Bibi and I both looked at each other with a sigh of relief and laughed.

"How is it that I missed this one when I was checking the jackfruits the other day?" she seemed to be speaking to herself as she leant over to pick the fruit up.

"Good thing the monkeys didn't get it," I added.

The two of us checked the other fruits hanging on the branches. Bibi went to the store room and got a bamboo pole. She prodded those out of hands reach to see if they were ripe enough to come down. There was one which was similar size to the one on the ground but not ripe yet.

"I am going get this one down too and leave in the store whilst we're away, otherwise Broken-hand and his mob will get it," she suggested as she twisted the stalk of the fruit with the split end of the pole and gently lowered it to the ground.

"Take this one and I will carry the ripe one back."

I picked up the fruit whilst Bibi carried the split one back to the house.

"As we are going to Purushpal we'll take it with us," Bibi suggested.

"Yeah! Boro Dada would love it," I replied.

Her brother had a sweet tooth just like my dad and they both shared a passion for jackfruit, the sweeter and more gooey the better, whereas I enjoyed the odd jackfruit here and there, eating too much would cause me to feel sick and bloated. We stored the semi-hard fruit spiking it with a wooden stake and covering it with a jute sack in a dark corner of the store room. This would ensure that when we came back the fruit would ripen enough to eat. We opened one half of the felled fruit and shared it with Bolai's family when she visited later in the day. The other half I lugged back to Purushpal to share with Bora Dada.

In the evening we put the chickens away in their pen, ensured we weren't leaving any valuables and packed our clothes into a couple of jute bags ready to leave the following day. Bibi went over to Bolai's mother to ask her to take care of the chickens. That evening we had an early night in preparation for the long journey ahead in the morning. We dined early and after Bibi had her customary betel nut and paan, and of course I had my share too, we went to our respective beds and fell fast asleep.

Jinns That Go Bump in the Day

Our trip back took us along the same route as our last visit. There were clear signs of the change in the landscape. Farmers had toiled the fields and planted rice seedlings in ankle high water, the plants looked as if they were drowning and a good rain could make it a reality. The full onslaught of the monsoon floodwaters was pretty imminent and soon enough it would leave the fields underwater for many months. The water level in the rivers and canals had markedly risen and the flow of water was much faster and stronger. Crossing the Lula River there were clumps of water hyacinths and other flotsam and jetsam being hurried along by the monsoon waters from the Meghalaya and Assam Hills in India. With Cherrapunji being the recipient of the highest rainfall in the world only forty miles northwest of Beani Bazaar the flood waters carried with them all sorts of debris. The swirling waters had a colour that was muddy and silt infused, bringing down tonnes of earth from the foothills of the Himalayas and beyond.

The skies overhead were dark and heavy with the monsoon rains and the ground underfoot was slippery and wet. Most of our journey was barefoot as walking with a pair of sandals on your feet was a sure enough route to landing on your backside. Eventually, we arrived into Purushpal and again I used Bibi as a shield when we passed the school. By the time we walked into the bari our feet were wearing shoes of caked mud and being clay mud from the latter part of our journey the task of washing it off was like trying to prize a leech from your skin.

With the rains the general atmosphere had changed in Purushpal. Back in Shupatola the rainwater pretty much came and went. Being hilly ground with sandy earth the water drained away fast and once the sun was out the air became dry and comfortable. However, here in Purushpal the clay earth did not drain the water so easily and the air had a constant wetness to it. I was forever washing mud from my feet, and water was visible everywhere and clinging to everything. Most of the time everyone stayed indoors to avoid getting wet from the rain and muddy from falling on their backsides, the latter tended to happen to me more often than not. Everyone attributed this to my Londoni feet that according to them were soft as cotton wool.

Nevertheless, I was quite happy to be back with my comrades, with whom there were many new adventures to seek now that the canals and the low lying fields had some floodwater to sustain one of Boro Dada's boats as transport.

Boro Dada had planted a variety of vegetables several months ago, such as chillies, tomatoes and groundnuts, which had now become ready for harvesting. These were planted on high ground close to people's baris or over on a plot of land on the south-western outskirts of Purushpal called Fulbari. Quite a few people from the village had a parcel of land near Fulbari, the area there was high ground and the soil was rich from the yearly alluvial deposits from the floodwaters.

Boro Dada had already harvested the groundnut, but the other vegetables were yet to be picked. One grey afternoon when Aman and Iqbal were back from school and the rains had slightly eased having drenched the land all morning, we decided to head over to Fulbari.

The *nowka* or boat was moored on the canal at the front of

the bari. Most of the boats used by villagers were the same design but varied in size and the ones used for transporting people would have a woven bamboo arch over the main section, where you could sit shielded from the sun and rain, these were called *gunti nowka*. The shape of the boats was that of a banana and they were painted with black tar to make them waterproof, with several seats in the mid-section. The rower would sit at the raised back end and would use paddles for the deep waters or a bamboo pole to punt the boat in the shallower fields. The front was also raised and if there was a second person he would stand up front and use the pole to direct the boat in shallow waters.

Iqbal and I went over to Boro Dada to get the key for the padlock on the boat and ask for permission to take it out into the fields. Iqbal suggested that if I made the request then Dada would not be too inquisitive as to why we needed the boat.

"Dada, have you tried the jackfruit yet?" I asked.

"Yes, Grandson, it is very delicious," he replied.

"Bibi and I spiked another one and left it in our house, so if you come back with us it should be ripe," I offered him. "Dada," I queried with a nervous inflection to my voice.

"Can Iqbal, Aman and I borrow the boat for the afternoon?" I requested.

"Where do you lot want to go?" he questioned.

"Nowhere really, just into the southern fields."

He looked at me, smiled and agreed, even though I felt if one of the others had asked he may have quizzed them further. It paid immensely to be the first and most favoured grandchild. Boro Dada would not see his own grandkids for at least another fifteen years or so.

"OK, but don't go too far, the waters can be fast and dangerous west of the village," he warned.

Having secured the keys to the boat Iqbal went off to get

two paddles and a pole, as I went to tell Bibi where I was going. I found her in our room with Old Auntie, she was grinding betel nut for her mother, whilst they chatted away in low tones.

"Bibi, I'm going over to the fields near Fulbari," I said.

"Who are you going with? And how are you getting there?" she wanted to know.

"Iqbal and Aman are going with me, and we're taking one of the boats," I explained.

"Yah! You're not going to go wearing that red shirt are you?" Old Auntie exclaimed.

"True! Wearing that shirt next to Fulbari, *Mamuzi* might get you," Bibi added.

"No! Nothing will happen, and we're not going into Fulbari, just past it," I tried to alleviate their superstitions.

Mamuzi or Uncle was supposed to be a jinn that lived apparently in the copse of Banyan trees in Fulbari. The story goes that Mamuzi would help lost travellers by the way of a lantern to direct them into the village at night time, or if he was feeling mischievous he would use the same light to lead travellers astray. By that he would take them far away from the village and way out into the fields, the traveller would come upon a lonely bari, where he would be hosted to a feast of kingly proportions. However, upon waking up in the morning the poor traveller would find himself sleeping on the cold earth floor with muddy hands and face, as well as dirt in his mouth. According to superstition, spirits such as Mamuzi did not take too kindly to the colour red and anyone who strayed too close to his place of abode wearing such a colour would get a taste of his wrath.

"Be careful then and keep any eye out for snakes and leeches," Bibi called after me as I bounded down the steps out of the house and towards the boat. Iqbal and Aman were already waiting there and Amad had joined us too.

"We've been waiting for you, why so long?" Iqbal asked.

"Bibi and Old Auntie are worried about Mamuzi and that he's going to get me," I scoffed.

"No need to worry about that, we're going nowhere near there," Aman added.

"Come on *sasa*, sit down," Amad ordered calling me uncle. "We've got the salt with us for the tomatoes."

"What do you mean?" I asked, thinking he's being a bit bossy for a little tyke.

"Well we're going to eat some tomatoes from the fields, with a bit of salt they're really tasty," Aman explained.

Unlocking the boat with Iqbal at the helm with a pole in his hand we moved off and out onto the northern fields. Aman and I had a paddle each, paddling gently on the either side to provide extra power. The whole landscape had completely changed, now that there was water everywhere as far as the eye could see. The field where we popped the rice grains passed underneath us in its watery grave. There were water based plants like hyacinths, lotus, water chestnuts and other numerous reeds and vegetation jutting from the surface in clumps here and there. Most of the plants just lay below the surface of the water, making it difficult to see the bottom. The water wasn't that deep, maybe up to my chest and with all the plants it was quite hard work to propel the boat forward.

We turned west having come out from under the bari and skirted the village on our left as we rowed towards Fulbari. Aman and I had pulled in the paddles as it was near impossible to use them with dense plant growth in the water. Even though there was no sunshine the air was very hot and muggy and overhead the clouds threatened to burst any moment. I sat back, sticking out my right hand to skim the water surface with my index finger and occasionally tugging on a plant head.

"Oh! Sasa, keep your hands in otherwise a snake or a leech

might get you," Iqbal warned. I retracted my hand as if a cobra had already made a strike for it.

"Yes, sasa, there's a particular type of snake that hides under some of these plants and if you touch it, the snake will follow you home and bite you," said Aman.

"Is that true?" I questioned.

"Yes! It's happened to quite a few people in our village," Iqbal added.

Trusting them, not knowing whether it was fact or myth and recalling what Bibi had said I kept my hand well inside the boat all the way. At the western end of the village we turned south and carried on until we came across the main path that emerged out of the village. There the path just disappeared into the water, leaving a channel that was about the width of two boats. I guessed it was more to allow the waters to pass between the fields on either side. The path carried on west into the fields before completely disappearing into the water about half a mile or so further down.

Aman and I steered the boat whilst Iqbal punted us through the gap in the path. We then turned east onto the river that came out of the village running parallel with the path. We shortly took another turn south into not so much a river but a channel that the waters had cut through the fields. Even though all the land was flooded the river and the channel were clearly visible, due to the fast flowing waters and the lack of any vegetation protruding from the water. Our ride became considerably smoother as the boat glided along, requiring only a gentle push from Iqbal every so often.

In the distance I could see the Banyan trees that were Fulbari, the copse being on the left side of the channel. As the boat approached it the land on either side began to rise from the waters, eventually leading to banks on either side of about three feet above the water channel. On the raised fields to our right I could see lush green crops about waist high. On some of the plants I could see red, orange, yellow and green chillies. Further along I could see tomato plants and on other plants there were no fruits or vegetables, just the green foliage.

"Where's our patch of crops?" I asked Aman.

"It's past Fulbari, just up ahead," he replied.

Approaching Fulbari I stared at the claw-like branches of the trees and their muddy colourless trunks, with dark nooks and crannies giving the impression of sockets missing their eyeballs. This sent a slight shiver down my spine and I was glad we were in the boat and not walking on the banks.

"Sabu's gonna get caught by Mamuzi," Iqbal taunted, breaking me out of my spell of gazing at the trees.

"Aarey! Sasa, I'm not scared of any Mamuzi or any other *buth*," I replied, the latter being another name for ghosts.

"You're the one with the red shirt," he retorted.

I put my hand in the water and sent a backsplash on him as he sat unaware behind me. The water caught him straight in the face, almost causing him to fall into the river.

"Hey!" he screamed, as the three of us up front burst out laughing. He couldn't splash me back because the rear of the boat was too high for him to reach into the waters. We settled back down chuckling under our breaths as the boat slid past Fulbari and the channel took a left turn.

"We're here," exclaimed Iqbal, as he turned the boat towards the right bank, giving the boat a rapid and hard punt which dug the front end into the soft, dark, grey silt.

Aman was already at the front of the boat and jumped off as soon as we hit land. Amad got off too and as I jumped off, my two feet sunk all the way up to my calves in the soft earth. I found I could not lift my feet out, no matter how much I struggled.

Iqbal seeing this laughed, "Hah! You wet me earlier, now it's my revenge."

He put the bamboo pole in the boat and came off the boat and even though his feet sank too, he somehow managed to lift them out without any problems. Iqbal then helped me get out of my sticky situation, letting me use his arms as leverage.

Meanwhile Aman had thrust one of the paddles deep into the soft earth and tied the boat chain around it securely. The four of us walked up to the fields and looked out west. Standing there, as far as the eye could see both west and south the crops seemed to go on for miles. In the far distance, to the south, I could see men in conical hats bent over working and beyond that I could see the billowing sails of a *gunti nowka*. I imagined it going somewhere exotic with its cargo of people or laden with goods for some far flung market.

Here on higher ground, away from the depression of the river channel, there was a cool breeze that flowed across the tops of the crops and ruffled our hair. Iqbal turned around to me and swept his hand across the fields in front of us.

"All these crops are ours, the chillies and tomatoes and further back there are other crops which are going to be picked over the coming weeks."

"The groundnut has already been picked," he continued.

"Come on, let's go into fields and find some tomatoes that are ripe," Aman said impatiently.

"Yes! Let's go," piped in Amad.

With Aman in lead we line marched along one of the gaps in between the rows of chillies until we came upon an earth ridge marking the end of the field of chillies. The next field was full of tomato plants, as we brushed along the plant leaves the smell of tomatoes permeated the air around us. We all sniffed in the fragrant air and each of us let out a "Vahh!" appreciatively. All the tomatoes were plump and almost all had turned an orange hue, whilst the odd one or two had become red. The first ripe tomato we found Iqbal picked, and to increase our chances of finding more, we fanned out into the field. Eventually, we had gathered a handful of tomatoes each and met up again at the edge of the adjoining chilli field. We sat on the ridge and laid out our tomatoes on the ground. Iqbal asked Aman to pick a few chillies, especially looking out for the darker green ones. Iqbal, for the benefit of me, then demonstrated the way to eat the tomatoes.

He took some salt from the packet that he had brought with him and placed it on his left palm then he took a tomato and rubbed it against his t-shirt and wiped it clean. He licked the tomato with his tongue and dipped it into the salt and followed that with a bite of the fruit. This he followed up with a small bite from a green chilli.

"And that's how you eat ripe tomatoes," he concluded as he wiped tomato juice from the edge of his mouth with his hands.

Aman and Amad had already begun biting into their tomatoes as I took one and followed suit. Biting into the juicy tomato was divine, as I had never tasted such sweet tomatoes ever and the fragrance danced with my nostrils every time I breathed out. The salt and the chilli added an extra dimension to the eating sensation, however I eventually just stuck to salt as the heat of the chillies was too much for me. The chilli that I did eat made my tongue go numb and caused tears to stream down my face. I had to inhale sharp intakes of breath to dissipate the heat. We then got our tomato supply and went back to the boat where we carried on with our tomato feast until we could eat no more.

"Hey sasa, do you want to go over to Fulbari and have a look?" asked Aman.

"Bibi and Old Auntie said that with a red shirt on Mamuzi will get me, so I don't know," I answered apprehensively.

"Come on, let's go, we can show you there's nothing to be afraid of, they're just old people trying to scare you, none of it is true," Iqbal encouraged.

"Alright then, let's go," I agreed, as being in the company of my uncles gave me a certain swagger.

We untied the boat and got back onto it, rinsing the mud off our feet by dangling them over the sides. We turned the boat around and headed back the way we had come and similarly parked the boat on the opposite bank under the branches of the Banyan trees.

There was about a dozen or so giant trees scattered along this area of high ground, the roots of the trees exposed to a degree with silt deposited around the edges. The trees were alive but had the look of deciduous trees during winter as if they had shed their leaves and gone into hibernation. All around and amongst the trees there was no vegetation and no one had planted any crops outside the wooded area.

"See, there's nothing here and no Mamuzi to get you," Aman said in a tone of bravado.

"Sasa is scared," Amad laughed.

"Get away! I wouldn't be here if I was scared," I snapped at him.

"Come on, let's go, there's nothing to see or do here," Iqbal interrupted.

"Yes! Let's go," I joined in.

So, with the two eldest in agreement we got back onto the boat and began the journey back to the bari. We made sure we took the long way back, by venturing into the northern fields relishing the freedom and open space which the watery fields offered. Even though I loved being in Shupatola and enjoyed the carefree life with Bolai as my buddy, there was something about being out on the open water under the great blue skies that exhilarated my spirit. The rain clouds racing overhead, the wind ruffling my hair, the fresh air and the silence and solitude of the plains underwater were breath taking.

We pulled into the canal under our bari and locked the boat, as a light drizzle began falling. As soon as we reached the porch of the house the wind had picked up and the skies fully opened up with a downpour. All the womenfolk of the bari went scurrying about bringing in clothes from the drying lines, fruits and vegetables that were out drying too, as well as ensuring anything light enough to be blown away was secured. We stored the paddles in the alley that ran between the four houses. I went into the house and put on my flip flops, using the rainwater falling from the roof to wash the last remnants of mud from my feet.

The last couple of hours of the day the rain drummed away on the roofs and the treetops swayed back and forth to the music of the wind and the rain. Everyone was pretty much housebound, Iqbal, Aman and I played marbles to kill time. However, as night drew in I wasn't feeling too good. I went back to my house just after dusk and lay on the bed, whilst Bibi and Old Auntie said their prayers. By the time they finished their prayers I was drifting in and out of a disturbed sleep and was feeling altogether very uncomfortable. Bibi put away her prayer mat and sat on the bed next to me with her rosary beads, then looked over at me.

"Sabu, what's the matter? Are you not feeling well?" she asked.

"I don't know, I can't describe how I feel but I don't feel too good," I replied as best as I could. She put her beads down and touched my forehead.

"Yah! Allah, you're burning up with fever," she gasped as Old Auntie leant over to feel my temperature.

"Yes my daughter, look at his face, it's gone all red," she pointed out to Bibi.

141

"Mother, you keep an eye on him whilst I go and get a cold cloth for his forehead."

My vision began to blur and I could feel droplets of sweat forming on my brow and my mouth and throat became parched. Bibi came back with a bowl of water and a swab which she placed on my brow and it kept it moist. With Bibi's return Auntie Rani and her sister Runi had heard that something was up and were also by the bedside.

"Bibi, can I have some water," I asked.

"Oh! Runi, go and get some water quickly," she ordered.

In the meantime my condition was worsening and I could only make out snippets of conversation here and there, catching a glimpse of the occasional face peering over at me.

"Where was he all day..." I heard someone say.

"Iqbal and Aman..." another voice replied to another question.

I think Iqbal and Aman were summoned to answer some questions. I heard their voices confirming that we had been near Fulbari. Then Bibi's voice gasped with horror saying that I had probably been touched by Mamuzi. I could sense that a lot of hustle and bustle was going on as other people came in to see what was going on. Finally, I could not keep my eyes open and just before I completely drifted off into a disturbed sleep I heard Bibi asking Boro Dada to go and fetch the Imam from the mosque.

In my dreams, or should I say nightmares, everything was distorted like a house of mirrors at a funfair. I could see people with distorted faces and limbs bent weirdly, in a funny way rather than grotesque. Colours looked like swirls on a painter's palette, mixing into a non-colour and then splitting away to its original hue. My eyes felt as if one minute they were sinking into my body then another minute they would bulge out like a frog's. The most frightening experience of the whole nightmare was a feeling of being held down by some presence, nameless, faceless, but ominous. I couldn't open my eyes, move my limbs or utter a sound, and I was in an eternal struggle for my survival, a fight that I had to win in order to live. After an almighty struggle that seemed to last for ages the being disappeared in a flash, and I was left alone with a feeling of being suspended in mid-air with no one around but me.

I woke up the following day around mid-morning, with Bibi sitting by my side having patiently watched over me the whole night.

"Bibi, water," I croaked.

"Here you are," Bibi put a stainless steel cup to my mouth, the water tasted like heaven.

As the water passed down to my belly it cooled my insides on its journey. I sat up and realised I hadn't eaten anything since the tomatoes and I was famished. I didn't have to say anything as one of the solutions to anything in Bengali culture is to eat first then worry. So Bibi went off to the kitchen saying that she was off to get some rice and asked whether I wanted rice with dhal or potato bhajee. I opted for the latter, and as she disappeared out of the doorway Old Auntie hobbled in through the rear door.

"What Sabu? You have woken up I see. How are you feeling?" she asked.

"Slightly better and not as bad as last night," I replied.

"Have you eaten anything?" she continued.

"No! Bibi's just gone to get some rice."

"We told you yesterday not to go near Fulbari with that red shirt on, last night you really were speaking some strange words," she said smiling.

"What did I say?" I asked impatiently.

"Wait till your Bibi gets here, she'll tell you," she said as she hoisted her small frame onto the bed adjoining to mine.

I looked out the window with an intricately patterned grill but no glass panes, which was directly aligned with the main path leading into the bari. The sun was out and it looked like a nice day, the heat was ever-present as usual and being a school day most of my accomplices were at school. Even Boro Dada would be out in the fields with the workers, either harvesting some crop or getting fodder for the cattle.

Bibi walked in with a plate of rice and bhajee, before she had put the plate in front of me I began harassing her to tell me what had happened.

"Bibi, what did I say last night?"

"Eat the rice first," she ordered.

As I began mixing the rice and bhajee, Bibi began to relate to me what had happened after I had fallen asleep. Boro Dada brought over the Imam, who upon seeing me drenched in sweat and moaning in my sleep declared that a jinn had taken possession of me and that he needed to act fast. He had the room cleared immediately except for Bibi, Boro Dada and Old Auntie, who being the elders would assist him. The Imam then read prayers in Arabic and blessed me over again and again. During the whole ordeal I was swearing and cursing in English and Bengali. I made no sense whatsoever to anyone.

The Imam left a *tabiz*, a small copper amulet containing a prayer for me to wear. I looked at my upper left arm and there it was, tied with black thread. After he had gone I settled down and slept with the odd moan and groan emanating from me that kept Bibi awake and diligently swabbing my forehead to hold the fever at bay.

"Really? Did Mamuzi get me then?" I asked Bibi.

"Well, the Imam said that something had gotten you, it could just have been the jinn's touch when you were out at Fulbari," Bibi explained.

"The Imam's coming back later to bless you again to ensure you get better properly."

Inwardly I was feeling like a swashbuckling adventurer who had survived the wrath of the jinns and returned a hero. Eat your heart out, Sinbad. I couldn't wait to tell Bolai upon my return, and even now I wanted to get up and tell everyone in the bari what I'd been through. However, Bibi ordered me to stay within the house until the Imam's visit. Bibi was feeling mightily relieved that I had pulled through successfully, I got the feeling she was concerned about how to explain it all to my parents if things got any worse than they did. Bibi left me with Old Auntie and went about her day of performing chores and helping around the bari. Old Auntie was almost housebound, apart from going to the toilet which she still managed on her own, she needed assistance when she went down to the pond to bathe and travelling was not really an option for her. She had lost all of her own teeth so her food had to be prepared with a baby in mind.

She sat next to me swinging the *panka* back and forth, trying to cool the muggy monsoon air whilst relaying stories to me about my dad and I. She was telling me how dad as a toddler rarely saw my grandfather who was away on the merchant ships between England and India. So, when he returned to the bari Dad would hide from him and needed to be coaxed by Granddad and pushed by Bibi to go to him. It's funny how history repeats itself, as the same thing happened to me. My dad was in England during my birth and I did not see him until I was close to two years old when he returned after the war of independence from Pakistan, when he and I went through the same motions as he did with his father.

My mum recalled how during the war of independence Purushpal was mainly inhabited by women, children and the elderly. Apart from the men who were overseas, the remaining adult males had to go into hiding for fear of being picked up by the Pakistani military and disappearing, never to be found again. She relayed to me how Pakistani fighter jets would scream overhead, sometimes firing randomly and other times dropping propaganda literature. This was also an opportune moment for many blood feuds to be settled and revenge taken out on enemies. Whereby one Bengali would betray another as being a *mukti bahini* – a freedom fighter to the Pakistani military, who would come and pick the informed man up and he would disappear forever. There were stories of men being chained to trees and machine gunned by the Pakistani military. There was one such story of an atrocity being carried out in Mathiura, where a neighbour informed on a neighbour.

On those occasions when the fighter jets flew by, all the womenfolk would run into the fields and hide in the paddy with their children. I along with all the other children being my uncles and aunts would scream and cry. Our parents would try and placate us long after the warplanes had disappeared. The whole routine would be repeated when the fighter planes returned on their next sortie. The nightmare of war lasted nine months, ending on 16th December 1971.

Maybe that's why my dad was quite willing to send me to Bangladesh for almost a year, not in a vindictive kind of way, but as the father and son bond had not developed during those formative years, he probably felt that I needed to grow up fast.

In the distance the muezzin's call to prayer began, the short Arabic recital being blared across the airwaves, which was so prominent to Bengali village life. Five times a day these calls would go out throughout the land like clockwork, notifying people of when to pray. Not only did they act as prayer calls, but in the absence of clocks and watches many people set their days by the calls. Apart from the devout and particularly elderly, few people actually went to a mosque to pray daily, however Friday was one day that all men and boys would be present for midday prayers.

Old Auntie looked out through the window, smiled and turned to me.

"Look who's coming up the path!"

I lifted myself up from the bed and looking out through the window I could see the familiar face of Uncle Naz striding up the path, holding the bottom end of his lunghi to prevent it getting dirty and muddy from the wet patches on the ground that were water logged. He walked across the courtyard and up the steps into the house. He greeted Old Auntie who had gotten off the bed and prepared herself to say her prayers.

"What son? What have you been up to this time?" he asked with a smile. I wondered should I go with the heroic jinn survivor story or a less dramatic approach to the story.

"No sasa, not much, just got a bit of Mamuzi's touch," I said modestly.

"So! You went to Fulbari," he stated raising his eyebrows.

"We only went to the look at the crops and then we only had a quick look at Fulbari," I didn't go into too much detail.

"Aarey! Sabu, what are we going to do with you," he said, not in a serious needing to find a solution kind of way, but rather how all the shenanigan's I was getting up to were building up, and how they would be taken by my parents. I supposed he felt partly responsible, especially as I was sent with him under his custodianship.

"I also heard you were selling fruits up in Beani Bazaar, a little while back."

"Who told you?" I said looking worried.

"Someone from the village," mentioned it.

Bibi walked in to the room and replied to Uncle Naz's salutation.

"Naz, you sit whilst I say my prayers," she said as she

walked over to the back of the room and placed her prayer mat next to Old Auntie's.

The two of us sat there quietly ensuring silence, so mother and daughter could complete their prayers without distraction. Bibi finished first and came and sat next to Uncle Naz and with her rosary beads in hand recited the various names of God in Arabic.

"Auntie, how are you? And what is this about your grandson being possessed?" he asked Bibi.

"I'm doing well, and don't ask about Sabu, he wore a red shirt and went to Fulbari so Mamuzi got a bit upset I suppose, and what's your news?" she asked him.

"So! so! But good overall, have you heard from bhaisab?" he asked referring to my dad.

"No, recently there have been no letters or anything, and even if there was a letter you never know someone may have opened it here," she replied.

"Auntie, you haven't been to my bari yet? Come one day whilst you're still here," he offered.

"I visited the other day but you were at the bazaar, but I will go. How's your wife doing?" Bibi asked.

"She's coping well, however I am a bit restless and want to get back to London. Hopefully her application will come through shortly," he said frowning. "When are you going back to Shupatola?" he continued.

"In a week or so," she answered.

Old Auntie had finished her prayers and joined us again.

"What Naz? Are you doing well?"

"Yes, Nani, is your health good?"

"Generally good, my age is creeping up on me, it's getting harder."

Uncle Naz got up from where he was sitting and went over to Old Auntie and grabbed her in a huge bear hug, almost lifting her up from her seated position on the bed.

"Get away, put me down, look Sabu, you're uncle has gone crazy," she laughed.

"Aarey Nani, I love you so much that I will give up everything and look after you," he said boisterously.

"No! You look after yourself and your new wife, I'll be fine."

Auntie Runi walked in with some tea and biscuits for Uncle Naz, when he saw her he quickly came back to sitting near me and became a well behaved young man. He acknowledged Runi's greeting and chatted with her, she asked how his wife was, and for him to bring her over for a visit. Even though visiting him and his wife was a matter of walking five minutes to Naz's bari, everyone was so preoccupied with day to day life that they rarely saw each other, especially the womenfolk. Due to culture and custom a teenager like Runi or any other lady for that matter could not go wandering to another bari, they had to carry an umbrella to hide their modesty, tell their parents and sometimes even be chaperoned.

Old Auntie, ever the sentry again, signalled the approach of another man up the path, this time it was the Imam. Both she and Bibi put their sari ends on their heads as a sign of respect and modesty and Runi did the same with her shawl and scampered across the courtyard back to the kitchen. Even Naz, who by now lay on his back on the bed next to me relaxing sat up straight.

The Imam was dressed in plain white lunghi and a tunic which was starched so heavily that his upper body looked like a cardboard cut-out. On his head he wore a white cap akin to those worn by Nehru and the obligatory beard, minus the moustache. He came into the room and was simultaneously greeted by everyone.

"Salaam alaikum," everyone hailed.

"Alaikum salaam," he replied.

"Sabu, how are you feeling today," he asked.

"I'm feeling much better," I replied.

"Did you get any more of a fever?"

"Today I'm doing OK, but my body is aching a bit," I explained.

"Well, you had a bit of a battle with a spirit so it's expected, I'll give you one more *fuu* and then you should be well again," he said referring to the blowing of air that was bestowed upon someone who has just been prayed for in such circumstances.

Uncle Naz moved away from his position next to me as the Imam approached. The Imam sat by me and began muttering Arabic prayer incantations under his breath, whilst I and everyone else in the room, including Boro Dada's wife and Mejo Dada's wife who were standing outside peering through the window, were deathly silent. The whole process took about five minutes after which the Imam blew his breath in a "chewfffff" sound on my head, and that was the *fuu*.

"Everything will be fine now, just be careful when and where you tread," he said as he got up to go. Bibi got up too and took him to the kitchen to feed him lunch, as was customary if it was a meal time, as well as paying him for his services.

Uncle Naz and I had lunch after the Imam had gone, by which time Boro Dada had also returned from the fields and he joined the two of us. I was definitely feeling better by the end of the day and as my chums returned from school I relayed to them what had happened and we had a laugh and a joke about it all, even though the elders did not see it as a matter to be taken lightly. Nobody questioned the whole jinn theory and no one even gave thought to the possibility of the whole incident being psychosomatic on my part. There was no question asked about eating unwashed tomatoes and chillies which may have been the cause, the power of the Imam and his incantations were believed irrefutably. I on the other hand, took it in my stride and was back to normal in no time. I followed my dad's view that most of these things were old wives' tales meant for children and to scare people.

Lazy Layabouts

Bibi and I had already been in Purushpal for a week and I was getting a bit restless and eager to get back home, however I could understand Bibi wanting to stay a little longer. All her life she had lived in Purushpal among her immediate family, as well as the extended family in the bari and village, and now here she was, miles away from home, lonely in a new bari with no one for company except her ten-year old grandson. Luckily, I had distractions to keep me busy for the extra week that we stayed.

Boro Dada, being the eldest of his three brothers, took most of the responsibility for the agricultural land belonging to the family. His youngest brother *Chuto Dada*, or 'Little Granddad' as I called him, was younger than my dad and was in London too and lived not too far from our home in London's East End. His other brother, who I called *Mejo Dada*, and yes, that simply means 'Middle Granddad', was in Dubai as a migrant worker. So the land cultivation was left in the hands of Boro Dada, who had the help of a couple farm hands, his two adult sons Hannan and Mahmod and Mejo Dada's teenage son, Shuwa.

However, the help that Dada got from his two sons, especially Mahmod, was like extracting healthy teeth from someone's mouth. He would drag his feet or disappear from the bari when it was time to perform chores with regards to farming. Hannan and Shuwa did help out on the odd occasion, but Dada still did the lion's share with the farm hands. The three uncles dreamed of going abroad like others who were doing so during the 1980's, they wanted Boro Dada to sell land if necessary and obtain work visas for the Middle East. To them it seemed that manual farm work was beneath them.

The irony of this whole battle between Dada's generation and his children was that the land produced ample cash crops, namely rice, potatoes, onions, as well as making their own cooking oil from the ground nuts they grew. This meant that they had a whole years' supply of food, plus surplus to sell for extra cash. Even my ten year old brain could deduce that with a little extra effort their farming could be profitable by producing more than the surplus they were already getting and selling at a great profit. However, like Dick Whittington, Dada's sons' and nephew dreamed of the gold paved streets of the Arab world.

So, over the remainder of the week I tagged along with Boro Dada as he went about his daily chores harvesting the crops near Fulbari, or getting grass for his cattle. One morning Dada, the farm hand Kotoy and I went off into the northern fields to get some grass for his four head of cattle.

"Grass! Where are we going to get grass? There's water everywhere?" I asked quizzically of Dada.

"You'll see Sabu, there's grass everywhere, it's just that you haven't been looking in the right places," he smiled.

I followed Dada out of the bari and onto the boat I had used to visit Fulbari, where Kotoy was already waiting for us. He was standing at the back of the boat with the pole and as we got on board he pushed off out into the fields. Boro Dada took a position at the front of the boat with another pole, therefore giving us extra muscle power and speed out on the open waters. In the boat there were a couple of sickles for cutting the grass, as well as two conical hats.

We headed north with Kotoy singing a traditional Bengali farmers song at the top of his voice. The sun beat down on the three of us and fat, rain laden clouds lumbered across the sky. He sang the song in a sad, lamenting tune, and it sent a tingling sensation down the back of my spine, causing me to shiver. The boat continued north until looking back all I could see of the bari were the greens of the treetops and other plants on the horizon. We were approaching the banks of the Kushiara River, where the land was rising and upon taking a closer look I could see fat, dark green blades of grass sticking out a foot above the water. The boat glided through the grass with a swishing noise, loud enough to stop Kotoy singing.

"Grandson, here's your grass," Dada said, sweeping his arms around him.

All the way up to the banks of the river, as well as up and down I could see a sea of spiky grass blades billowing in the gentle breeze, as if they were dancing to a tune only played for them by the wind. The boat was brought to a halt and Kotoy planted his pole firmly into the bed of the field and then tied the boat to it with a jute rope. The two men then retied their lunghis around their waist so as to give them plenty of length towards their ankles. Then, they lifted the bottom of the lunghis, gathered it towards the front, tightened the whole length under their groin over their back and tucked the end into the back of the lunghi. The two of them now looked as if they were wearing nappies but which gave them great mobility in the waters they swiftly jumped into.

"Grandson, you sit while we cut the grass," Dada said taking the sickle from the boat, with Kotoy following him suit.

The two men started close to the boat by leaning into the waters with their hands, grabbing the base of the grass and severing the stalks from the roots. They went around cutting the grass and placing them in the boat, which were easily three or four feet in length. I could see further along the bank other people doing the same as us. During the wet season such grass provided vital fresh fodder for cattle that could not graze freely due to a lack of dry grazing land in the low plains around Purushpal.

I was so tempted to jump into the water, but the water level was high enough to reach my chest and with the river nearby underwater currents could easily pull me away. So I stayed onboard restively, playing with the grass stalks or just chewing on blades of grass, which were as sharp as a razor. I understood from that day why "a blade of grass" was exactly that, by the end of the day I ended up with minute lacerations on my tongue and lower lip.

Soon the boat was stacked high with grass and Boro Dada got back onboard the boat, however Kotoy was not cutting anymore grass, but picking something from the surface of the water. He came back with a handful of *bhet*, a variety of Lotus flower whose core, when ripen, is edible. Returning to the boat he handed me the lotus flower buds and hoisted himself onto the boat.

"Here you are nephew, I've got some *bhet* here, try them."

With little or no use of the word 'thank you' in everyday Bengali life and me being a Londoni, I blurted out, "Thank you, *sasa*" with a big grin on my face. I don't think he understood and I realised I wasn't in England, he laughed.

"What did you say son?"

"No *sasa*, I just said *dhanyavaad*," which was the Bengali equivalent of thank you.

However I had never heard it being used in any situation so far. Even though I hadn't made errors as such that often, I knew I had to be aware of what I said sometimes, especially when I was wrapped in a moment of happiness or the odd temper tantrum.

"Turn the boat around Kotoy," Dada asked as we headed back to our bari.

I sat there facing our direction of travel and opened one of the *bhet*. Inside hundreds of black seeds were wrapped in a fluffy, transparent coating. I took a mouthful of the seeds, which once open started to fall apart due to their delicate composition. The texture was that of candy floss and had a nutty, fragrant taste, it was divine. I offered Dada and Kotoy one each, the latter declined but Dada took one and savoured the delightful flower seeds. I continued to enjoy the one I had opened, saving the others for later.

Halfway back to the bari a few specks of rain started to dust us, the wind also picked up and the rain came and went as it was blown hither and thither.

"Give it a good push Kotoy, the downpour is going to be here soon," Dada said, as he plunged his pole into the water. We picked up speed and made it into the canal beside the bari, as the rain came pouring from the heavens. Fortunately, we were under cover of the bamboo branches and other trees that protected us temporarily from the rains. Eventually, the rain droplets made their way through the leaves and branches and found their prey, drenching us just as we moored the boat.

Dada and Kotoy began grabbing armfuls of cut grass and walking up the path to the barn on the left. I joined them, grabbing puny amounts compared to them and walked precariously up the slippery muddy path. Dada asked me not to as they would be done quickly anyway. I insisted on helping so he let me continue with the task until all the grass was stored away. I ran back to the house by which time I was literally soaked, water droplets fell from the locks of my hair into my eyes and from the end of my nose into my mouth. I waited for the rain to stop before going down to the pond for a bath. I walked out to the porch, taking my wet t-shirt off and hanging it to dry on a clothes line. I began drying myself lightly with a towel and couldn't help but start scratching my arms with fervour. I looked at them wondering why they were itching so much. The inside of my arms had extremely fine cuts all over them and each one was crimson red and throbbing to be scratched. Boro Dada came up the path and saw me scratching vigorously.

"What's up, Sabu?"

"My hands are itching really badly," I replied continuing to scratch my arms.

"If you carry on, you'll make it worse, look the rain's letting up, why don't you go and have a bath and then come and see me," he suggested.

I went back into the house, got a soap bar and ran barefoot out to the pond, the risk of wearing a pair of sandals and falling onto the muddy path was too great and I could always rinse my feet once back. At the ghat there were some of my aunts who had gone down to wash their clothes. I dunked myself in the water and gave myself a quick lathering of the soap and rinsed as fast as I could. The rains having cooled the water temperature considerably did not make it too comfortable to hang around in the water for long. I dried myself and put on a lunghi and carefully walked back to the house. Boro Dada was waiting in my room and he had a bottle of oil in his hand.

"Here, give me your arms," he applied viscous mustard oil all over my arms. "Apply some over your legs and feet as well."

Even though the itching had subsided a tad since washing, upon applying the oil the initial stinging gave way to a soothing relief. I recall my mum telling me how when I was a baby Bibi used to slap on so much mustard oil all over my body after bathing that visiting relatives would have to wipe me prior to holding me, else they would have permanent oil stains on their clothes. I guess Bibi had a good reason for doing so, and today I became aware of one of the oil's benefits.

The remainder of the day and into the night the rain came and went, but never fully stopped. This meant that I, as well as my uncles when they returned from school, were housebound. We broke the boredom with the odd game of marbles and roasting some of the recently harvested ground nuts in the kitchen hearth. We took the nuts and wrapped a cotton blanket around our shoulders, sitting on my bed next to Old Auntie, cracking the shells and crunching on the kernels whilst the rain drummed away on the roof. When Aman or Iqbal got a bit boisterous or noisy Auntie hurled a caution in their direction with little effect, however I could see that it was just as much fun for her to see we were enjoying ourselves as it was for us. Her cautions or reprimands were always accompanied by a smile that she tried to conceal.

Old Auntie had a look of serenity and peace on her wizened old face that made her look almost saintly. Her skin had become almost translucent with age and she had a permanent cheeky smile in the corner of her mouth. It was as if she knew something that we didn't and she was not going to reveal what it was. I guess she had reached her own form of enlightenment on planet Earth and she was enjoying watching her progeny in their youth all around her having fun and growing up fast. Everyone loved her and I never knew her to raise her voice or say an unkind word.

That night before the evening meal Aman and Iqbal had gone back to their house to do a bit of homework, whilst I lay on my bed as Bibi and Old Auntie said their prayers. Next door I could hear Boro Dada and his wife having a slightly heated discussion. Initially, I couldn't tell what they were talking about. Suddenly, Dada came out with an outburst that made Old Auntie and Bibi jump in the prayers.

"Those sons of *gulams*," he cursed, I guessed at Hannan and Mahmod, referring to them as no better than serfs.

Bibi, being second in seniority after Old Auntie finished her prayers as quickly as possible and got up to go next door to Dada's house with me following her.

"Don't say too much my daughter," Auntie warned Bibi.

Bibi walked into the room where Dada and his wife were having their argument.

"What's the matter with the two of you?"

"Your two nephews think they do not need to work around this bari and that the food on their plates appears by magic," Dada said, completely confusing me.

"What have they done or not done?" Bibi asked.

"Your brother asked Hannan and Mahmod to go with him tomorrow evening to Asirkal Bazaar and help him sell the groundnuts," Boro Dadi said nodding towards Dada.

Another oddity in Bengali marriages is that people of Dada's or even my parent's generation, never call each other by name. It's usually 'your mum...' or 'your dad...' or in this case 'your brother...'

"But they do not want to go, apparently they've got things to do," added Dada.

"Now, I cannot make them go," Boro Dadi pleaded with Bibi.

"You've been too easy on them, and now they will not obey me at all," Dada blamed his wife.

"This means I go and do all the work while they sleep with their backsides in the air expecting life to bring everything to them."

"You might as well stop for now, as they're not going to agree to do anything if you carry on like this," Bibi said trying to end the argument.

"Look, it's getting late and if you've said your prayers you may as well go eat your rice."

Bibi then turned to Boro Dadi.

"You go and heat the curries and we'll be over shortly."

Bibi and I left Dada to calm down as his wife went off to the kitchen to prepare dinner. Boro Dada wasn't the argumentative kind of man and he usually shies away from confrontation, so it must have been really upsetting for him to get to that position. I could feel for him as all his life from about my age he had done nothing but work on the family land, and his sons did not even want to accompany him to the market for one evening. The sad thing was that the two of them were neither in further education, nor did they have any other jobs so the only reason I could think they had would be to loaf around on their own or with friends.

Later on Bibi and I joined Dada for dinner, only his daughters were visible around the bari, his sons were nowhere to be seen, I guessed keeping a low profile somewhere. Dada had calmed down by the time we got to the kitchen and he was his usual chatty self, even though Boro Dadi avoided any sort of conversation with him apart from asking if he wanted any more curry or rice.

After dinner I went and sat with Dada as he sat on his bed and dragged on his *hookah* – a water-based smoking pipe. He gave me a couple of puffs which were more than enough for me to turn green at the gills. This wasn't my first time or the last attempt at smoking the hubble-bubble, and by the time I went back to England I was able to take a few puffs without choking.

"Dada, when are you going to leave for Asirkal tomorrow?"

"Just after *Asar* prayers," he replied, which was about a couple of hours prior to sunset.

"Are you going to sell all the groundnuts?" I continued.

"No! Half of them we're going to keep to make oil," he replied. "Why Grandson?" he questioned.

"Dada, can I come with you?" I looked up hoping he would say yes.

He took a drag of his *hookah* and mused whilst looking at the smoke drifting up towards the ceiling, where it lingered momentarily before disappearing into nothingness.

"You can come as long as your Bibi is happy about it," he answered smiling. I was over the moon to say the least.

"I'm going to ask her now Dada," I said as I dashed off in search of her.

"Bibi! Bibi! Where are you?" I ran into my house shouting.

"Hey! What is all this yelling?" Old Auntie asked.

"I'm looking for Bibi, where is she?"

"I think she's in the kitchen."

Without another word I shot off down the steps and across the courtyard, taking care not to slip on the mud and into the kitchen. There was Bibi in a corner on a short stool chewing on betel nut, whilst all of the womenfolk, Mejo Dadi and Boro Dadi with all their daughters sat around the bamboo mat eating their evening's rice.

"Bibi, can I go to Asirkal Bazaar tomorrow with Boro Dada?" I fired off like a machine gun without taking a breath.

"Why?" She asked worriedly.

"For no reason, I want to help Dada sell the peanuts and see how the nuts are sold," I replied. "I've asked him already and he said if you're happy then I can go with him."

"Eh! Sabu is becoming a true bazaar-man going to all the main markets and selling things," Auntie Safa teased. She was one of Mejo Dada's teenage daughters' who was always quick with the quips.

"Alright then, you can go, just don't bring back any jinns or buths," Bibi joked.

With the answer that I was looking for I rushed back out of

the kitchen, not giving anyone else a chance to say anything, I ran over to Boro Dada's place and gave him the permission that I had just received.

That night going to bed I was full of excitement and went to sleep imagining what the market would be like, how big it would be and what sorts of people would be there. The following morning began with a bright and sunny start, I went to the pond to clean my teeth and wash my face. With my supply of toothpaste having depleted about a month after I arrived I began using black tooth powder with my right index finger as an implement for cleaning my teeth. The powder was basically the ground up remains of the charcoal from the kitchen hearth. It was only possible to clean the surface areas of the teeth with little effect in between. Once cleaned up I went over to the kitchen, where Bibi had prepared breakfast which varied depending on what was available. Most days it was either *muri koy* or *seera*, rice pops or rice flakes respectively with milk, other times it would be paratha or steamed rice cakes with a curry dish. My favourite was paratha with hot dhal, it would set me up for the day like no other and today was one of those days. A couple of the aunts were in the kitchen preparing the parathas and as everyone came in they were given a couple of pieces of the bread with dhal.

After breakfast I looked for Boro Dada to see if he needed any help but I could not find him, I asked Boro Dadi where he was. She allayed my fears of missing out on the trip, saying that he had gone to the fields with Kotoy to finish some small jobs and would be back by noon. A bit disappointed I sat at the steps of the house looking out towards the path as Iqbal, Aman and other children from the bari headed out to school with their books and slates under their arms. With the sun at the back of the house the courtyard was under shade and was pleasantly cool. Bibi walked out of our house and stood next to me.

"What are you doing?" she asked.

"Nothing," I replied.

"Do you want to go over to your Uncle Naz's bari later in the morning?"

"Yes sure!"

"Let me just finish up some odd jobs then we'll go."

With that she picked up a broom from the porch floor and began sweeping the front of our house and the room within.

The remainder of the day I was fidgety, unable to wait to get under way to the bazaar. Our trip over to Uncle Naz's bari broke the waiting, where Bibi and I found Naz's father Ali sitting on the porch of the kitchen smoking his *hookah*. He greeted us and we asked him where Naz was. We found Uncle Naz in the kitchen with his mother and wife having a late breakfast.

"Hey! Auntie is here, give her and Sabu something to eat, sit down the both of you," he asked his wife and making a fuss over us.

"No son, we've had breakfast, don't make anything for us," Bibi insisted, which didn't work as Naz's wife gave us some milky vermicelli dessert and tea.

We sat on muras that were brought over by a maid who was also going about her duties in the kitchen. Through the rear kitchen door in walked Uncle Feer, and as I got up to greet him he came over and gave me a big bear hug.

"My Sabu, has come," in a lisp and a slight stutter.

"Uncle, what's your news? Are you well?" I asked.

"Yes! Have you eaten?" he asked. And before I could reply he turned to his bhabi, Uncle Naz's wife and yelled. "Hey! Give my Sabu something to eat and drink."

Feer was in his mid-teens but only slightly taller than me, yet surprisingly he was sharp as any other person in the room, only that he needed that special love and care in a country that did not have basic medical facilities let alone cater for the needs of people with Downs syndrome. Feer sat beside me while Bibi chatted with Uncle Naz and his mum. Occasionally Naz would joke with me, and Feer would come to my defence, sitting with his right arm over my shoulder.

We got back to our bari shortly after midday to find Boro Dada having returned from the morning's work. He had already bathed and was heading to the mosque for prayers. As he was walking out I caught up with him and asked if I needed to do anything or did he need any help to get ready for this afternoon. He assured me all was in hand and that we were pretty much set to go.

After lunch the weather turned a bit grey and gloomy and didn't look as if the clouds would hold much into the late afternoon. With the return of Aman and Iqbal from school I hung around with them, telling them about my trip with Dada. Neither of them seemed too interested in travelling to a bazaar to sell nuts, but I didn't let their lack of enthusiasm for adventures dampen my spirits. For his late afternoon prayers Dada did not visit the mosque, instead he prayed at home.

As soon as he was finished we went out to the boat and Dada began loading the eighteen sacks of groundnuts. With no trolley or carrying equipment it was a case of loading the sacks one by one from the barn onto the boat, by the end of which Dada had worked up a sweat and I did so just by watching him working so hard. He grabbed a bamboo pole, two paddles, two conical hats, two oil lanterns and one umbrella. We both had a glass of water each before we boarded the boat for our journey to the market. Bibi came and waved us good luck and asked Dada to keep an eye out for me.

"Bibi, nothing will happen, I will be fine," I said assuring her that I was old enough to take care of myself.

"We are going now," Dada said as he pushed off the banks of the canal.

Bibi stood there and watched us as we glided into the northern fields. I was so excited sitting at the front of the boat with the cargo behind me in the middle and Dada at the back end. I had never been to Asirkal Bazaar and the thought of going there on business with Dada made me feel grown up. However, the key motivation for me was the adventure, again here I was out doing something I had never done and I didn't know what the night ahead was going to be like. For me every bend in the road, every fork in the river, every hill, village and bazaar held an opportunity to see new faces, places, sights and sounds.

Getting out of the fields around the village we took the same route as if we were heading towards Fulbari, however once we had passed through the break in the road Dada turned the boat west on the canal. Here he put his pole away and took up one of the paddles and sat down to steer us in the fast flowing waters rushing to join the Kushiara River. Shortly afterwards the road to our right disappeared into the watery fields, which apart from the channel of the canal, all became one body of water.

Joining the Kushiara, Dada had to be careful as it was much wider, deeper and the currents faster. Where the canal joined the Kushiara little eddies were created and with our boat laden with valuable cargo, Dada had to slowly and carefully join the bigger river. Once we joined the Kushiara and the boat was positioned squarely in the centre of the channel we travelled even faster, with Dada doing little or no rowing apart from the odd directional steering. We travelled south for a considerable time following the rivers twists and turns, the further we travelled we were joined by more and more river traffic from tributaries and homesteads lining the banks.

There were some *gunti nowkas* carrying passengers, other boats like ours were ferrying cargo and then there were boats that dwarfed us carrying sand, stones and other raw materials. Soon enough the darkness began chasing the sun over the western horizon, whose blades of red tried to fight back the black hands of the impending night. Pinpricks of lantern light could be seen along the river banks as the villages began preparing for the night. Wood fires were lit with the smoke and smell drifting out over the waters, reminding me of similar activities going on back at the bari. Dada asked me to light one of the lanterns which I did and held by its handle. The noises of the night also began in earnest, the chirruping of the insects and the croaking of the frogs being the most distinguishable.

"We are almost there," said Dada.

"If you look ahead in the distance you can see the cluster of lights, that's Asirkal."

I held the lantern slightly off to the side so I could see into the distance and sure enough there was a mass of what seemed to be hundreds of lights on the left bank, like fireflies dancing in the dark velvety night.

As we neared Dada steered the boat closer to the bank and turned into a tributary flanking the bazaar. There were numerous boats moored and tied against tree roots, bamboo poles and to each other. Dada rowed against the current until he found an empty space to moor the boat, and as he pushed the boat up into the bank beside a huge mango tree he asked me to jump off and tie the chain around its roots. I waited by the tree as Dada stowed away the paddles and pole, he then lit the other lantern and came on shore with both of them.

Handing me a lantern, Dada said, "Wait here Grandson, I need to go and get us a space to sell. I will be back soon."

Behind me the bazaar was bustling with people going about their business. There were elderly men in the lunghi, starched shirts and caps on their heads, younger men in groups laughing and joking. The traders in their work clothes looking the grimiest of the lot, who walked passed me and into the melee of the bazaar. Lit lanterns were hung on poles and ceilings of the small wooden stalls, mobile vendors of snacks, cigarettes and betel nut went about yelling a melodic tune to sell their wares. Dada came back, minus the lantern.

"I've got a place for us, I'm going to take the sacks over and I want you to stand guard here."

"OK, Dada," I replied.

Both of us were barefoot to enable ease of walking on the muddy paths in and around the bazaar. Dada used one of the paddles to tie two rope nets at either end and then put a sack in each of them. He then hoisted the paddle onto his shoulders and went to drop them off in the bazaar. When he was ready with the last two sacks I followed behind him as we wound through the throng of people and the odd stray dog into the bazaar. Arriving at our pitch Dada was glistening with sweat, which he wiped with a large piece of cloth tied to his waist. With the bulk of the sacks behind us Dada opened a couple of them to display the nuts in front, and we began our night of trading.

Dada was hoping that he could get a trader to bulk buy his whole lot, even though there would be less money. However, he knew we would sell all of the stock by the end of the night. Standing there I looked around our place which was amongst other traders selling onions, potatoes, chillies and a whole host of other produce in bulk. The Asirkal, once a week, was a wholesale bazaar, as well as the normal retail trading that went on, many farmers and retailers came to bulk buy goods. Opposite our section was the fresh fish area where fishermen, speaking in a tongue not from the Sylhet region argued, bartered, discussed and sold their prize catches to customers. There were beautiful silvery chandpuri hilshas, glistening black catfish, some of them almost as long as me. Then there were the smaller fish in batches, some of their colours would stand a good chance of competing with a rainbow. All around us the whole market was lit with lanterns and oil lamps, the smell pervading the air with little chance of any other aroma or smell to be noticed.

Our first customers were two men who looked about Dada's age, they were neatly dressed, with beards and prayer caps on their scalps, with the scent of rose oil wafting over from their clothes. This caused me to pinch my nose and hold my breath. Rose oil was favoured by Muslim men of a certain age, who wore the scent when going to Friday prayers or just going out and about.

"Oh! *Sasa*, what are these like?" one asked Dada, wanting to know the price.

In Bangladesh you always referred to any stranger as a brother or uncle, depending on age and circumstances, it was considered kind and friendly, hence these two referred to Dada as an uncle.

"Seventy taka, per sack," Dada replied.

"What uncle? That's a bit dear, isn't it?" they smirked.

"These are from my own crops and they are very good, I've even kept some myself to make oil and to use as seed next season."

"No uncle, the price still is too high," one of the men rebutted.

"Do you have any real intention of buying?" Dada questioned, trying to provoke a better price.

"If the price is right then we'll consider about six sacks."

"Well what sort of price are you looking to pay?" Dada asked.

"We were thinking of forty five per sack," this made Dada laugh quietly.

"If I sell at that price I might as well go home now and use them for myself."

This banter went back and forth for a while and eventually the two men walked away. However, it wasn't long before they were back again, this time with a third man. I thought to myself "Oh no, not again," the third man took one of the nuts and cracked the shell open and tasted them. His face displayed a sign of approval even though he never said anything. One of the first two men began the bid at a fifty taka per sack. Dada would not accept anything less than sixty taka, which we eventually agreed on and sold six sacks.

"See Sabu, it is even hard work trying to sell stuff," he looked exasperated.

"I had the same problem in Beani Bazaar."

"Yes! I heard about your antics in Beani Bazaar, it was very brave of you," he stated.

I did not reply and on that note he asked me to watch the stall as he went off to buy something for us to eat. He came back with some steaming hot *shingaras* – samosas – and some lentil patties. We washed it all down with two cups of water he had also obtained from the cafe. By the time he got back from returning the cups there were several people at our stall who were asking questions about the price and quality. This time we sold fewer sacks but more people began to buy. With no clock or watch I had no idea of the time and did not know whether it was eight in the evening or midnight.

By the time the muezzin's final prayer call of the day went out from the local mosque, Dada and I had sold all the nuts and were pushing off the boat and heading back home. The ride home was slower, with Dada hugging the banks and punting upriver. Everything was exceptionally dark now and even some of the baris had put the lights out for the night. The cloud cover had increased by the time we reached the northern fields.

We pulled into the canal under the bari in Purushpal and chained the boat to a tree root. I was dead tired and eager to get to bed.

Bibi was up waiting for us, seeing how tired I was she accompanied me to the pond to have a quick wash before a very late dinner. At dinner Dada and I chatted to Bibi, Boro Dadi and Aunt Runi about our evening. Dada made one comment that did not get a reply from anyone.

"You see, my grandson here helped me out today, whilst my own flesh and blood could not even be bothered."

Back in my bed shortly afterwards I related the story of the whole evening to Old Auntie, who said that I was indeed growing up fast and learning a lot about Bangladeshi life. She joked that I should forget about going back to London and stay here for good. We continued to talk as Bibi said her prayers, then eventually my eyelids were too heavy to keep open and I drifted off into a deep slumber.

The Tooth Fairy

A couple of days after my second experience as a trader Bibi and I went back to Shupatola. We were quite fortunate as the going was good and the weather held throughout our journey, with the sun beating down on us interspersed with racing fluffy cotton white clouds. We walked up the path and into our bari and the first thing we noticed was a huge gaping hole at the base of the house where the storage room was. The hole looked freshly dug as if by an animal scraping the earth away with its paws.

"Yah! Allah, what's happened here?" Bibi exclaimed.

We could hear the chickens clucking nervously in the house. We rushed up to the main door and Bibi frantically opened it, letting out two weeks' worth of stale air. The two of us walked into the house and went into the storage room. The chickens were huddled as far away from the opening as possible and upon seeing us they started clucking even more vocally. Before opening the cage Bibi made a quick count and unfortunately there was one missing. Bibi sighed.

"Bibi, what's the matter?" I asked worriedly, my adrenaline pumping and my heart beating faster than normal.

"One of the chickens is missing."

"Who can make a hole like that?" I asked.

"It looks like a fox might have done it, can you go and get Bolai's mum?" she asked.

I went off to Bolai's bari, and by the time I returned with

Bolai and her mum in tow Bibi had released the chickens into the courtyard and they were running around like they were released from a penitentiary after two weeks of incarceration.

"Oh! What's the matter sister?" Bolai's mum said with a worried look, having seen the hole at the side of the house.

"It looks like a fox has got one of my chickens, do you know when this happened?" she asked.

"I came round yesterday and fed the chickens and everything was fine," she replied.

"I suppose this happened overnight or early this morning," said Bibi, talking more to herself than anyone else.

"Or was it a thief?" Bolai's mother went on.

"It doesn't look like a thief, because they could easily break the door down and why would they spend so much effort on digging a hole into the chicken coop," Bibi rationalised. "What's happened has happened; I may as well mend the damage."

"Do you need anything?" asked Bolai's mother.

"No, not at the moment," Bibi replied anxiously.

Bolai's mother went back to her bari and ushered her daughter to go with her, but Bolai decided to stay behind. Bibi went into the store room and came back out with two spades. I took one and the two of us began shovelling back the earth into the hole with me getting help from Bolai. Once we had packed the earth around the base of the wall Bibi decided to plant a few lime bushes around the edge of the house to prevent any further intrusions by any wayward foxes.

The rest of the bari and the house was intact and everything in its place. Bibi was more than convinced that it definitely was a fox which smelled the chicken and thought he would try and feast on them. The mangoes were on the verge of full ripening and in amongst the green leaves I could see cheeks of red, yellow and pink displaying themselves teasingly. Jackfruits were also plentiful and many were ready for picking, unfortunately the one we had left over a fortnight ago didn't fare too well even though it had ripened, as the fruit was too gooey. It had a whiff of fermentation to it and an alcoholic taste, so we had to throw it away. Worst of all was the lychee trees; they were stripped bare of all fruit by the monkeys, with not even a single lychee in any of the trees. Alas, I would have to get some from the bazaar.

Bolai and I spent the rest of the day together in my bari. I missed the bari so I took her along with me, wandering around the place with an inspector's eye in mind, just ensuring everything was fine. I relayed to her my jinn experience and my venture into Asirkal. Her eyes lit up as I told her all those stories, I always wanted her to come with me to Purushpal but her parents never let her go. I knew that she would have been welcomed with open arms and we could have had a great time with all the other uncles and aunts who were our age.

That evening Bibi and I carried out a patrol of the courtyard and perimeter of the house. This was more to warn any fox brave enough to return that there were people back in the bari. so they can go elsewhere with their chicken stealing ideas. Bibi kept a lantern burning throughout the night on the porch, just in case of any unwanted disturbances. However, our fears and protection were overkill as there were no disturbances, even though we did hear the odd fox howling on the hill opposite us throughout the night.

The following day was very busy with a string of visitors, vendors and neighbours. Word must have got round that the Londoni owners were back so they thought let us go and visit them. The day was very hot and sunny with the odd wisp of cloud scampering across the blue heavens as if late for some prior engagement.

First of the visitors were Makoy Haji's wife. I knew full well that she wanted to engage in a trade to stock up on her supply of betel nut. I've got to admit, I am no betel nut connoisseur but the one's from our bari did seem to have a sweeter taste, and it wasn't just Makoy Haji's wife who had a particular fondness for them, but every time someone from Purushpal or Sreedhara visited they would take a bagful.

I left the two ladies to chew on their betel nut and to catch up on their gossip and made my way over to the pond to do a bit of pole fishing. My fishing rod was a simple implement, a bamboo pole about six feet in length with a fishing line and hook at one end. The buoy was a piece of cork tied towards the hook end of the line. My bait was cold rice clumped together and a few spiders that I took from their cobwebs around the outside corners of the house. I removed the limbs of the spiders, leaving only their plump bodies as bait.

"Bibi, I'm going over to the pond, if Bolai comes tell her to go over," I said and walked over to the pond.

At the ghat of the pond I placed the pot of rice and spiders beside me as I scoured the surrounding trees, shrubs and bushes for any signs of Broken-hand and his mob. With no cackles and screams to indicate their presence I sat down beside the ghat, hooked a rice ball and gently lowered the pole into the water. I maintained a watchful eye and an attentive ear for any unusual sounds, as well as keeping vigilance over the floating cork. A couple of times the cork was gently tugged and I lifted it to find my rice had disappeared, so patiently I re-hooked some more rice and flung out the pole again.

After what seemed like ages, which it always does when pole fishing, I heard a scrunching of grass behind me. With a sharp turn I looked around to find Bolai making her way over to me.

"What's your news Bolai?" I asked.

"Nothing much," Bolai replied predictably. "Any more foxes come round last night?" she asked.

"No, but I heard a few of them howling away on the hill."

"Have you caught any yet?" she enquired about my fishing. "What are you using?" she continued without waiting for an answer.

"So far rice, but I've got some spiders as well, which I think I'm going to swap to." I lifted the hook out of the water and sure enough the sneaky devils had nibbled away the rice. "Here, do you want to have a go?" I offered.

"Yes! Definitely," she beamed, hooking a spider then walking further along the bank away from the ghat and sitting down.

I walked around to her side and watched silently whilst toying with some twigs and leaves. Shortly the cork disappeared and Bolai yanked the pole over her right shoulder with a silvery fish wriggling and dangling at the end of the line. She put the pole down and ran over to unhook the fish.

"It's a *futi*, quick go and fill the pot with water," she ordered.

I poured the rice and cadavers of the spiders on a leaf and rushed down the steps of the ghat to fill the pot halfway with pond water. I came back to Bolai where she was fighting a near losing battle to hold on to the slippery fish. She put the fish into the pot and wiped her hands on the grass to remove silvery specks of scales that had stuck to her hands. I looked into the pot where the *futi*, which was like a large goldfish but silver coloured, was swimming about in its new temporary home. From the top it had a dark grey, almost black spine, however when it turned in the pot the sun caught its silvery scales that twinkled like little diamonds on its flanks.

"Yah! You got a huge one," I yelled.

"They like spiders more than rice, here you carry on and I will go and see if I can find bigger spiders," she said and walked off towards some trees behind us.

I hooked another spider and was determined to bag myself a fish before she got back. The spot Bolai had chosen must have been quite lucky, because not too long afterwards I bagged a fish too.

"Yeah! Another one," I shouted.

My yelling brought Bolai running back with a handful of black spiders minus their limbs. We continued to fish for the remainder of the morning, bagging ourselves half a dozen fish.

"Ohhh! Sabu," Bibi called from across the other side of the bari.

"Whaaaat!" I shouted back at the top of my voice.

"Come here quickly."

With a slight frustration I threw away the remaining spiders and rice into the pond and noticed a flurry of fish causing a huge squabble as they fought to eat their heaven sent feast. Bolai carried the pot of fish and we hurried back to the bari. Walking into the courtyard there was a throng of people on the porch with Bibi: there was Makoy Haji's wife, Bolai's mother, some straggly children in shorts, bare feet and no tops. Putting away the fish and the pole in the kitchen I came back out and joined Bibi on the porch.

In the middle of the group sat two strange ladies. The two women were dressed in the most spectacular way. They had colourful beaded necklaces as well as bright decorations in the hair. Their wrists were jingling with the sounds made by copper, gold and silver bangles that came almost up to their elbows. Their ears had numerous piercings from the lobe all the way to the top with a string of earrings of different colour, shape, size and material framing their ears. Their clothes were also multi-coloured and they seemed to be wearing something not too dissimilar to a skirt that went down to their ankles, instead of a sari. As they sat squatted on the porch, in front of them they had a circular jute basket each displaying their wares.

These ladies were *bezneen*, a group of women who were like gypsies, they went around from bari-to-bari selling jewellery, adornments and accoutrements for women, who could buy things for themselves without the embarrassment of having men around or having to travel to a bazaar, again where men were ever present. They also plied themselves as palm readers, dentists, voodoo practitioners amongst a range of other skills that preyed on the superstitious beliefs of villagers. I was pretty sceptical of people like this and tended to avoid them at all costs. So, I was a bit suspicious of having been called over, especially with these folk in our bari.

Even Bolai was taken by their wares and she was busy fingering and trying the bangles, rings and other cheap jewellery items on display.

"Here's my grandson, can you do something?" Bibi offered. I looked up with a flight or fight mode taking over, and thought *what on earth is going on here.*

"Bibi, what's going on?" I said quite tersely.

"You said you had a toothache, so I've asked these ladies to help you out," she explained.

"No, it's not needed, I'm fine," I said, not wanting to take any funny medicine or have any of these ladies peering into my mouth. One of the bezneen ladies piped up.

"Don't worry son, I will not hurt you," in a dialect so alien to me that I only grasped one or two of the words she uttered and completed the rest through logic.

Bibi again pleaded, saying that it might ease the pain.

True enough, for about a month one of my left molars was causing me a dull pain, not continuously, but on the odd occasion. With no toothpaste to use for cleaning my teeth and the water being straight from the tube-well, I could understand the reason why I had the pain. Plus, my last visit to a dentist was back in Worcester prior to moving down to London in 1979.

Bibi pleaded and all the other ladies joined in, I could even see Bolai giving me a look to say grow up. I conceded, deciding to give the bezneen the benefit of doubt and sat down next to one of them. She pulled out some cotton wool and asked me to open my mouth. She placed a ball of cotton wool into the left side of my mouth which I was asked to promptly close. She then got a small root of some unknown plant and ran it along my cheek and recited some weird incantations. I was asked to re-open my mouth and she took the cotton wool out as I tried in desperate vain to pull out the remaining threads of wool from my tongue. The lady opened up the ball of wool and there wriggling in the middle was a milky coloured maggot with a black head. The lady began saying something but I yelled and jumped up and onto the courtyard.

"Hey! You pig, you put that thing in my mouth, aarrrghhh!" as I spat and cursed, livid that I was tricked into this. I ran off into the kitchen to get a glass of water continuing to curse the lady. "You dirty, filthy spawn of a pig," I continued.

I came back out and I was still in a rage and was pacing up and down like a crazed animal, wanting the lady to get out of my sight. The woman looked at me with dagger eyes, which Bibi cottoned onto so she began placating her.

"No, my dear daughter, don't be angry, he doesn't understand, he's from London, please forgive his language."

I could see that Bibi was getting fearful of what I had done and thus was keen to prevent the bezneen placing any spells or voodoo magic on me, her and the bari. I wasn't too bothered because my dad always disregarded spells, magic and other superstition as nonsense, which he instilled in me but I could see the shocked looks on the faces in the crowd, especially the likes of Makoy Haji's wife and Bolai's mum, who used the ends of their saris to cover their mouths.

As stories go, apparently there have been tales of bezneen placing such spells on people and their possessions, like jilted lovers exacting their revenge in a cold and calculated manner. People in villages around the country tended not to upset these travelling jewellery stores, in case they were to bear the brunt of their wrath.

Bibi paid them for their so called dental services and everyone else gave the two women some space so they could pack their stuff into their baskets. Once they were ready they hoisted the baskets onto the tops of their heads and walked off in an angry huff. The other ladies also left and Bolai's mum grabbed her by the hand and dragged her away too. They all looked back as if we were doomed and our bari was cursed. After everyone had gone, the bari was deathly quiet and Bibi turned to me, a bit annoyed.

"Why did you do that?" she asked.

"That lady put that maggot in my mouth, I don't have a hole in my teeth she was trying to con us," I blurted out, trying to make Bibi realise that I wasn't the one in the wrong.

"Well, I just hope they don't put a curse or anything on us," as she walked into the kitchen.

I did not reply and changed the subject to the fish Bolai and I had caught to appease Bibi. In the kitchen Bibi, even though upset with me, approved of the fish we had caught. I sat down beside her and watched her prepare the fish for lunch. My tooth still hurt every so often, but not to the extent where I was in agony or anything, so I never gave it much thought and I didn't mention it to Bibi, just in case she wanted me to be seen by the next charlatan that walked into our bari.

Later in the afternoon Boro Dada visited with some provisions for us, which consisted of rice, spices, oil, onions, tea, biscuits, soap and other day to day requirements. Bibi told him about the fox stealing one of the chickens and how I insulted the beznen. Upon hearing this all Dada could say was "Hai re Sabu!" and shook his head as if to say I was a lost cause. Yet, I knew he was only joking and it wasn't a serious indictment of my behaviour.

Once he had rested after a spot of lunch and the obligatory betel nut, Bibi asked Dada if he could cut a pole to pick the mangoes from the trees behind the house. I joined Dada at the bamboo grove where he searched for a perfectly straight specimen of the plant. He found an emerald green and beautifully straight bamboo that was even the right girth for me to hold and chopped it at its base.

"Hey! Sabu, look!" Dada pointed at some pointed shoots sticking out of the ground around the base of the grove. They looked like ears of corn growing out of the ground.

"What are they?" I asked.

"Those are *koril*, which will grow into a new bamboo plant," he referred to the bamboo shoots. "You can also cook them with fish, do you want to try some?"

"Yes, why not I'd love to give it a try," I agreed.

The shoot was deceptively small above ground but Dada dug deep into the ground with the hooked machete and extracted a large, pale coloured shoot. We went back to the courtyard and putting the bamboo shoots on the porch he went about topping and trimming the bamboo pole. He then made a V-shaped incision at the top that could be used to twist the fruit from their branches.

With the tool ready for use we made our way onto the earth

wall behind the house and craned our necks upwards to seek out those fruit on the lower branches. We spotted several clusters of mangoes that were reachable with the pole, which Dada put to good use. The fruits came crashing down through the branches, landing with a dull thud on the grass and dried leaves strewn across the floor. I dutifully collected them and placed them in a neat pile until we were done.

In my excitement, however, I wasn't paying attention to any creatures that may be lurking in the undergrowth, and soon enough I was howling in pain as angry red fire ants that came down with the mangoes crawled up my legs and began biting me in earnest. I brushed them as best as I could and jumped off the wall onto the courtyard to get some respite. The stinging was excruciatingly painful and my howls of pain and cursing brought Bibi out back. Dada also stopped the fruit picking and came down from the wall. Both Bibi and Dada looked at my legs and saw that the ants had gone, but there were some angry red bite marks.

"Don't worry, Grandson you'll be fine, it's not gonna kill you," Dada slapped me on the back.

Bibi and I collected our small harvest and went over to the porch to check the fruits. The mangoes looked perfect for consumption, Bibi and Dada selected two of the ripest ones to try out, save a few which Dada was going to take back with him, and the rest we stored away. The mangoes were delicious. Not overly ripe but enough to have the natural sweetness and juicy enough to dribble down one's hands. With the tool Dada prepared for us, every few days Bibi and I, as well as Bolai on the odd occasion, would pick the mangoes. It was a continuous battle against Broken-hand and his mob, some days we would find that they had beaten us to the fruits and on other days we would pick as many as we could and store them.

Dada stayed the night and over dinner under the dim light of the lanterns, he asked, "Have you ever been to a *Roth*?"

"No Dada, I haven't," I replied.

The *Roth* or *Roth Jatra* as it was officially known was a famous Hindu festival celebrating the journey of Lord Jagannat and Vishnu in a chariot to the sea. Even though it was a Hindu festival, Muslims joined in and enjoyed the festivities just as much.

"Well, do you want to go tomorrow? It's not far from here," Dada offered.

"Yes, Dada I'll go and can we take Bolai with us?"

"As long as her parents are OK about it, sure," he said approvingly.

Bibi did not even bat an eyelid, the only thing she said was, "Keep away from the *Mandir* and ensure no jinn gets you again," referring to the temple. Muslims in Bangladesh had this superstition that Hindu Mandirs were places where spirits, ghosts and jinns resided. So, they were to be avoided at all costs.

"I think the jinns will be scared of my grandson," Dada laughed. "After what he has been up to every jinn, buth, spirit, ghost and Satan himself will stay away," he continued.

Bibi smiled as we finished off our meal and she went about cleaning up the plates, pots and pans.

The next day was bright and sunny and weather-wise a good day to visit the Roth festival. We were going to leave for the festival late morning, so I went over to Bolai's bari to get permission from her parents. I walked over to the kitchen and there on the porch sat Arzomond and his wife enjoying the gentle warmth of the morning sun. After midday the sun would become unbearable and shade would be sought by all.

"So what brings the little monkey Sabu to our bari?" asked

Arzomond, as Bolai emerged from the kitchen. She had soot on her hand and her hair looked a bit straggly. She looked like Cinderella taking a break from her kitchen chores.

"Nothing Dada, I wanted to ask if Bolai can come with me and Boro Dada to the Roth?"

Hearing this Bolai's eyes lit up and I could see she was interested and wouldn't say no.

"Ahh! So your Dada is here, how is he?" Arzomond continued.

"He is good," I replied.

"The beznen will be at the Roth and they will kidnap you, since you upset them yesterday," joked Bolai's mum.

"No, they won't," I scoffed.

The *Roth* would explain why the beznen were around. The festival provided a great opportunity for them to sell their wares, amulets and charms for a few takas.

"Can Bolai come with us then?"

"Do you want to go Bolai?" asked Arzomond.

"Of course I do," she said impatiently, as if they needed to ask!

"Well come by before noon then and we'll go with Dada."

When Bolai arrived later on she had cleaned up and did not look like one of Fagin's street urchins, even though the two of us could have fitted into that motley crew very easily. Bibi watched as we left the bari through the southern exit and walked west along the path. The rainwaters meant the path was a bigger stream than normal and in some parts the water was up to our ankles.

Shortly afterwards we turned south onto another path, delving deeper into the Shupatola hills. The path was almost devoid of light as the overhanging branches created a thick canopy. The air was distinctly cool and refreshing under the shade, although the darkness and silence was a bit disconcerting. We walked for about quarter of an hour before turning left onto another path on which we were joined by other Roth-goers. At the far end I could see the path opening up as sunlight beckoned us to come into the open. I could hear drums and musical instruments, as well as a fusion of voices.

As we stepped into the light the greeting was a kaleidoscopic explosion of colour, sounds and smells. We emerged at the top of a rise, looking east below us was a flat area of land with a small lake in the middle. Every inch of space was covered by vendors and attractions that I had never seen before. We walked down into the melee of people. Again, there were mainly men, boys and girls. The only adult women to be seen were Hindu women who were distinguishable with the red *tikka* or *bindi* on their forehead. Interspersed amongst the traders was my tooth fairy nemesis, the bezneen. They walked around with their stalls on their head. The ground underfoot was wet and muddy and almost everyone was walking barefoot. Those who wore sandals ended up struggling to walk properly and their back was speckled with mud that was flicked up by their footwear.

The profusion of merchants and attractions was extraordinary. Whereas a bazaar had the traders selling daily necessities and foodstuffs, here everything being sold was fun and luxury. There were multi-coloured bangles, rings and assortments of jewellery being sold. Other vendors had stalls with colourful toys made of wood, metal and strings. Kites, yoyo's, spinning tops, wooden scimitars and dolls were amongst an assortment of play things being hawked, to entice youngsters like me.

I could smell a mixture of sweet and savoury foods that would not be eaten every day, but here it was all that was offered. I could see pink candy floss as well as *ghee cham cham* and freshly fried *jilebi*. There were woks of fried snacks being peddled, from shingaras to dhal bhora. My eyes turned the size of saucers as I looked over at Bolai, who shared the same expression as me of wonder and awe.

All of these attractions seemed to detract from the main reason for the gathering, the *Roth Jatra*. Even though there were Hindu people going about carrying out their religious rites, going into and coming out of the Mandir. The main patrons of the festival were Muslim men and boys.

"Would you like something to eat?" Dada asked.

"Yes Dada," both of us blurted out simultaneously.

Boro Dada took us over to a dhal bhora seller and brought three portions wrapped in old newspaper, akin to how fish and chips were wrapped back home in England. The three of us walked around the festival quietly, content with our snacks. We stopped by a man who was selling glasses of sugar cane juice and had a glass each. The cane juice was nectar that only nature could concoct, delicious sweet and refreshing. The festival was edged by the main road going to Beani Bazaar on its eastern flank. Dada bought us some candy floss and a yo-yo each. Whilst Dada was paying for the yo-yos a man walked up to us.

"Hey Bolai, what are you doing here?" he asked.

We turned to see Bolai's brother Lukman. He was in his late teens and skinny like a garden rake. He was also un-schooled and did nothing but laze around his bari, living off the earnings of Arzomond.

"Nothing, I am here with Sabu and his dada," she replied.

"What's news Lukman, how are you?" Dada turned and asked.

"Salaam alaikum Dada, is Bolai with you?" he questioned.

"Yes, I wanted them to see the Roth."

"OK Dada, I'm going," he replied nervously and scooted off.

Dada looked at him quizzically and then handed us the yo-yos. Lukman did not look comfortable in Dada's presence and he disappeared into the throng of people almost as quickly as he appeared behind us. Bolai and I were too occupied with our candy floss and new toys to worry too much about Lukman.

As with all good things, before we knew it Boro Dada announced that it was time for us to head back to the bari. We contended our way through the crowds that had grown and headed back the way we had come. By the time we got back it was *Asar* prayers. Dada went off to carry out his ablutions prior to saying his prayers, Bolai went back to her bari. I asked her to come by later if she could. Whilst I played with the yo-yo trying to make it spin, Bibi and Boro Dada said their prayers facing west on mats adjacent to each other. Dada and I had a late lunch while I relayed to Bibi what I had seen and the goodies that Dada bought us. It was quite ironic that the Muslim population in the Beani Bazaar area were more into the festivities of the Hindu religion and the two groups enjoyed a good level of peaceful co-existence. Without the religious aspect, the two groups of people were racially and culturally identical. It's amazing how a belief system can generate so much animosity, literally between brothers.

After our meal we did not get a chance to settle down for betel nut before we heard a commotion on the path between our bari and Bolai's. The three of us walked out of the kitchen and out to the path to see what was going on. By the entrance to Bolai's bari there were a couple of policemen in khaki uniforms, wearing black boots and black berets on their head. They both had long bamboo canes in their hands and were in a heated argument with Arzomond.

Their accent indicated they were not local officers, but stationed in Beani Bazaar from another part of the country. Boro Dada walked over to Arzomond to find out what was going on. I stayed with Bibi and could see Bolai behind Arzomond standing alongside her mum.

From what I could gather the police were asking to enter their bari and they were looking for Lukman. Arzomond was arguing that they could not come in and that his son was not in. Eventually, to avoid getting a beating from the police and listening to Dada's and his wife's advice, Arzomond let the police in. They went into all the houses and came out empty handed. They warned Arzomond that they would be back and if he was hiding Lukman then both father and son would be arrested, as they walked away north along the path.

"What's the matter?" Bibi asked Dada who was standing next to and still talking to Arzomond.

"The police are saying that Lukman stabbed someone at the Roth."

Bibi put the end of her sari to her mouth and muttered in horror, "Oh! My dear mother."

Arzomond went back into his bari followed by his wife and Bolai, whose attention I tried to get but she was ushered away. Dada walked back and explained that Lukman was involved in an illegal card game involving money. He got into an argument with one of the other players and stabbed him. The man was not fatally wounded but enough to require hospital treatment. Lukman had run off and was nowhere to be seen and Dada got the impression that Arzomond had sent him hiding.

Boro Dada did not stay too long after popping a small packet of betel nut and paan into his mouth and taking another for the road leaving for Purushpal. Bibi and I got a mura each and sat on the porch as the late afternoon sun started to fade.

"Dear Allah! Where have I come to with neighbours that are murderers, gamblers and criminals," Bibi said to herself as she rotated a *panka* to keep both her and myself cool.

Many years later Lukman would lose his sanity and one day take his own life. On the southern road approaching Beani Bazaar he would go into one of the hillocks, douse his entire body with petrol and burn himself to death. By the time he was discovered he was just a charred human remain.

Bloody Leeches

The monsoon was still ever present, every day it rained and in the instance where it was a particularly heavy downpour the paths circling our bari would be deluged, making us an island. Once the rains stopped the sun would bake the land dry and the paths were reclaimed as the intended thoroughfare for cattle, people and of course the odd bezneen. On those occasions when they ventured into our bari, I'd keep my distance and throw dagger looks at them, not that the same ones visited after my outburst.

One such day just after midday a visitor came strolling up to our bari. "Anybody in the bari?" a man shouted.

Bibi was out at the pond and I was sitting in the shade of the porch, trying to engage in as little movement as possible to avoid sweating. In the stifling muggy heat even breathing made me sweat, every item of clothing clung to my body like superglue and on a day like today with no wind, globules of hot air went in and out of my mouth. As such I was only wearing a pair of shorts and no top, nor sandals. I turned towards the entrance to the bari and there was Uncle Babul striding onto the courtyard.

"Salaam alaikum, Mama," I greeted him.

"Alaikum salaam," he reciprocated.

Uncle Babul handed me a bag of biscuits and fruits and I got him a mura which he took and sat beside me. He was donned in pants and long sleeve shirts, sweating profusely with dark wet patches under his arms and on his back and chest.

"What's news, Nephew? Are you well?" Uncle Babul asked.

"Yes, I'm well. How's everyone back at Nana's?" I returned.

"They're all doing good, they've missed you and they would like you to visit sometime soon."

"Oh, I will go one day," I replied.

"Where's your Bibi then?" he asked

"She's down at the pond, she'll be back soon," I replied.

I couldn't have timed it better as Bibi walked into the courtyard. She was greeted by Uncle Babul and whilst replying she hung up a washed sari on a clothes line on the porch. Bibi asked him how his family were and went into the kitchen to fetch some water for him. Uncle Babul guzzled the water and I could see his Adam's apple yo-yoing as he finished the drink in one gulp.

Bibi excused herself from us, "Let me just read my prayers and then we can eat rice."

In Bangladesh no one referred to having lunch or dinner, it was always "let's eat rice". The grain is entrenched into the psyche of the country, so much so that if a native of the country does not eat rice they feel out of sorts. Once a meal of rice has been had the world is all well.

Uncle Babul lit a cigarette and asked me if I had heard from Mum and Dad. I told him that I hadn't, to which he didn't reply.

"You know your Nana isn't too well," he said solemnly.

"What's the matter with him?" I asked.

"Doctors cannot say for sure, but he is getting weaker and weaker," he continued.

"We've written to your mum, that's why I was asking if you had heard from her."

"Is Mum coming to see Nana?" I asked a bit excitedly.

"I don't know, we'll have to see how your nana fares over the coming weeks and months."

Bibi came out from the house and ushered us into the kitchen for lunch. Whilst eating Uncle Babul told Bibi about his father's condition and how he wasn't too well, she told him that we would visit tomorrow morning. I wanted to see Nana and how he was, however a part of me just did not want to go. I stayed quiet and agreed with a nod of my head. Uncle Babul suggested that I go with him and then I could return tomorrow with Bibi. At hearing this my ears pricked up like a cornered animal and my adrenaline began rushing through me, causing my heart to beat faster with me wanting to flee into the bari.

Bibi looked at me and asked, "Do you want to go?"

"Come on *bagna*, you might as well?" he requested affectionately, referring to me as nephew. Being put in such a difficult position I had no option but agree to go.

After lunch I got a day's worth of clothes ready for the trip and Bibi put together some betel nuts and mangoes to take to Nana's bari. Uncle Babul and I headed off to Sreedhara via the bazaar. At the bazaar we stopped at a general store and rested for a while. The proprietor gave the two of us sweet, milky tea infused with cinnamon and bay leaves, accompanied by Nabisco biscuits. The owner was an uncle of Babul's from Sreedhara.

"Have you heard the news?" the owner leant over and said to Uncle Babul in a shocked tone.

"What? What's happened?" he replied.

"Well, just outside a bari on the road to Bordesh someone was murdered last night," he delivered gravely.

"Apparently the man was slaughtered like a cow," he continued shaking his head.

"Have you heard who it is?" Uncle Babul asked.

"I haven't heard the full details, but something that never happens is now on our doorstep. Ya Allah! People in this world have gone crazy."

"I might go by and see if I can find out who it was," Uncle Babul added.

In a community this small like elsewhere in the world, where marriages are between families that only live few miles apart, eventually it comes to a situation where almost everybody is somehow related to each other. So it was with a look of concern on Uncle Babul's face that we left the shop and instead of cutting through the back country lanes to Sreedhara we walked through the bazaar to its northern end and then turned east onto a road leading towards the village of Bordesh.

Once we entered the hills of Bordesh, just like my village the trees and bamboo soared into the sky, blotting out most of the sun, where only the odd ray of light penetrated onto the road we were following. We eventually arrived at a fork in the road and followed the smaller one going left. A few minutes later we rounded a bend and there, ahead of us, a group of men had congregated, blocking the path and the view. I could also make out the khaki uniform and beret of two policemen keeping the crowds at bay. We joined the crowd and I pushed myself in between the lunghi adorned legs of the men to the front.

To the left was a bari with a small half earth and tin walled house with a tin roof. The path was lined with plants that backed onto the house. On the right was an earth wall slightly taller than me but the top of which was sloped upwards, giving it an even greater elevation. Ahead and beyond where the police blocked the path there was a crimson red squirt of blood cutting the thoroughfare diagonally from left to right. It looked as if someone got a washing up liquid bottle full of blood and then squirted it onto the path. The blood, where it pooled in places, had coagulated into a dark crimson colour. The path smelled of death and iron from the blood permeated the air so much so that I could taste it. The corpse was nowhere to be seen, it transpired that it was already being prepared for burial. The two policemen with handlebar moustaches that looked a bit too big for their bony face and almost skeletal bodies stood around twirling their bamboo batons lazily.

Uncle Babul behind me asked one of the men in a hushed tone what had happened.

"Last night some men came by to this bari," he said pointing to the house, "...they then asked to speak to the man who lives there, apparently they argued with him. They grabbed the man and pulled him onto the path, held him down and slit his throat," the man gestured with his index finger moving from one ear to the other. "The police haven't caught anyone yet, the ones who did this will most probably get away with it by paying a bribe."

"What's the man's name?" Uncle Babul asked.

"I don't know brother," he replied shrugging his shoulders.

Fortunately it wasn't anybody related to or known by Uncle Babul, as the bari was not somewhere he had connections with. We did not hang around too long and left for Sreedhara.

"Are you OK, Nephew?" Uncle Babul asked me as we walked back the way we come.

"Yes Uncle."

"Don't be scared, it's just that some people are mad in this world and the police will get them," he comforted me.

I was glad to have left this place of death behind, the atmosphere was beginning to suffocate me and if truth be told I was scared witless. The thought of the man being killed by having his throat cut gave me nightmares for many months. But that day I walked away with the bravest of facades.

Once we got to Nana's bari we found him sitting up on his

bed, reciting prayers with rosary beads in his right hand. I greeted him and he acknowledged me with a weak reply. I sat at the end of his bed being joined by Nani, Elder Mami and Samad on her hip. Uncle Babul picked up Mithun, who was wandering around the room uttering new words that she was picking up but were indecipherable to adults.

"Nana, what's happening about your illness?" I asked.

"The doctors don't know Sabu, they've just given me some medicine which helps a bit, but I don't think they can cure it," he replied.

"You'll be OK, you'll be better soon," I said positively.

"We'll see," he did not believe that he was going to get better, and his face gave away resignation to his symptoms and a fate of death.

"Bring my grandson something to eat and drink," he ordered both to Nani and Elder Mami.

Mami scurried off into the kitchen where she already had some milk on the stove being heated gently. I chatted with Nani and Nana for a while. Nana's household had a sense of impending doom as if something was about to happen and I did not feel comfortable at all. I patiently put on a brave face and kept telling myself that I would be going home tomorrow.

That evening I accompanied Uncle Babul to the bazaar to get some fresh fish and vegetables, which helped alleviate the boredom and the doom and gloom ever-present at Nana's bari. After the evening meal, for which Nana did not join us, having eaten something light earlier and gone to sleep, I chatted with Nani and Mami under the light of oil lamps. Then one by one we all fell silent and I fell asleep beside Nani.

The following day Bibi arrived late morning, I was sitting at the ghat of the pond and was glad to see her walking up the path. My heart lightened and I beamed a smile at her. I knew I would be going back home. I accompanied her to the kitchen and carried the jute bag she was carrying with her, she had brought some biscuits and fruit for Nana.

Nana was surprisingly quite well compared to the previous day, and was seated in the kitchen on a mura. He was a slim man and with the daylight streaming through the open kitchen door he looked almost skeletal, his lunghi was draped over his legs accentuating his knee bones and legs that lacked muscles. His granddad shirt exposed his collarbone and he looked extremely pale and weak. Bibi greeted him and we both took a mura each in the kitchen where Nani and Elder Mami were preparing vegetables and spices for lunch.

"How are you, sister?" he asked Bibi, his voice seemed stronger than yesterday, considering how he looked.

"I'm doing well, what's your news?" she asked.

"Ahh! When you get old this is what becomes of you," he answered.

"Are you taking any medicines or anything?" Bibi continued.

"Yes and today is the first day I've felt good in a week or so. It must be because my grandson has visited me," he smiled as best as he could.

"Is your mum coming over?" he asked me.

"Nana, I don't know, I haven't heard from them in a while."

"I'll see if I can find someone who's going back to London recently and send a message by mouth," Bibi offered comfortingly.

Mum was Nana's favourite and she loved him just as much. I could see the pain in his face as he thought about mum.

"I'm going to die soon and two of my children are not going to be here to bury me," he referred to mum and Uncle Nurul in Pakistan. In Bangladeshi culture life and death are talked about openly with no taboos about discussing the latter.

"Don't talk such nonsense," Bibi said. "With Allah's grace

195

you will live many more years, and you *will* see your children."

"No, my sister I just do not feel good this time, I think it's my time to go," he continued.

Such morbid talk about death – especially about oneself – is common among all people, especially the elderly, unwell and infirmed. Even though a person may only suffer from a minor ailment and make a full recovery, they will still talk about how they are knocking on death's door. Understandably people in Bangladesh live life on the edge, forever at the mercy of the elements and diseases, parasites and other killers that are prevalent in the absence of clean water, basic hygiene and elementary medical facilities. As such life and death come and go as the seasons come and go. With six seasons in a twelve month period that cycle of birth, death and regeneration is even more rapid and stark.

Bibi remained in the kitchen with Nana, Nani and Elder Mami chatting about various aspects of village and farming life. Talking about everyday life seemed to give Nana a small reprieve from his illness. I went into the adjacent room and sat with Mithun and Samad who were being looked out for by Uncle Babul. I engaged in some light baby talk with the two as Uncle Babul lay back looking at the ceiling in a contemplative manner. I suppose his thoughts lay with the future and what would happen if Nana were to pass away. With the absence of his brother Nurul, the responsibility of the bari would fall on his shoulders. He looked like someone who was going to be forced to take responsibility for something that he wasn't ready for or did not want to accept.

Bibi and I stayed for lunch, for which Nana couldn't join us as he had fallen asleep. Later in the afternoon after Nana was awake again Bibi raised the subject that we should be leaving, without causing offence. Nana asked Bibi to leave me behind for another day.

"Sister, I do not have long to live and it would be good for me to see my grandson for a little longer," he pleaded. Bibi looked to me to see if I wanted to stay.

"Nana, I will come and visit, but I should go today," I replied. Nana did not have the strength to engage in the tug-of-war. I felt bad for not staying, however I could not face staying another night.

Uncle Babul accompanied us to Thri-Muki Bazaar where Bibi and I walked over the bamboo pole bridge over to the Koshba side, the adjacent village, and walked back home through villages and back country lanes. This was a short cut, the use of which enabled us to avoid Beani Bazaar altogether. Over the coming weeks Nana's health oscillated between improvement and deterioration. Some days he would be well enough to walk accompanied to the mosque and other days he would be bedridden. Thus, it was with increased frequency that Bibi and I visited, but returning the same day.

Once we had returned back home, Bibi asked me to write a letter to my mum and dad on her behalf. She gave me a blue aerogramme on which I wrote a letter for Bibi and the second half I used to write my own letter to my parents. In it I mentioned Nana's condition and how he was asking about Mum. Once I had written the letter Bibi said she would ask Boro Dada to find someone who may be going back to London soon and ask them to hand-deliver the letter.

When Dada visited again about a week later he took the letter with him. This 'black market' mail service was quite prevalent in the Bangladeshi community abroad, and it worked both ways. The postal service in the country was notorious, letters would get lost, take months to arrive and worst of all the letters arriving from abroad would get opened and tampered with. For example, there were instances where money orders or cheques sent by people in the UK were removed from the letters which were then resealed and sent on their journey to the recipients.

One afternoon Bibi was pottering about the bari trimming a branch here, cutting back a bush there with a machete in hand. It was Bibi's industriousness that meant the bari looked less a jungle and more of a home. I was following Bibi around removing the branches and twigs as she chopped them from the trees overhanging the path. We were near the lime grove when we saw a figure through the bushes coming up the path and then turn into our bari's courtyard.

"Go and see who it is," Bibi asked.

I walked back into the courtyard and there was Uncle Fozlu from Bordesh, peeking nervously into our house checking where we were.

"Oh! Uncle," I yelled from across the courtyard.

"Where are you and your Bibi?" he asked as he turned around to see me approaching him.

"We're over there, chopping back some of the bushes," I said pointing to where Bibi was still working. "Come on over," I said as I walked back.

Uncle Fozlu was about four years older than me and had a permanent puppy dog look of sadness in his eyes. He had a fair complexion and was extremely bashful, always avoiding eye contact with his elders. He would stand on the sidelines and engage in conversation only when someone asked him something. Yet, he was a very kind person and I liked him from day one when I met him during Uncle Naz's wedding.

He greeted Bibi, who reciprocated. "I'm just going to tidy up here and then we'll go back to the house," she said as we picked up the branches and headed back to the courtyard.

"Do you want me to help you with anything?" Fozlu

offered. He was forever a helpful individual and sometimes people abused his kind and helpful nature.

"No! We're fine," Bibi replied.

Back in the courtyard we placed the branches at the southern end to dry for later use as firewood. We got ourselves three muras and sat on the porch and fanned ourselves to cool down. Once we had caught our breath, Bibi went into the kitchen to fetch a jug of water and three glasses. Even though the water was not refrigerated it was cool enough to be extremely refreshing.

"How's your mum?" Bibi asked Fozlu about her younger sister.

"She's well," he replied.

"You should have brought her with you, it would have been a nice break for her," she suggested.

"She will visit, but at the moment she's a bit busy with everything, actually I'm here to take the two of you to my bari."

"It's not really a good time for me to go," Bibi replied. "Maybe Sabu will want to go," she said looking at me.

"You come too Auntie," he insisted.

"No, a few weeks back when we returned from Purushpal a fox had almost killed all the chickens, so I cannot leave the bari empty anymore."

"I'll go uncle," I added.

"Well that's good, because I wasn't going to leave unless you came with me."

Bibi and I laughed and Uncle Fozlu joined in too. Bibi offered tea to uncle Fozlu, but ever the helping hand he did not want to impose and instead offered to make the tea himself.

"You sit and relax Auntie, I will make the tea," he said, heading into the kitchen. Uncle Fozlu was a self-trained chef in Bangladeshi cuisine, having worked in his family's restaurant in Beani Bazaar ever since he was my age if not younger. He made some of the most wonderful parathas, curries, samosas and bhajees I have ever known.

After having sipped our teas I packed a week's worth of clothes for the trip. The clothes that I packed for most of my trips consisted of t-shirts, shorts, a lunghi and the sandals on my feet. So it was a quick affair for me when getting ready to go somewhere.

Bibi bid us farewell, saying that she would most probably come round in a week or so, she also gave me some money, even though the need would be minimal apart from the odd sweets or snacks. She privately had a word in Uncle Fozlu's ear asking him to keep a particular eye out for me. We left the bari with Bibi watching, I could see a frown on her forehead, I'm sure she thought about whether I was going to be okay. Knowing the experiences that have befallen me and what I have been engaged in, I guessed she was expecting the worst.

Arriving into Beani Bazaar we headed north, walking past College road, then the high school on our left atop a hill which overlooked the town's football field. At the end of the bazaar was the main bus terminus where all the buses for Sylhet, Srimangal, Dhaka and other destinations departed from. Walking pass the terminal was like dodgems of humans versus buses. All the vehicles were intricately designed and colourful with over simplified drawings of actors in handlebar moustaches, a scantily dressed damsel, a sunset, a village scene or some other painting that was completely out of perspective and lacking any dimension. One thing the buses had in common was the words *'ma'* or *'bismillah'*; 'mother' or 'in the name of God' respectively, inscribed on the front. I suppose with the roads being potholed and treacherous driving any vehicle meant the drivers relied not on their skills but on the Gods to look out for them and their mothers' prayers, be they Hindu or Muslim.

Young boys my age or slightly older hung off the open doorways like gibbons on a branch, one hand clutching a fistful of takas, yelling destination names out to prospective passengers. All the buses were windowless and passengers leant out for some fresh air in the hot and humid afternoon.

A cloud of black, smoky diesel billowed behind one vehicle as it lumbered south and we stepped up our pace to avoid getting crushed by the metal behemoths, manoeuvring cumbersomely in an attempt to leave the terminal or find a parking spot. To our left was the police station sitting atop a hill looking deadly quiet, there were no officers in sight and no members of the public either. Apart from seeing the two policemen at the scene of the murder and outside Arzomond's bari, the police in Beani Bazaar were almost like mythical creatures. People talked about them and referred to them but they were never to be seen anywhere and when one was seen he was avoided like a plague, with people crossing onto the other side of the road. In the bazaar when a crime was committed, which was usually theft, justice was meted out in the form of a good beating by locals and bystanders and by the time the police arrived the culprit would be lying in a bloody mess, all beaten and battered. The police would look around to get witnesses or a statement and all they would get is a wall of silence.

We shortly turned off into the hills of Bordesh and as with Shupatola the interior was a cool haven, with trees shading the road from the glaring heat and light from the sun. The road meandered left and right up hills and down into small clearings where people had sown taro plants that thrive in boggy, wet land. Eventually, we emerged from the village where the road took a ninety degree left turn and straight ahead was the *Muriha Haor*, a vast expanse of water that spread across into India. The land dropped away from the road and as far as the eye could see there was water. A gentle breeze tickled the surface, creating little waves that danced in the sunlight. In the horizon there was the odd island jutting from the water as if gasping for air. These were perfectly oval shaped and covered with grass, I could just about make out a man with a fishing net and a small boat moored on one of the islands.

By this time I had lost all bearing as to which direction we were travelling, so I just followed Uncle Fozlu as he reassured me that we were nearly there. To the left of us were the entrances leading up to the individual baris and on the banks of the lake peopled had tethered the odd cow or bullock that grazed lazily on the fat, green leaves of grass. There was one calf that was ripping away at the grass with its mouth. It had a rope around its neck which was tied to a small tree. We watched the animal as we walked up to it and by the time we were next to it we could see something wasn't right. On one of its hind legs just above the hoof was something black and glistening. When we got close enough we recognised it as a leech, it had obviously been sucking on the blood of the poor animal for a very long time, like an alien creature latching onto the calf with its sucker like maw and feeding on it. Occasionally the calf would raise its hind leg and brush it against the side of its face, but to no avail. We stopped beside the animal and Fozlu broke off a small branch from the tree, he asked me to face the calf and calm it as best as possible. He, in the meantime, got down on his knees and put his mouth quite close to the leech and began spitting on it like a pellet gun.

The salt in his spit seemed to have done the trick and the leech dropped off, curling into a little ball. Blood began to trickle from the open wound on the calf's leg, but not heavily enough to cause any problems. Fozlu then took the stick and pierced the leech through its middle, popping it like an overripe berry with dark blood spurting onto the grass. Then like a sacrificial warning he stuck the other end of the stick into the ground far away from the calf. It was akin to warring armies spiking their foes heads and putting them on display as a sign of victory and warning to others. I asked Fozlu why he did that, to which he replied that in the hot sun the leech would dry and wither away almost instantaneously. We left our kill writhing in its final death throes and our beneficiary, who was totally oblivious to what had just transpired, carried on with the important task of munching on grass.

We continued on our journey along the banks of the lake eventually arriving at uncle Fozlu's bari. We turned left onto the path skirting the back of his homestead and then right onto another path leading onto the courtyard.

One of his brothers saw us walking up into the courtyard who yelled musically, "Sabu has arrived!"

With the heralding of my arrival Fozlu's mother and father, his elder brother Abul, his two sisters Hasna and Sufi, and what seemed to me like an army of his younger brothers rushed out to greet us. His three younger brothers were all junior to me and all looked alike, namely Alta, Aplu and Dilu. They were all slightly darker in complexion than Fozlu but all had the droopy eyed, sad look of their mother.

"What's your news, Sabu?" asked Fozlu's mother Kutina.

"Salaam Alaikum Granny, I am well how are you?" I greeted her.

I liked Kutina Granny quite a lot, she was Bibi's youngest sister and was extremely kind to all people. She was short like Bibi and just as slim, except she had straight hair, unlike Bibi's curly locks.

"I am well Sabu, how's your Bibi?" she asked, coming up to me and asking one of her younger sons to take my bag containing my clothes.

I was taken into their kitchen which was of simple mud

construction and I was seated on a mura. Auntie Hasna poured Fozlu and me a glass of water each from the earthen water pots stored neatly on a rack like wine bottles in a dark corner.

Again I found myself sitting in a position of being the centre of attraction, with all the uncles and aunts, Granny and Granddad asking about me and Bibi and my family and if I missed them. Even though I knew they meant no harm and they were just being kind, I could not help but feel a bit annoyed going through the whole process of relating to people my innermost feelings. Whereas the first and foremost thing on my mind was I now had play pals, namely Fozlu and his younger brothers with whom I just wanted to get out and explore the lake. As everyone in the kitchen talked about Shupatola and Purushpal my mind raced with all the adventures I wanted to get up to whilst here.

Fozlu's bari was on a small hillock and akin to all other homesteads his family and his uncle shared a couple of houses at one end of the bari, whilst there were other family homes set apart from them. Fozlu's house occupied one end of the bari that overlooked the Muriha Haor, which was approached by a path winding down to the waters where the boats were also chained to tree trunks. Bordesh, literally meaning 'big country', was a very large village and was spread out with baris dotted on hills around the lake. During the monsoon the baris that backed onto the lake were often cut-off from main roads and transportation by boat was the most convenient way to get about. During the dry season the water almost completely disappeared to leave rolling pastures for the farmers to cultivate and their livestock to graze along the exposed edges of the lake. Like Shupatola the earth was red and sandy in texture in the hills of Bordesh.

I ended up staying for about a week at Fozlu's bari until

Bibi came by to collect me. During my stay I was on a Huckleberry Finn style adventure every day, either fishing, swimming, looking for wild fruit bearing trees or helping uncle Fozlu and his brothers with chores around the bari.

On the third day Uncle Abul, Fozlu, Aplu and I went out on a fishing trip. Muriha Haor had been beckoning me ever since I arrived. Even though I went out onto the lake with Fozlu and Aplu we did not venture out too far from the fringes of the bari. The weather during monsoon could change so rapidly, boats were known to be lost and people drowned. We were warned by Kutina Granny and Granddad not to venture out too far from the bari's edge. So, during my initial trips we gently glided along the banks picking berries from low hanging tree branches, whilst Fozlu would whistle country song tunes with a word or two thrown in here and there. Sometimes we would moor the boat and go swimming, jumping off trees into the water and yelling at the top of our voices.

On the day of the fishing trip the sun was out with a few storm clouds that raced overhead as a breeze ushered them onto far and distant lands. We gathered together our tools for the trip, namely a punting pole, three paddles, one 'Y' shaped foldable fishing net and one *ural zaal*, literally 'flying net', as they were thrown out into the waters before being dragged in with the catch. We also carried a couple of hand held, curved, broad knives also known as a *daa*, for any cutting or chopping needs.

All prepared, the four of us made our way down to the boat, Kutina Granny and Auntie Hasna and Sufi followed us to the water's edge, to bid us good luck. The three youngsters boarded the boat one by one whilst Uncle Abul held the boat steady with the pole. We sat on the boat so as to spread the weight out as evenly as possible.

Once we were all settled Abul pushed the boat off into the

waters as Granny yelled out, "Keep a particular eye out for Sabu, and don't let anything happen to him."

"Nothing is going to happen, Granny," I yelled back and turned to face the direction of travel.

When we reached deeper waters Uncle Abul put the pole in the boat and picked up one of the paddles. He sat down and began to row and steer the boat further out into the lake. Fozlu and I took up the two other paddles and began rowing on either side of the boat. The boat picked up speed and we exited the channel with baris on either side and onto the bigger expanse of the lake.

As soon as we entered the main body of water the wind cut in from the left of us and blew our hair in all directions. The wind was a comforting relief from the stifling heat of the bari. The four of us remained contentedly silent with only the rush of the wind playing in our ears as we rowed further out into the lake. Out in the open waters a sense of freedom and excitement overcame me and my heart felt as light as a helium filled balloon lifting into the sky. Even though I was living in the rural countryside, my bari in Shupatola being in the hills never gave much opportunity to come across wide open spaces under a large azure sky as today, so out here in the boat I wanted to carry on rowing and go as far as I could, visiting the ends of the earth.

The lake seemed to stretch for miles in all directions and in the distance there was the odd boatman dotted here and there. We eventually approached a small hill jutting out of the water. Uncle Abul increased the speed to get the boat as far up the rise as possible. "Hold on tight," he warned us, as the boat sliced into the rise and we came to a bumpy halt.

We all got off and Abul used the punting pole to moor the craft securely on the island. The island was bare apart from a covering of short grass and was small enough to walk around in less than a minute. On the opposite side of the island the waters were quite shallow, with depressions in the earth forming mini pools where we could wade through up to our waist.

"Right, I'm going to use the *ural zaal* to catch some fish on this side, why don't the three of you head over there and see what you can do with the *feloyn*," he instructed us, referring to the 'Y' shaped bamboo framed fishing net.

Aplu was already heading off into the mini pools of water with one of the bamboo baskets to carry the fish, whilst Fozlu and I got the fishing net out and carried it over to join Aplu. Fozlu looked at the pools and assessed how far we could go without jeopardising our chances of losing the net and losing our footing underwater.

"Uncle, you follow behind me with the basket whilst I push the net into the water, Aplu you stay on the shore," he said, having decided the best way to go about catching some fish.

Fozlu placed the open end of the net into the water and then used the handle to drive it forward and into deeper waters. I followed behind him with the basket and when we reached deep enough waters up to our waist Fozlu lifted the net out by digging the handle into the earth and hoisting the front slowly upwards. As he lifted the net I could see small fish dancing at the base as they struggled in vain to escape, their silvery scales sparkling like diamonds.

Fozlu asked me to hold the basket while he scooped the fish, which were quite similar to goldfish, into the basket. The catch wasn't that big, but it was a sign that we could catch more.

Aplu from the shore shouted, "Have you caught something?"

"Yes! Only a few small ones though," I yelled back.

Fozlu and I carried on going from pool to pool and also working around our edge of the island. Our prize was diminishing slowly so we decided to head back to the other side where Abul hopefully was catching bigger game. Fozlu explained that because the water in the pools was quite warm many of the fish would be in deeper waters. Uncle Abul saw us approach him, and it looked as if he was also about to call us to move to another fishing spot.

"It's not that good around here for catching any fish today, let's go onto another spot," he said as he took a couple of brown catfish and put them in the basket Aplu was carrying.

All of us boarded the boat again and pushed out to new fishing grounds. By this time the sun was almost at its zenith and intensely hot, I could feel the back of my neck burning and I could see the others also feeling the heat. As Abul gently rowed away from the island I scooped handfuls of water and dabbed my neck for temporary respite. We did not have any drinking water with us either and even though I was thirsty I did not complain for fear of looking weak. We also filled the bottom of the boat with enough water to keep the fish in the basket alive, who wriggled away, jostling for space and water.

We moved from island to island and spent the day continuing with our fishing expedition, which was proving eventually bountiful. However, apart from Abul, who was in the serious business of fishing, we three youngsters were swimming and having as much fun as we could whilst fishing with the net.

By the time we headed back to the bari it was late afternoon and we were all tired, hungry and very thirsty. Our hands and feet were wrinkled from spending all day immersed in water. As Abul rowed the boat back to the bari a slight breeze picked up, which helped dry the water from our bodies but made us shiver at the same time.

We approached the bari with the sun already dipping

behind the trees lining the western horizon. At the ghat we hauled ourselves out of the boat carrying the fishing nets, baskets and paddles. Abul secured the boat to the trunk of a tree and we climbed the steps up to the bari, where at the top stood Kutina Granny expectantly. I wondered how she knew we were coming, or how even my Bibi knew when I was coming and going. It must be a parental or guardian's instinct.

"What Sabu, did you catch a lot of fish then?" she asked as we approached the top.

"At first there wasn't much, but later we did get to catch some," I replied.

"The fish are not that big either, they're hiding out in the deeper waters," Fozlu added.

We walked onto the courtyard as Granny took the fish and went into the kitchen to prepare them for dinner. We laid all the tools and equipment out on the courtyard to dry and then went off to the pond to wash ourselves.

After bathing we sat around the porch of the house as the sun went down and the lanterns came out and were placed by doorways and steps. The night was clear with no wind and the only noise that could be heard were the frogs and crickets noisily going about their nocturnal activities. Around the branches of trees the odd firefly would glow here and there as it navigated towards its secret destination unknown to us humans.

Fozlu was telling scary stories to me and his younger brothers and we lapped it up with gusto. The story being told tonight was of the *kusudora*, the story goes that every so often this being or thing called the *kusudora* would go round terrorising the villages of Bangladesh. It would go round the villages seeking victims to abduct before cutting them up for their organs. Some people said it was a man who sold the organs to buyers and others said it was an unknown creature seeking children in particular. This *kusudora* character was used by adults to scare children when they were naughty. Hearing the story raised the hairs on my neck and as the story was wound down I consciously made a note not to go wandering alone anywhere at night.

We were eventually called by Kutina Granny to go and eat our evening meal, which was a noisy affair like those scenes at camp, with a group of children all piling into the kitchen for food. Me, Fozlu, his younger brothers, as well as his eldest brother all made our way into the kitchen area and squatted on the bamboo mat, waiting to be fed. Tin plates were laid out in front, glasses of water were fetched along with small side plates with rock salt, chillies and thin wedges of Jara Lebu. We were served plain rice that had a thin vein of red colour running through it, as one of Fozlu's brothers passed a bowl of cold water round to wash our hands.

Kutina Granny had fried the small fish in a dry, spicy masala and then curried the larger fish and there was a side dish of potato chutney and a Bangladeshi version of salsa. We tucked in ravenously, savouring the deliciously spicy fish and the side dishes that complemented the fish extremely well. As was the tradition in a patriarchal society like Bangladesh, Granny and her two daughters had their meal after the men and children had eaten.

With bellies full we all sat around the lanterns and oil lamps on the porch, chatting in low tones and as usual in such gatherings stories began. This time it was Kutina Granny. She was telling the story of her childhood in Purushpal with my Bibi and her other sisters. As Granny was relating her story my attention broke off to a slight irritation on my backside. I put my hand down the back of my shorts and scratched my lower back. There was nothing to my touch that was obviously a foreign body that shouldn't be there. However, the irritation was still there, but this time I could feel it in between my buttocks.

As the storytelling continued I got up without trying to raise too much suspicion and walked into the kitchen with a small oil lantern where there wasn't anybody around to have a closer look. Having got my privacy I pulled down my shorts and I put my hand in between my buttocks and almost fainted when my left finger encountered a wet and cold lump around my anus. I shrieked in horror and pulled up my shorts.

I couldn't go anywhere before everyone that was sitting out on the porch rushed into the kitchen, with Uncle Abul leading the way. "What's the matter Sabu?" he asked with a shocked look on his face.

"There's something on my bum," I replied with embarrassment.

"What do you mean and where?" Kutina Granny came forward bringing with her another oil lantern.

"I've got an itch on my bottom and when I put my hand in my pants to check I felt something wet and slimy," I added, with my uncles and aunts looking on trying not to laugh.

Uncle Abul shooed his siblings and mother away and asked me to pull down my pants to have a look. I leant over as he looked in between my buttock cheeks, which was the most embarrassing thing in my life so far.

"Don't move, I see something," he added.

"What? What do you see?" I yanked my head back to look to at him.

"Well get back down so I can see," he said, sounding a bit irritated.

I could not see exactly what he was doing but I could from the corner of my eyes see one of the younger uncle's sneaking a peak through the door leading into the kitchen. Uncle Abul then stood up and dropped a black glistening leech on the floor, which was oozing my blood through its mouth. Uncle Abul asked me to wait whilst he went over to one of the cupboards and got a small dab of limestone paste – which was used as a condiment with betel nut and paan. He then applied the paste around my anus which stung like alcohol on an open wound. I yelped in pain and everyone rushed back into the room again.

"Yah! What's going on?" let out all the uncles in one go.

The leech was writhing on the floor, bloated, having feasted on my blood, for how long I didn't know.

"A leech was feeding on Sabu, he must have got it whilst we were out on the lake today," Uncle Abul relayed to everyone.

"Yah Allah, so much blood," Kutina Granny exclaimed.

In the meantime Aplu had rushed over and got some rock salt and sprinkled it all over the leech, which liquefied, forming a pool of blood and mushy leech flesh on the earthen floor. Granny, annoyed at the mess Aplu had made, shooed him out of the kitchen. She then gave me a glass of water to drink. I was definitely shaken up and must have looked like a ghost.

"Uncle, that thing could have gotten inside you and eaten you from within," Aplu described in gory detail.

"Hey, get away and stop saying such things," Granny said raising a threatening hand at Aplu. "Now, all of you get off to bed," she ordered.

"Sabu needs to rest, and Sabu you will be fine, do not worry about the leech, we got it in time."

In time, in time! I was going crazy thinking how close I was to having an alien like creature inside me, I could have been dead. The doctors would have had to slice my gut open to get the damn monster out. I kept my emotions in check and whilst my uncles bantered with me I kept calm and did not expose my anxiety of nearly having a leech tear away inside me.

All of us slowly made our way off to the various rooms in

the house across the courtyard and going to bed. I think the leech was enough excitement for one night. As I lay down next to one of the uncles my thoughts went back to the leech. I had assisted in ceremoniously killing his brethren whilst coming to Bordesh, I guess this was revenge from the brotherhood of leeches.

Lying Letters

The story of the leech incident was told and retold for the last few days I was at Bordesh and when Bibi arrived to collect me, she had nothing to say but shake her head. Bibi stayed for one night and then we made our way back to Shupatola on foot. I was sad to go as I would miss the camaraderie of having other boys of my age group to hang out with. As Bibi and I turned onto the path heading out onto the main road running through Bordesh, I looked back over my shoulder to see Kutina Granny and all her children waving us goodbye.

Back in Shupatola everything seemed a bit slower and quieter, but having been in the hubbub of a large family like that of Uncle Fozlu it took me a few days to re-adjust back to my 'lone wolf' type of living. Not going to school as well meant that the friends I had were limited to Bolai. So, back home I was pretty much left to my own devices, to make and engage in my own games and entertainment.

A few days after Bibi and I returned from Bordesh we had a visit from Boro Dada's eldest son, namely Uncle Hannan. He was at least a decade older than me. With such an age gap I didn't have much in common with him and I never really liked him as an individual. There was something about him that made me very uncomfortable in his presence. So, apart from the niceties required for uncles I would avoid any contact with him.

The day Hannan visited it was late afternoon and I was

helping Bibi tidy up the bari, getting the chickens and ducks into their cage in the store room. Bibi was sweeping the porch and putting away clothes that had been dry roasted in the blazing summer sun. Uncle Hannan walked up the path into the courtyard with Lukman, who was of similar age. Hannan called out to Bibi. "Oh Auntie, where are you?"

"Who is it shouting?" Bibi questioned back looking out towards the path.

"It's me Auntie, your Hannan, salaam alaikum."

"Alaikum salaam, what's your news? How is it that you are this way?"

"No! I was just visiting the bazaar, so I thought I'd come and see you."

"Come and sit down, Lukman you come and grab a mura too."

I came over from the far corner of the courtyard and greeted Hannan. "Salaam alaikum Uncle," I said respectfully.

"What news Nephew, are you well?" he asked as he sat down on a mura on the porch with Lukman taking one too.

"I am well Uncle, what's news with Dada?" I asked about Boro Dada.

"He's doing fine he said that he would visit soon. So, have you heard anything from your mum and dad?" he continued as Bibi came out of the kitchen with two glasses of water.

"Here you are, drink some water while I get the tea ready."

"Don't fuss over us Auntie," Hannan protested, by which time Bibi was already halfway to the kitchen.

"I am here because someone has arrived from London and there's a letter from your mum and dad," Hannan continued with the conversation. I was excited to hear that my parents had written and eager to find out whether he had the letter with him. "Have you got the letter?"

"No! I am going to get it later and then I'll come by again."

I was a bit deflated that I had to wait for the letter, still I was happy to be able to hear from my parents and find out how my brothers and sister were doing. Bibi came back out with cups of tea for all of us. She sat down on a small wooden stool and I took a seat at the edge of the earthen porch step. All of us took our cups of sweet, milky tea and began to dunk our biscuits into the hot liquid.

"Did you say that there was a letter from Sabu's parents?" Bibi enquired.

"Yes! Auntie," Hannan replied.

"Where is the letter then?" she asked.

"I haven't got it yet, I'll bring it round later," he replied.

"So, who did the letter come with?" she queried further.

"No! Just someone east of the Bazaar," he answered without further elaboration, which I thought was a bit odd.

Usually when someone arrives from London everyone knows who it is, especially in those days of the late 1970's and early 80's when there were very few Bangladeshis abroad. After drinking their teas both Hannan and Lukman left saying they would be back later. By this time dusk was starting to close in and the evening prayer calls would be starting soon, so Bibi gave me a few tasks to tidy up and help her secure the bari for the night. Just as we were finishing up our chores, the prayer calls from the various mosques had come to an end and we had lit the lanterns for the night and hung them around the house, allowing us to navigate without bumping into each other or other inanimate objects. The only sounds that could be heard were the odd quacks and clucks of the ducks and chickens as they lay to roost for the night. Out in the foliage of the bari the crickets were beginning their nightly chorus.

Once Bibi had finished her prayers she came out onto the porch where I was sitting on a mura. The night was quite warm and dry with the moon casting a bluish hue over the land through a light scattering of clouds. Bibi had her customary betel nut thali with her. It contained a couple of ripe nuts, some emerald green paan leaves, the limestone paste, as well as the dried, flavoured tobacco leaves. Bibi began the process of making a tiny parcel out of the ingredients. Firstly, she took a whole paan leaf the size of her palm. She then applied the limestone paste with a small bamboo spatula, then she sprinkled the finely cut betel nut into the centre of the leaf, followed by a sprinkling of the tobacco. She then neatly folded the leaf into a triangular parcel like a samosa and popped it into her mouth.

For Bibi and the millions of other people in Bangladesh this routine was second nature and the concoction of ingredients was not out of the ordinary. However, any uninitiated newcomer to the ritual of chewing betel nut, would, within minutes, suffer from constriction of the throat, flushing of the face and gasping for breath and water.

"Where is Uncle Hannan?" I asked impatiently of Bibi, getting up from my seat and looking out towards the entrance to the bari, which showed no signs of life except the odd lantern flickering across Bolai's courtyard.

"He will come, just be patient," Bibi replied.

With impatience being one of my faults I began pacing up and down the porch.

"Here, come help me in the kitchen to prepare something for dinner, instead of stomping around crazily," Bibi said as she got up and headed into the house.

I followed her in, taking the lantern from the porch with me to provide extra light. In the kitchen Bibi got a two-legged *daa* and placed it on the floor. She then placed a low stool and sat in front of it, holding the *daa* secure with her right foot. Beside her she had a basket of small, red potatoes and red onions. I guessed she was going to be making potato bhajee, which I've got to admit I had a great fondness for. An aluminium pot contained some small, freshwater prawns which Bibi had purchased from a bari-to-bari fish salesman. Out in the rural areas fishermen, when they caught their catch for the day from the various rivers and lagoons, passed through the baris on their way to the market selling whatever they could. It provided a convenient way for many womenfolk to buy fresh fish without having to go to the markets or trying to find someone who could do the job of going grocery shopping.

So Bibi put me to task peeling the shells from the prawns, which were so tiny that I had difficulty in holding and peeling the grey shell off them. The extremely tiny ones I was told to leave as there would be nothing left once the shell was removed. It was an easy task but my fingertips started to wrinkle and after I had finished the smell of freshwater prawns lingered on my fingertips.

Bibi, having prepared the onions and potatoes, got a cast iron wok ready on the wood burning stove and a small pot for the prawns. She added the spices to the hot oil and the aromatic smell wafted throughout the kitchen and beyond. The prawns she prepared with a gourd type vegetable, using a lot of sauce and the potato was a dry dish with a simple flavouring of turmeric, salt and coriander as garnish. By the time we had finished cooking my stomach was rumbling with hunger and I had forgotten all about Uncle Hannan and the letter from my parents. Out from the darkness of the porch walked Hannan, with the light from his Chinese made aluminium torch dancing ahead of him.

"What Auntie, are you eating already?"

"No my dear boy, we are only cooking the curries," she replied.

"I hope this is not all because of me."

"We do need to eat too, you know," she added as Hannan grabbed a low stool and squatted beside me.

"So Uncle, have you got the letter?" I asked impatiently.

"Yes son, I have."

"So, let's hear what it says?" I continued.

"After eating I will read it to you," he said, making the whole process unnecessarily longer than needed. At this point I was getting a bit angry to say the least.

"OK then," I said quite strongly, before getting up and walking out to the porch in the dark.

Even though I tried to disguise my anger I felt that Bibi and Hannan were both aware, which in a way made me feel good, as I wanted them to notice.

"What Sabu? Where are you going?" Bibi called after me.

"No, I'm just going over to Bolai's, I'll be back."

"It's nearly time to eat, you can go afterwards."

"I'm coming," I yelled from across the path as I headed into Bolai's bari. I headed towards her kitchen where I could see the most activity and light.

I walked in to find Bolai, her mum and her elder sister squatting around the hearth, stirring pots and pans preparing their evening meal. The spices sizzling away in the pots reached up into my nostrils, making me squint and wrinkle my nose to prevent a sneeze. The smell was mouth-watering, even though a bit strong.

"So what brings you around here Sabu?" asked Bolai's mother.

"He must be hungry," her sister joked.

"No! I just thought I'd visit Bolai and see if she can come over later on," I countered the allegation of hunger.

"Yes! I can come over after dinner if you want, any reason why?" she asked.

"Nothing really, just haven't seen you today and I've got an uncle visiting so it's a bit boring listening to him."

"Well why don't you stay and have something to eat with us," offered Bolai's mother.

"I can't, Bibi has cooked and they're waiting for me," I shrugged. I loitered for a little longer, just to ensure that Hannan in particular got the message that he should not be messing with me before deciding to go back. "I'll see you later Bolai," I expressed, walking out of the kitchen and towards my bari.

I got back to see Bibi had already placed the three white tin plates on the bamboo mat with three stools behind the plates. The bhajee and prawn curry was dished up in small serving bowls and placed on the mat. I silently took my place. Bibi passed a bowl with the water jug for washing our hands. Uncle Hannan took his place and the three of us took our meal initially with silence but eventually the conversation started and by the end of the meal the earlier events had become a distant memory.

After dinner we sat back out on the porch with three of us taking betel nut and paan according to what our palates could handle. I sat there on a stool chewing on the nut and paan and sucking on the addictive juices. The bluish light from the moon washed over the courtyard and the green foliage giving the night an eerie glow.

Bibi and I turned towards Hannan as he began rustling something in his shirt pocket. At the same time I looked towards the path upon hearing movement and hushed voices, to see Bolai and her mother coming towards the house.

"You're here then Bolai," I asked.

"Yes! What are you up to?" she asked.

"Nothing, just sitting here with Bibi and Uncle Hannan," I replied.

"Sister, come take a seat," Bibi offered Bolai's mother.

Bolai came and sat on the porch next to me while her mother took a seat with Bibi. Even though Bolai's mother had a cheek full of betel nut and her lips were blood red, Bibi offered her the thali with the Betel nut which she took and proceeded to put more nut and paan in her mouth.

Uncle Hannan had got the letter out now which was of the blue airmail variety. It looked a bit crumpled and somehow it did not look like the typical aerogramme letters the post office in the UK sold. Anyway he carried on preparing to read the letter. "Sabu's dad has written a letter, so listen," he postured, I felt.

> *"Sabu, I hope you are well and your Bibi is well too. Your mum and I send you and your Bibi our prayers. Kindly give our salaam to your Bibi.*
>
> *I hope your health is well. How is the bari in Shupatola? Is everything OK there?*
>
> *Are you going to school and behaving and not giving your Bibi any trouble? Make sure you listen to your Bibi, your dada and your uncles."*

As Hannan carried on my ears had gone hot and I could feel my face flushing as I felt embarrassed, as well as angry. Especially with Bolai and her mother present I felt chastised not only in front of Bibi, but strangers as well. By the time I had recovered my composure and my anger had subsided, I could hear Uncle Hannan coming to the end of the letter.

> *".. and give our salaam to your Bibi"*

I looked at Bibi and then Hannan and asked, "Can I read the letter?"

One thing my dad ensured was that I learnt how to read and write Bengali fully. Back in England on top of my English schoolwork, my younger brother and I had to learn Bengali, as well as the daily Arabic lessons at home. With English and Bengali my dad would make us write out the alphabet over again and again until we could write it perfectly. Whilst we performed our writing in a robotic manner, Dad would maintain a nearby presence to ensure we did not slack or falter from our learning. Hence, through the practice of copying both alphabets over again and again during my early childhood not only had I grasped English very well, but also Bengali.

I took the blue aerogramme from Uncle Hannan and looked over the letter. For some reason it did not feel right, the letter seemed lighter in colour, even under the light from the oil lantern. The paper felt thin so I looked at the writing on the inside and immediately I could tell this was not a letter from my dad. My dad always wrote in black and his writing was one that was heavy and bold. All his Bengali characters would have a slight lean towards the right and usually you could see the figures on the reverse side of the paper, due to how much pressure he applied when writing. Immediately I jumped out of my stool and shouted. "This letter is not from my dad!"

"Yah! What are you talking about," exclaimed Hannan.

I got the distinct impression that whatever plan he had was about to be unravelled as he looked nervous and began to increase the volume of his voice to match mine. This made me even angrier and I started swearing all sorts of profanities.

"You mother fucker, you are lying, this letter is not from my dad," I spewed.

In my irate state I lost all focus of people around me and I heard Bibi faintly questioning, "Hey Sabu, what is this you are saying?"

Even Bolai's mother piped in trying to calm me. Uncle Hannan made things worse by saying that he had permission to discipline me.

"You son of a pig, who are you to me to say that?" I continued and began stomping off out of the bari.

I heard Uncle Hannan follow me out saying, "Hey boy, I'm going to teach you a lesson tonight."

This made me rattle off a tirade of more swear words at him and each subsequent swear had a greater severity and cutting insult than the last, all of them referring to his parents. By the time I had reached the path Hannan caught up with me and picked me up of the ground. I began to struggle with all my might to get free but had no luck. He took me into Bolai's bari and into the house on the left as you entered her place. This was where Bolai's brother Lukman stayed and I could see that there was someone in the house as the light from a lantern could be seen in between the cracks through the window shutters and door.

I could hear Bibi in the distance say, "Hey! Hannan, let him go, it'll be impossible to control him later on."

As Hannan took me into Lukman's house I was screaming like a banshee and continued with my effort to get out of his hold on me and was desperate to get away. From the corner of my eye I could see Bolai and her mum walking back to their house across their courtyard. Bolai's mum asked Hannan to let me go but I got the impression that she wasn't too concerned and ushered Bolai away in the opposite direction.

In Lukman's room I carried on swearing at Hannan and calling him all the vulgar words that I could think of, I even surprised myself a little at how much I came out with.

"What's going on here?" Lukman asked a bit surprised and

awoken from his slumber by my swearing and the resulting commotion.

"No! Nothing's going on, this boy needs to be taught a lesson," Hannan replied.

So there I was, placed on the bed and pinned down by Hannan still struggling and swearing. Hannan and Lukman lit a cigarette each and began chatting about things in which I had no interest and wasn't paying much attention to as I was too busy trying to break free.

I stopped struggling even though the odd swear word would escape my lip in defiance and anger, accompanied by a wriggle. Hannan may have been the son of Boro Dada and knowing how much I loved Dada I couldn't forgive Hannan for bringing a fake letter to me telling me how to behave. What did he think I was a stupid kid who did not know his dad's handwriting? I began to think that this was some sort of conspiracy against me. Certain people were up to no good to try and make me go to school and behave. It wasn't that I was bad or doing things that would bring 'shame' to my family. Things like stealing, lying, creating mischief or even smoking cigarettes. All I did was stick to myself and just lived like a ten year old would without parental control and no responsibilities, a life almost out of Rudyard Kipling's Jungle Book. Okay, I admit I wasn't going to school or going to the local mosque for Arabic lessons. Maybe I wasn't listening to Bibi all the time, but I wasn't disrespectful to anyone and never with Bibi. I would never harm her or let any harm come to her. So, it was beyond me why Hannan had done what he had done and who else was behind it?

While I was musing over the turn of events tonight I had stopped struggling to set myself free, mainly because I was worn out. Hannan released me from his grip, setting me free and told me to be on my way.

"Make sure you behave in the future son," Hannan ordered.

I jumped off the bed and as I walked out of Lukman's house I did not look back at either of them, but muttered a profanity at Hannan under my breath as I left.

Back at my house I was met by Bibi. She asked me if I was alright to which I responded in the positive but with a frown and looking menacingly enraged. I wanted Bibi to say something else, but she realised that I should be left alone. Even so I began ranting at her, telling her that I would kill Hannan if he did that sort of thing again and that he wasn't welcome to my bari ever. Bibi accepted what I was spewing out and asked me to calm down over again and again, saying that Hannan would hear and that I shouldn't swear using Dada's name.

Eventually I calmed down, by which time it had become quite late and my throat was quite hoarse. I got myself a glass of water from the earthen water pot in the kitchen, gulped it down and went to bed. However I was having trouble sleeping, initially because I was so worked up. Then, as I started to think a bit more I thought what if the letter was from my parents, written by someone else. What if news had got to them that I wasn't going to school but living more like Mowgli? I began to worry about what my dad would do when he saw me next. As I tried to banish those thoughts from my mind, I began to think about Hannan. From that day on I never trusted Hannan again, he looked like a weasel and he fit the persona of one in my estimations because of what he did.

That night he stayed with Lukman only to return late in the morning. Bibi gave him breakfast, I did not even want to look at him, nor be in his presence so I went out towards the pond and sat there at the steps for a good few hours. When I returned he had gone back to Purushpal, for which I was glad. Many months later after I had returned to London and asked my mum about any such letter she assured me that neither she nor my dad had sent any letter with such contents. From that day on I gave Hannan respect only because he was my elder and my dad's cousin, but for no other reason.

Arrival of Mum

A month or so had gone by and a telegram arrived from my parents. The monsoon was coming to an end and slowly the waters would start receding from the fields. Bibi and I were in Shupatola when Boro Dada walked up the path and into our Bari.

"Oh! Sabu, where are you Grandson?" I heard him call out from where I was just outside the courtyard watching Broken-hand and his mob stream down from the eastern hill and onto our bari. I dared not confront them in such large numbers so I turned back into the courtyard. Dada was wearing his obligatory topi, a white cotton tunic and a dark chequered lunghi, carrying a shopping bag and sweating profusely in the mid-morning heat.

"Salaam alaikum Dada, what's your news?" I asked smiling, happy to see him as I rushed and greeted him.

"Nothing much Grandson, I have news for you though."

"Oh, really?" I replied excitedly.

By this time Dada had taken a seat on a mura on the porch and Bibi, who had been hanging some washing up, walked over. "What's up sister?" Dada enquired of her.

"No, nothing much, what news have you brought us?"

"Well, Sabu's mother is coming to Bangladesh soon."

"Really! When is she coming?" I asked in excitement.

"Well, your father said that he will send another telegram once he has booked the tickets."

"Is she coming to take me back?" I continued.

"Yes I suppose and also to see your Nana, he's been very ill lately as you know and there's talk that he may not live for much longer," Dada said solemnly.

I saw Nana several weeks ago and even though he was able to talk he was bed ridden, he looked extremely gaunt and almost as thin as a sheet of paper. At that visit I did not even contemplate that he was so close to death's door. Now that mum was coming over to see him it made me realise that Nana's situation was graver than I thought. However, the severity of Nana's situation was overridden by mum's imminent arrival. I was excited to learn that she was coming and that I would be going home shortly. However, after my initial euphoria had subsided, I started to think about the potential admonishment that could be coming my way. I was convinced that all the things that I had been up to would have reached the ears of my parents, and my mum upon her arrival would take me aside and have a serious talking to with me, with the prospect of a couple of clips round my ears to put me straight. Thinking about such an encounter put a downer on meeting my mum. I would be quite happy now for her not to come, but I could not delay the inevitable.

"Who else is coming Dada?" I enquired, not so cheerful anymore.

"It doesn't say in the telegram, but I think it might be your mum and only your younger brother and sister," he replied.

Hearing that my siblings would be coming too made a slight improvement in my mood, but not by much.

"They're going to be staying in Purushpal so we had better get back down there and get the house ready," Bibi told herself more than Dada and I.

Dada stayed that night but my mind was preoccupied. I had begun to think of all the possible repercussions that could happen over my behaviour and actions over the last ten months. My sleep was restless and butterflies were playing havoc in my stomach. The following morning Dada left straight away after a breakfast of puffed rice, tea and biscuits. He said that he would come by to accompany us back to Purushpal prior to mum's arrival. I was sad to see Dada leave as he was the messenger bringing the telegrams with news of mum's arrival, so with him going I felt disconnected from that news line.

Over the coming days I went about my days half-heartedly, expecting the wrath of my mum when she arrived. I didn't say anything to Bibi or anyone else for that matter. I don't think Bibi noticed my melancholy and even if she did she did not say anything to me.

Less than a week after Dada's visit a message arrived through Arzomond. He had been to Beani Bazaar on his daily visit, usually to top-up supplies for his doctor's practice. On some of these occasions he would also pick up shopping for us and any news from Purushpal. With no telephone and public transport being rare and dangerous, people would leave messages at the bazaar which would then be picked up by someone else and carried onto its final destination.

Arzomond arrived at our bari early evening just before the evening prayer calls began to hit the airwaves over the village. He sat on a mura on the porch, chewing on the last remnants of some betel nut.

"What are you up to grandson?" he asked. I referred to him as grandfather even though there was no blood connection, because he referred to Bibi as a sister.

I liked Arzomond as he would always joke with me about giving me medicine to cure my madness. He was a slim man probably a few years younger than Bibi and had the beard of all elderly men, but lacking the moustache.

"Nothing Dada," I responded.

"Well, it looks like your mum is finally arriving," he announced.

"Really, what's the news?"

"I was walking past Kutub Tailors and one of your uncles called me over. The message was from your Boro Dada. Your mum is going to be here in less than a week's time and you and your Bibi should go to Purushpal."

Bibi was just walking back from the pond with some washed clothes in one hand, a trail of water droplets followed her into the courtyard where she hung up the washing before coming over to join us.

"Bibi, Mum's coming this week, we've gotta go to Purushpal!" I yelled excitedly.

"What bhaisab, is that right?" she directed at Arzomond.

"Yes! Sister, that's the news I got at the bazaar," he reconfirmed.

Bibi came over to the porch and offered him some betel nut, which he accepted gladly.

"Sabu's mum is due to arrive on Sunday and your brother said that you should get to Purushpal as soon as you are able to. He was going to come and help you get back but has been tied up with chores," Arzomond continued.

We were pretty much waiting for this news to come anyway and Bibi had kept the bari tidy and ready to be left at short notice.

"We'll head off tomorrow, can you ask Bolai's mum to come over later today?" she asked of him.

Arzomond left as the prayer calls ended and the long shadows of dusk began to draw in around the house. He left chewing on the betel nut and spitting a jet of red juice from his mouth as he walked out of the bari.

"Right, you might as well get your things ready for

tomorrow," Bibi suggested as she headed into the house.

That evening the two of us were busy tidying up, getting our clothes and putting them into jute bags. We were going to walk back to Purushpal, so we had to take only what we could carry. Later on Bolai and her mum came by, whereby Bibi asked Bolai's mum to keep an eye out on our bari.

Bolai and I sat on the porch away from the elders. I spent the evening relaying to her the news about my mum arriving with my kid brother and sister. I explained that I would most probably spend all of my time now in Purushpal before going back to London. She was saddened to hear that I would soon leave for England. Even to me it seemed alien, the thought of going back to England. I had not contemplated it at all after my initial sense of homesickness had disappeared. I wasn't even sure how long Mum was coming for and when we would go back to England.

"When will you come back to Bangladesh," Bolai asked gulping on tears that she was trying to hold down.

"I don't know," I replied sadly.

We sat there in the darkness with only the oil lantern providing light but not enough, as I could not see Bolai's tears as she looked away periodically. I avoided eye contact so as not to embarrass her. My insides were in turmoil and I did not know what to do or not do. Having not felt such feelings before I was a bit confused and at a loss for words.

Our silence was broken when her mum came out of the kitchen, "Come on Bolai, let's go."

As mother and daughter walked into the darkness of the night and across the path to their bari, I had a sense of loss welling inside. A friendship that was one of the best I'd ever had was coming to a close. After Bolai and her mum left, Bibi and I closed the house down for the night and both of us took to our beds.

In the morning the sun rose strongly in the late summer sky.

It was going to be a swelteringly hot day by the look of things. After breakfast I looked around the bari to see what I could take with me. I got several Jara Lebu from the thorny bushes, and a few papayas from the tree at the back of the house. I was ready by mid-morning and eager to start the journey. I was always keen to commence a journey, no matter how near or far or how often. For me the journey was the fun part, the sights, the people, and just being on the open road. Sometimes the destination may be an old familiar place and the route trodden many times, but the journey through the fields and beneath the overhanging branches of palms and bamboo of the villages on the way I always found refreshing.

With the house locked from the outside I carried two oversize bags slung over my shoulders, Bibi had one bag whilst carrying an umbrella in her free hand. We were as ready as we were going to be so we headed onto the path. Bolai and her mum were at the mouth of their bari watching as we left. Bibi repeated her request to Bolai's mum to keep an eye out for our place. Bolai stood by her mum's side, looking as sad as she did the night before.

"Bolai, I'm going," I said.

"OK," she replied in a barely audible voice.

When we got to the bottom of the path and turned left to head west towards the Lula River, I looked back, both at the bari and Bolai. Deep within me I knew that a chapter in my life had come to an end and that my friendship with Bolai and my stays at our bari were over. With a heavy heart I quietly followed Bibi, both of us barefoot, as we made our way past the mosque and out of Shupatola.

Little did I know that this was that last time I would see Bolai before I left for England, and I never actually got to know her real name. Bolai was a loving name parents called their children by. It was a name that could be used just as easily for boys as girls. We had departed with no hugs, no kisses, just a simple statement of farewell and our friendship ended.

We arrived in Purushpal just after the midday prayer calls were dying off over the village. The midday prayer call would spur people into having their daily baths at the communal ponds. This was followed by prayer facing Mecca to the west. The men would go off to the mosque with the women praying at home. Upon their return lunch would be had first by the men and children, followed by the women. Most of the farming duties would have been done in the morning, with the farmers and their workers getting up before sunrise, which was roughly around six in the morning. So, after lunch people tended to relax on their porches chewing on betel nut. Later, as early evening drew in, the men would go off to the bazaars to buy the groceries, whilst the women began to close the baris down and start preparing the evening meals.

As Bibi and I walked up path to the bari in Purushpal, Boro Dada was making his way to the mosque.

"Salaam alaikum, Dada," I addressed him.

"Alaikum salaam Grandson, you here already. Go in, I'll be back soon," he replied as he headed off towards the mosque.

Walking into the bari we were greeted with Amad's loud voice. "Uncle Sabu has arrived," he cried out, his dark face smiling and his white teeth gleaming in the sun.

By this time both Bibi and I were hot, sweaty and very uncomfortable. I had rivulets of warm salty water running down my forehead into my eyes and mouth. We walked into the kitchen and had a long, cool drink of water. The two grannies and their daughters were all in the kitchen tidying up the cooking before going off to the pond to bathe.

233

One of my aunties joked about my mum's arrival, "Oh! Sabu, your mum's not coming at all."

"No, my mum *is* coming," I replied defiantly.

"Stop being silly," Boro Dadi cut her daughter Rani short. "Leave him alone," she scolded.

Auntie Rani was a bit of a joker and she would always play the joke with me and I would always fall for it. Even though afterwards I would say that I would never be a sucker when she joked.

"Sabu come, let's go and put our things away," Bibi said as she walked out towards our house.

I followed her to find Old Auntie saying her prayers, so I quietly unpacked my clothes and stuck them on a wooden clothes horse in one corner of the room. Whilst Bibi carried on getting her clothes sorted out I dashed out of the house. "I'm off with Aman and them," I shouted as I exited the room.

Amad was already waiting outside I asked him where his brother Aman was.

"He's already at the furki," he stated.

We both ran off down the narrow path at the back of the house towards the pond. As we approached it I could see water being splashed with the droplets dancing in the bright sunlight. The splashing was accompanied by lots of shouts and yells of joy as Aman, Iqbal and other children from the bari were having fun. Amad and I scuttled down the stone steps where I took my top off and jumped into the water.

I was overjoyed to be back in the company of Aman and Iqbal and they reciprocated equally. Even though I enjoyed Shupatola and the company of Bolai, there was something about being with boys in my age group and just being raucous. It just felt as if I was at a permanent holiday camp, not that I was doing anything in Shupatola which would suggest otherwise.

There was a fruit tree that bore edible black berries in one corner of the pond. The berries looked like cherries and tasted a bit like blueberries but with a slightly acidic twist to their flavour. All of us swam over to it, climbing its overhanging branches to get to the berries, as well as diving into the pond from the topmost branches.

I cannot remember for how long we played in the water but it was the calls by Bibi and her sisters-in-law for us to go and have lunch that eventually got us out of the water. I ended up with stings on my stomach from belly-flopping onto the water and my eyes were red. I had water go up my nose and into my ears, plus I had swallowed enough water that I felt like a whale. My fingertips were wrinkled from the prolonged exposure to water, but as I headed off into my house to change into dry clothes I had a sense of happiness and elation that beamed from within.

The remainder of the week went by in a flash, most days I would stay within the confines of the bari until Aman and Iqbal arrived from school and then I would join them in the adventures and pursuits around the bari and in the flooded fields beyond. The water out in the fields was receding fast and there were many people from the homesteads out catching fish, which were disappearing rapidly along with the waters. On the day of Mum's arrival Bibi and I stayed behind whilst Boro Dada and his son Mahmod went to the airport to collect Mum and my siblings. They were going to be gone all day and I was feeling anxious and a bit on edge. Uncle Shuwa asked me if I wanted to go out fishing with him. Aman and his brothers were at school and as usual without thinking twice or needing any encouragement I agreed. Shuwa was the eldest son of Mejo Dada and he was a quiet and reclusive character who didn't socialise much with anyone, but he, akin everybody else, liked me as a nephew and always had time for me.

Shuwa got a fishing net from his house and a bamboo

basket to carry our catch in. He was a lean and strong teenager who didn't say much, usually keeping himself to himself. I liked him as an uncle and more so because he was quiet and treated me with kindness and respect without being bossy. He was like Boro Dada, always out in the fields as much as possible, taking care of the cattle or farming the land, more so than Hannan and Mahmod.

We went out to the canal under the bari and got into one of the boats. The two of us headed off out into the northern fields with Shuwa punting the boat northwards towards the banks of the Kushiara River. The sun was out and the day was quite hot, but bearable, with a gentle breeze ruffling the tops of the grass protruding out of the water. Halfway to the banks of the river we came to a stop. Putting the punting pole in the boat Shuwa then tied his lunghi under his legs and into his rear waist before sliding into the water, which only reached up to his waist. I took my t-shirt off and followed suit and gently lowered myself into the water. The water had been heated slightly by the sun and was a perfect temperature for a bath. With me, though, the water reached almost to my chest and I had a slight struggle to move around without falling over.

Where we had moored there was no grass or reeds sticking out of the water, so there was a slight current tugging at my legs as I manoeuvred about trying to get a secure footing. Shuwa had no problems.

"What Nephew, will you be okay?" he asked, seeing me struggling.

"Yes Uncle, I'll be fine," I replied bravely.

He then got the net out of the boat and passed me the bamboo basket and we walked westwards through the water with Shuwa towing the boat with us, as we moved carefully. I stayed behind Shuwa as he began to throw the net high into the air, which would then land on the water in front of him with hundreds of ripples forming a circle where it landed. The net then slowly sunk to the bottom, followed by Shuwa slowly dragging the net back out of the water. He then put the net in the boat to see what we had caught. Unfortunately, nothing but a few minnows, not even worth a second glance let alone putting in the basket.

We continued to move westwards and every so often Shuwa would launch the net for the next attempt to catch fish. We meandered through the water for what seemed ages, with little success. We had caught some fish, mainly small, grey black *Koi* fish. These were tough little buggers and if they weren't handled properly their spine could inflict a nice gash in your hand. We were quite far west of where we started when we came across another lone fisherman with a similar net to ours. He had his fishing basket tied to his waist, but no boat. Shuwa struck up a conversation with the man who also didn't seem to be having much luck with his fishing endeavours. Shuwa and he agreed to go into partnership to increase their yield. I was confused as to how they were going to achieve this.

The partnership involved tying one end of their nets together to create a greater catchment capacity. Then, with Shuwa holding one end of his net and the man his end they would drag the net across the waters and see what results they got. My job during this manoeuvre was to go round the side of the two men and throw clumps of mud which I would grab by clawing at the ground underfoot, this usually meant I had to dive beneath the water's surface and end up getting a good soaking.

During the first sweep of the net I was frantically splashing the water around the side of Shuwa and then the other side. It was very tiring, especially having to wade through water that was almost up to my chest in places. When the net was raised and put back on the boat we could see that our net had trapped a far greater number of fish than the stranger's. We had caught two fairly large catfish. The two fish were silvery grey in hue, with pink coloured whiskers. The creatures opened and closed their mouth as they struggled to break free. We also had a few more *Koi* fish. The stranger was not happy with his lot as he had only netted some small minnow like fish. I could see the envy and disappointment in his eyes. We did one further sweep before deciding to call it a day. I think Uncle Shuwa stopped because the man was not very happy that we were doing better out of our little partnership.

Back on the boat we rinsed our feet and washed our hands and face with the water from the fields. As the sun dried my arms and legs I was caked in a film of dried mud and my hair was matted. Shuwa punted us back to the bari, and as we pulled into the canal I could hear a commotion as well as throngs of people out on the path leading into the bari.

"What's the matter, Uncle?" I asked.

"Don't know, we'd better go and see," he replied, shrugging his shoulders.

I picked up the basket where the fish had gasped their last breath and lay silently at the bottom. Shuwa secured the boat to a tree trunk and picking up the punting pole walked towards the bari. I followed behind him and as we walked up the path I could see Boro Dada in the courtyard, which caused my heart to jump into my throat. I gulped with fear and joy and quelled a tear trying to break through. I realised Dada had returned back from the airport and my mum and siblings were somewhere in the throng of people.

"I think your mum has arrived," Shuwa stated.

"Yes Uncle," was all I could say.

I could hear people asking where I was, but nobody seemed to know or was too engrossed with my mum and siblings to look. I walked through the crowd which had now moved with my mum up onto the porch of our house, and then walked out in front of my mum. Someone shouted, "There's Sabu," to which my mum looked down and grabbed me in a hug and started crying. I tried not to cry but could not stop the tears rolling down my cheeks.

I knew I was muddy and now it had rubbed off onto my mum's sari. I asked her to let me go so she would not get dirty, however she held onto me tightly. I then noticed my sister Sheli and youngest brother Gulz by Bibi's side, as they looked around, bewildered by this scene of chaos. I rushed over to the both of them and hugged them as tightly as I could without hurting them. I kissed them both again and again. They both looked far more grown up than when I left them and they stood out like beacons of light with their fair skin in a sea of chocolate coloured people. Sheli was four years old now and Gulz was three, both looking healthy and well, a total antithesis of me, who was skinny, sun burnt and muddy. I realised that someone was missing. It was Alom, who had not arrived.

"Mum, where's Alom?" I asked.

"Your dad decided to keep him back with him," she replied dismayed.

This was not atypical of Dad, some of his actions went in the face of all logic, no matter if God himself came in front of Dad he would not budge from his decision. A trait that I would realise later in life I inherited.

Eventually the crowds dissipated as Mum went into our house and Bibi asked or shooed the stragglers away so that she could unpack, get herself organised and take care of Sheli and Gulz as they started to look uncomfortable. I stayed with my siblings, chatting playfully with them, as well as keeping them company.

When Mum eventually got her breath and most people had left us alone, she looked at me and said, "What is this state that you are in?" referring to my filthy urchin look.

I looked away and muttered, "Nothing."

I felt embarrassed and anxious, the latter mainly due to my suspicions that had begun when news of Mum's arrival became apparent. I thought to myself, *Oh no! Here it begins, I'm going to get some serious ticking off from now on.*

However, Mum didn't say anything further and I took the lead by going down to the pond and cleaning myself up.

Nana's Farewell

That evening Uncle Babul came by, having heard of Mum's arrival. Upon brother and sister meeting there were tears all round and a lot of hugging and sobbing. Seeing this did not help keep Gulz and Sheli quiet, they began to join in on the crying. Having not seen each other for over five years meant that both were overcome by their emotions and this was exacerbated by the fact that Nana was knocking on death's door. Bibi eventually stepped in and asked Mum to calm down and I assisted by trying to keep Gulz quiet, with Bibi taking Sheli.

Uncle Babul wiped his tears and Mum did the same with the edge of her sari. They both took a seat next to each other on the edge of the bed and Mum began asking about Nana. In between further bouts of tears Uncle Babul relayed the message which Mum dreaded: Nana did not have long to live. The doctors said that his insides were raw with sores and that he could not eat or drink and so was wasting away. They had also said that there was nothing left to do and it was now a matter of time.

Upon hearing this, Mum burst out crying, even I felt a twang of sorrow. I had a feeling of guilt beginning to play on my conscience as I had not bothered to visit Nana, not only during the days when he was healthy, but also when his health deteriorated. I liked Nana but I just could never bring myself to visit as often as a grandson should have. With this sense of guilt playing on me another thought crossed my mind. Mum would ask me if I had visited Nana during his last few days and weeks when he was lucid and able to comprehend what was going on and who was around. This further compounded my internal struggle with the possibility of serious repercussions due to my erroneous ways. This made me shrink further away from my Mum and throughout the short duration we remained before leaving for London I always sought the company of others to avoid her. The fear of being reprimanded was too great.

Uncle Babul stayed the night as we were going to Sreedhara with him the next day. The impending death of Nana cast a sombre mood that hung over my family and I felt awkward, not knowing what to say or not to my mum. My siblings, due to their youth, were oblivious to what was going on and I wished I could escape through innocence. After dinner, Sheli and Gulz were put to bed, for which they did not need encouraging, as they were jet lagged and already half asleep.

My mum performed her prayer ablutions and after prayers, began reading the Koran. I left her to her recitation and spent the rest of the night with Aman and his brothers, before we all fell asleep lengthwise on the floor in one of their rooms. The warm night meant a more comfortable sleep was affordable on the floor covered with a bamboo mat and a light blanket on top.

The following morning I awoke and went over to my house. I left Aman and his brothers getting ready to go to Arabic lessons at the mosque, after which they would head off to school. At my house Mum was already up and so were Sheli and Gulz, all three suffering from jet lag with their bodies not knowing whether it was dawn or dusk.

"Are you up then?" Mum asked.

"Yes," I replied.

"Get ready quickly and get something to eat, we need to leave to get to your Nana's place," she hurried me along.

I didn't want to go but I had no choice, my life was now back under parental control, so I left and went over to the pond to wash my face and clean my teeth. After, I went over to the kitchen where Bibi was with her two sister-in-laws toasting plain rice cakes. Seeing me, Bibi got a tin plate and filled it with some curry sauce just off the heat with trails of steam rising gently towards the soot blackened ceiling. I sat down with a melancholic slump of my shoulders, not saying anything to anyone. Bibi also put half a dozen small toasted rice cakes on a plate in front of me. I took one, breaking it in half and then dunking it in the curry sauce before placing it in my mouth. Normally I would taste the spices and curry flavour and smell the aroma as I chewed on the cake. Today however, I munched without tasting, swallowed without savouring and ate not out of a desire to eat but more a necessity for nourishment.

Boro Dadi looked at me whilst Bibi had returned to the wood fire to toast more cakes and said, "Grandson, what's the matter with you? You should be happy your mum and brother and sister are here."

"No, nothing's wrong," I replied.

"So I hear you are going to your Nana's bari today?" she continued.

"Yes, we'll be leaving soon," I replied grumpily and then asked Bibi, "Are you going to Sreedhara too?"

"I will go, but I won't stay," she came back.

"Why?"

"I need to go to Shupatola and check on the bari in general," she replied.

"Can I go with you?" I asked, hoping for a yes.

"No! You need to stay with your mum and be there for your brother and sister," she said, dashing my hopes.

I looked down at my plate and didn't say anything further and neither Bibi nor Boro Dadi continued with the discussion. I left after finishing only the second cake. As I walked out of the kitchen, uncles and aunts streamed into the room for their breakfasts.

Back at my house, with Uncle Babul's help Mum was almost packed. When she saw me coming into the house she asked me to get my belongings ready. I did so in between tumbles with Sheli and Gulz, who were running around their new environment like spring lambs in an open meadow. Our home in London was a terraced house, so all this open space must have been liberating for them. Once I was ready Mum went off to look for Bibi so that she could also get ready for the journey, whilst Uncle Babul and I kept an eye on Sheli and Gulz.

Old Auntie was chewing on her ground betel nut and smiling as she watched the two of them run around the house. She had a look of contentment on her face and I guessed because she was seeing her first group of great grandchildren running around her. Unbeknown to her we would be the only set of great grandkids she would lay eyes on before her time on earth came to an end.

Mum and Bibi came back shortly and Bibi, in her usual green sari, took another white sari from her wardrobe and went off to get changed. I could sense a slight tension between the two. I had a feeling Bibi was not too keen on going either and Mum must have had a few stern words, which would have been along the lines of, *"I've come to see my dying father and I need your help with the children, but you seem to want to not come with me."*

My mum and Bibi had a good relationship compared to

other mother and daughter-in-laws, particularly in this part of the world. However, on the odd occasion even their relationship was tested. As Mum, Uncle Babul and the three of us went out onto the porch waiting on Bibi, a small crowd of the bari's inhabitants had gathered around us. The elderly women offered prayers and words of kindness to my mum. I was feeling a bit claustrophobic and walked down the steps with Gulz and stood out on the courtyard, which was being gently warmed by the morning sun. By the looks of the strength of the sun's rays it was going to be a hot day and the journey would be pretty exhausting.

Bibi came out of the house carrying the obligatory jute bag containing her travelling gear as well as an umbrella for shade, with a consignment of betel nut and paan being the most important cargo. As Uncle Babul ushered us towards the path and out of the bari a posse of women and children followed us out. We walked out onto the main path and headed east out of the village. We walked silently, with Uncle Babul and Mum exchanging an odd word here and there. Uncle Babul carried Sheli and Mum had Gulz on her hip, whilst Bibi and I trailed behind.

Walking through the village we were shaded by the leafy boughs of the trees lining the path. The air was nice and cool, but as we exited the village we were immediately hit by the blazing sun overhead and the light reflecting from the path blinded me temporarily. It took a while for my eyes to adjust. The walk to the main road that ran through Mathiura was about a half mile away. Even though I was used to the heat and travelling by foot over long distances, I still felt the sun burning my back and became uncomfortable as the sweat began rolling down the middle of my back. My mum and siblings were struggling under the immense heat, having arrived from an autumnal October in England.

My brother, being very fair in complexion, was the colour of a tomato and sweating profusely, even though Mum was shading herself and him with an umbrella. I could also see my sister struggling. Luckily, we were going to be getting onto a couple of rickshaws once we hit the main road. I could see some rickshaws waiting at the main road, which was a normal sight as many people from the village would walk up to the road and then continue their journey by rickshaw to the Eid Ghah Bazaar, from where they could take motorised transport.

We all took a much welcomed breather at the intersection whilst Uncle Babul negotiated with two rickshaw drivers to take us to the Eid Ghah Bazaar. Bibi had got her betel nut and paan container out and was preparing her usual strong concoction of nuts, tobacco and limestone. Mum and I took a small paan pouch each and saved one for Uncle Babul. Once we boarded the rickshaws, with Mum and her brother in one with Gulz and Sheli and Bibi and I in the other, we sat back and let the cool breeze dry our damp foreheads. The wiry man powering our rickshaw was sweating as if a hosepipe had been turned on within him and the water was leaking out through his pores. His chocolate brown skin glistened in the sun as he motored onwards.

As we approached the bazaar the density of people increased as traders and public alike were heading to the market. Our rickshaw drivers jostled and shouted their way into the bazaar. Whilst we waited in the relative safety and comfort of the rickshaws, Uncle Babul went and got us a baby-taxi. All around us the usual bazaar chaos ensued with people, animals and vehicles vying to get through the tiny main thoroughfare. Uncle Babul came back and ushered us towards a waiting baby-taxi. Mum, Bibi and my siblings sat in the back whilst Uncle Babul and I took either side of the driver, who screeched away before our bums could hit the seats.

Motorised transport gave us speed but at the price of comfort as our entire frames were shaken to the last bone in our bodies. The unpaved road was merciless as we headed towards Sreedhara. At the Thri-Muki Bazaar Mum asked Uncle Babul to buy some fruit for her father, even though he would never touch them. I guessed Mum wanted to be comforted by doing the normal things, even though she knew in her heart of hearts it was futile. She must have felt terrible coming home to her parents for the first time since going to London and it had to be to visit her dying father.

As we approached Nana's bari I could feel a sense of anxiety and uneasiness in the vehicle. Everyone was silent as the noisy two-stroke pulled to a stop at the mouth of the path leading into Nana's courtyard. There were some people milling about in the courtyard, someone saw Uncle Babul exit out of the baby-taxi and shouted, "Sabu's mum is here."

With that announcement a throng of people burst out on the courtyard like a swarm of hornets angered out of their nest, whereas this was more out of expectation rather than anger. At the head of the party was Nani, followed by Elder Mami with Mithun on her hip. Mum dashed towards Nani whilst carrying Gulz, they both embraced each other and burst into tears. Seeing this, Elder Mami did likewise and my siblings could not help it either and they also began crying. In their case I guessed it was more a case of all the strange faces and seeing mum cry.

Bibi and I followed Uncle Babul, who was carrying Sheli into the courtyard. I could hear mum sobbing and asking where Nana was, as they disappeared into the house. I followed suit into the dark interior where my eyes had to readjust from the glaring light outside. Nana was lying on a single bed so small that it looked more like a cot for an adult. The bed lay directly in line with the door at the opposite end of the room. He looked so gaunt that it was only his head at the other end of the bed that indicated that someone was lying in it. His body had almost disappeared into the bedding and his face was emaciated and ashen.

Mum was already at his side crying and stroking his head, touching his face as tears rolled down her cheeks. I don't think Nana was lucid enough to understand what was going on. Everybody else had gathered around Mum and various people were trying in vain to calm and quieten Sheli and Gulz. Bibi was in the melee with them, but she was having little luck. I stood several feet away from the foot of Nana's bed, totally bewildered and disorientated. I felt like crying, with tears trying to well up to surface, but I grit my teeth and watched everything that was going on quashing any emotional uprisings. I had never experienced anything like this before in my life and I felt lost, confused and afraid. Thankfully, everyone was too engaged in their own personal turmoil to notice my anxiety and fears.

Eventually, Nana seemed to come out of his comatose state and looked around with glazed eyes. He uttered in a barely audible voice, "Is my Mina, here?" referring to Mum.

Through her tears and sobs Mum replied, "Yes Baba, it's me, Mina."

A smile passed across Nana's lips as he slowly took Mum's hand and held it without saying anything. At Nana's bedside was a small tin cup containing water and a small teaspoon, which Mum picked up and began spooning water into his mouth. "Here Baba, your granddaughter and grandsons are here to see you," she said referring to Sheli, Gulz and me. Mum asked us to go near so that Nana could see the three of us. Whether there was any recognition in his eyes was hard to say, but he gazed in our direction. Sheli and Gulz recoiled back from Nana, I guess his gaunt and frail look scared them. I eventually moved away and Mum passed my siblings back to Bibi and Nani.

There wasn't much movement from Nana, only the odd inaudible word asking for water. Slowly everyone began to leave and Nani asked Mum to get changed and eat some food. With Sheli and Gulz feeling hungry, tired and irritated, Mum had to leave Nana's side to take care of their needs too. Bibi joined in by going into the kitchen and helping Elder Mami with the cooking and preparation to feed what seemed like an army of people in and around the house.

I, on the other hand, met up with my cousin Babor, who was my mum's elder sister's son, and wandered around the bari in an aimless manner. Babor was older than me by about seven years and even though I had met him before I did not bond with him but tolerated being with him, as he was my elder cousin. I did not want to be here and to me everything seemed too serious and scary, where a kid like me could do nothing. The children, apart from the very young, were shooed away from underfoot, whilst the elders and an Imam from the village mosque prayed at Nana's side.

A dark cloud hung over the whole household and the adults knew that Nana was probably waiting for Mum before departing. Even though no one was saying it out loud that Nana was going to die, I had a feeling that was what everyone was preparing for. There were no doctors coming to visit Nana and everybody seemed surprised that he had hung on for so long, especially as his illness was preventing him from taking any sustenance in either solid or liquid form.

As evening drew in most of the people from the surrounding baris had left, with the odd person staying behind to assist as required. Nani and Elder Mami went around lighting lanterns as a hushed silence fell across the bari and the evening prayer call went out, causing all the women to pull the ends of their saris over the heads. Uncle Babul went down to the pond to perform his ablutions before going off to the mosque.

I was getting fidgety and restless, finding no private space for myself to do anything or just laying down and doing nothing. So, I kept my brother and sister company as Mum went and said her prayers. Nana's condition was calm and stable, with someone keeping a vigil by his side and tending to his needs.

That night ended with a silent meal for everyone, with no chatter or discussion about Mum's life in London as everyone prepared for a night of vigil over Nana. As there were so many visitors, sleeping all of them was going to be a task. Mum, my siblings and I got to sleep in the room with Nana, for Mum to be close to her father. Babor and his mum were sleeping in the adjacent room. Uncle Babul was going over to another bari, Nani, Elder Mami and her kids would make sleeping arrangements on the floor.

The following day Bibi decided to go and said that she would be back in a day or so. She wanted to go to Shupatola and check that all was in order with the bari and then she would return. Mum wasn't too happy, as she would have liked Bibi to stay to assist with Sheli and Gulz. I was hoping I would be allowed to go, through an offer from Mum or Bibi's request, but neither came and I never raised it. Uncle Babul escorted Bibi to the bazaar to get her a rickshaw, and as they walked out of the bari I watched glumly from the banks of the pond.

The day was pretty uneventful for me but Nana did seem to perk up a bit for a brief moment when he spoke to Mum and stroked Sheli and Gulz's heads. Whether he had the faculty to recognise his grandchildren nobody could tell. However, his brief improvement did put a smile on Mum's face and other members from Nana's household. He also asked for people by name, he particularly asked for Uncle Nurul.

"Where is Fonki?" Nana asked by his son's nickname.

"He's abroad and he is alright," Nani reassured him. "He said he will come over soon," she continued.

Hearing this he turned his head away sadly. Mum, being ever present, saw the distressed look on his face and soothed him by stroking his hands and saying, "Baba, don't worry, you will be better soon and Brother will come and visit."

"No my dear, I fear I am going to be leaving soon and I will not see my eldest son," he replied.

"No Baba, you will get better soon enough."

Mum tried to hide the tears which were rolling down her cheeks, luckily for her Nana's head was facing away from her. Throughout the day Nana came in and out of lucidity and his situation in general deteriorated. The tension within the house increased and more and more relatives and well-wishers visited. Emotions were like a yo-yo; when Nana showed some signs of comfort everyone would breathe a sigh of relief, when he began to breathe erratically or groan and moan in pain then everybody began to increase their praying and trying to ease his pain. This was accompanied by an ensuing pandemonium as someone would yell for the Imam to come. The day ended on a similar note and I was feeling even more anxious and tired, wishing I was away in Shupatola or Purushpal. Even though I was tasked with looking after my siblings, the duty only provided a temporary respite from hanging around without having anywhere to get away from the impending death.

The following day Bibi arrived with Boro Dada, who went via Shupatola to pick her up. By the time they had arrived it was late morning. Nana's bari was thronging with people milling about, some weeping, some praying and some doing nothing more than loitering.

Boro Dada and Bibi could hardly have caught their breath

when someone yelled, "Quick! Where is the Imam, Fonki's father is going."

We all rushed into the house and I could see Mum, Nani, Uncle Babul and a whole host of other bodies around Nana. There was bedlam as the Imam pushed through to read the last rites. I could see Sheli and Gulz on someone's hip crying, Mum was crying which was all too much even for a ten year old who had never experienced death, let alone in such a chaotic way. Tears started to roll down my cheeks as I stood at the end of Nana's bed and I wiped them just as fast as they came welling up. Then, just as suddenly as the Imam turned up he turned around quietly, said a prayer and announced that Nana had died. This led to an increase in volume of those crying, who began to call out to Nana according to whatever relation they held with him. The crying was followed by a chorus of prayer recitation, obligatory upon the death of someone.

The Imam took Uncle Babul aside and asked him to get all the people out, leaving only the immediate family, and to start preparing for the funeral. There was no doctor present and no medical people were called. Uncle Babul, fighting back his tears and emotions, took Mum aside to get her to take control of all the ladies whilst he along with his cousin from across the bari decided to clear the house of any menfolk.

It was with amazing speed that the house was cleared and a handful of core men, along with Boro Dada, were kept behind to bathe Nana's corpse. Mum, Nani and the other women went down to the pond for ablutions, so that they could read the Koran and pray. Someone came along and lit incense sticks in the corners of Nana's room.

Nana's corpse was bathed behind closed doors by Uncle Babul, Boro Dada and other male relatives of Nana. Once they opened the door, Nana was covered in a white cotton shroud and perfumed oil was daubed over the shroud which emanated pungently through the air. Uncle Babul had instructed someone to arrange for the grave to be dug on land which was specifically owned by Nana's family at the local cemetery. The cemetery was a short walk away on the road to the bazaar and was overgrown with bamboo and other foliage. I had to get away from the house as I became tearful every time I saw my mum and my siblings cry. I decided to go over with one of numerous uncles to have a look at the grave being dug. When we arrived at the site, two men who were as dark as roasted coffee beans were barefoot and bare chested, except their lunghi which was wrapped like a loincloth, were making a clearing underneath the bamboo. Their bodies glistened with sweat as they toiled away and began digging. The men were from Noakhali, which I ascertained from their accent. Most of the people from that region who were employed in Sylhet worked predominantly in fishing and earth-work, thus the Sylhetis called them Noakhalis in a very derogatory manner. I, however, loved their accented Bengali. It was very fast and musical and whenever I had the opportunity I would engage in conversation with them.

The two men took a good few hours to dig the hole in the ground. I had left long before they had completed their task, after being called over to get ready for the funeral. Back at the bari, mourners had arrived from near and far, including Uncle Naz and a group of other uncles and grandfathers from Purushpal. All the men wore skullcaps and their best clothes in preparation for the funeral. By now it was getting near to late afternoon and time for Asar prayers. Uncle Babul, Boro Dada and four other men related to Nana hauled his shroud covered corpse onto their shoulders and carried him to the mosque. An entourage of male relatives, friends and general mourners followed his body. Everyone was wearing white tunics, pants and white skullcaps as they snaked their way through the village path to the mosque. Even all the women wore white, who stayed back in the bari.

Once in the mosque, Nana's body was placed at the front. The Imam led the main Asar prayer which was followed by the funeral prayer. Afterwards, the Imam raised his hands, cupped at chest level, to bless Nana in the afterlife, he was accompanied by the all-male congregation. Looking around I could see Uncle Babul and other close male relatives crying into their palms. Boro Dada had his eyes closed as he prayed with the sincerest of looks. There were so many people that countless had to sit outside on the hard earthen floor of the path and the mosque grounds.

With the prayer over, the same six men who carried Nana to the mosque re-carried him to the place where he was to be buried. Once there his body was gently placed in the grave as the Imam said prayers, with everybody else saying prayers in quiet muffled tones. A platform made of bamboo was placed about a foot or so above Nana's white shrouded body. I asked Boro Dada, who was standing next to me, what it was.

"It's a place for your Nana's soul to rest before being questioned by God about his time on earth and before he can make his way to heaven," he explained.

I was gobsmacked and didn't know what to say. I hadn't realised that death was such a serious business, even in the afterlife. Uncle Babul then placed the first handful earth over the bamboo platform and then everyone else one by one placed a handful too. Some stayed back and then watched as the Noakhali workers shovelled earth over Nana's grave until it was fully covered and a mound was formed over his burial spot.

I could see Uncle Babul shed tears and on the path leading to Nana's bari Mum, Nani and other womenfolk had gathered, watching from a distance as the burial took place. It wouldn't be until the following day that the women made a visit to Nana's grave. Once the burial was over we all headed back to the bari. The mood was sombre and one of reflection, with people visiting and talking about how Nana was as a person sharing stories about his kindness and generosity.

Uncle Naz came by and said hello to Mum and I, he stayed a while and played and joked with Sheli and Gulz. Other mourners from Purushpal stopped by to offer their condolences and subsequently left as quietly as they had come.

Tricky Telegrams

Nani, being now a widow, was going into forty days of mourning, which comprised of her going into 'hiding', whereby for the duration of the mourning she would stay veiled from the outside world and only immediate family and other female family members could have access to her. I thought it was a bit over the top but who was I to question centuries of religious doctrine. During this period she was also required to engage in prayers five times a day, which is expected of any practising Muslim anyway, and for her to recite the Koran in private.

The day after Nana's death most visitors and relatives had gone or were departing. Boro Dada and Bibi headed back to Purushpal, whereas I remained with Mum. As Bibi and Boro Dada walked out of the bari and onto the main road I felt like a prisoner whose last chance of freedom was walking away into the distance. I had imagined that I would be able to go back with them and grasp the last few days and weeks of a rapidly waning Huck Finn existence, something that I had gotten used to over the last ten months.

Over the coming days Nana's bari was one of prayer and reflection and conversations took place in hushed tones. Few visitors came and those who did respected Nana's family's prerogative to mourn in their own way. I became the custodian of my siblings during this period, ensuring Mum had time to read the Koran and say her prayers. Sheli and Gulz did not cause much in the way of nuisance for anyone and it was only when they were hungry or needed some tender loving care from mum did they cry or whine. Sometimes when I was lying in bed next to my brother and sister on the verge of falling into deep sleep, I could hear both Mum and Nani crying softly as they prayed, or when they spoke to each other about Nana, I could see in the shadows their quivering lips and tear streaks.

On the third day after Nana's passing a ceremony called the *shinni* was held. This was a bit like a funeral wake held by Christian families. Friends and relatives from all over came with a mass prayer held at noon at the mosque. A goat was slaughtered and various curry dishes were prepared, most of which were done by Mum, Mami, Nani and other women from the bari, as well as surrounding homesteads. Sweet meats and desserts were prepared alongside the curries.

Boro Dada and a few uncles came from Purushpal, they attended prayer at the mosque with Uncle Babul and myself, as well as other relatives and villagers. After, we stood outside the entrance to the mosque donating food to the departing congregation, beggars and other poor people who had come by hearing of the news that food was being distributed in honour of Nana. Aman and Iqbal, having arrived from Purushpal as well as a few uncles from Sreedhara, stood with me until all the food was distributed. Once our job was completed we headed back to Nana's bari, where the courtyard was a sea of men in white tunics and skullcaps squatting on bamboo mats with their heads bobbing up and down as they ate mutton curry and rice.

Amongst the men I could see Boro Dada sitting next to the Imam who had led the prayers earlier. I could also see a few other recognisable faces from Purushpal and many other uncles and grandfathers from Nana's side of the family. At one end of the row I could see several beggars who had been welcomed and seated to join in on the meal. They were easily distinguishable as their clothing was raggedy and under their arms they had jute bags for collecting alms and donations.

I went into the kitchen where I saw a few female beggars with sunken eyes and saris like tents on their skeletal frames, holding out bowls for food. A couple of the women had naked children on their hips; for some reason the kids' bellies were unnaturally swollen, and they had around their waists a black string with a small metal tabiz. I looked at my arm which still wore the tabiz, since the Fulbari incident.

Mum and Nani were handing out food to the women and any other poor womenfolk from the village. The ladies and their children took a seat just outside the kitchen, where they ate their meal before washing the food down with a glass of water. It made me extremely sad to see this level of poverty, especially when women could not feed their children. I had been here almost a year now and the shock of seeing such hunger made me embarrassed and angry. As I looked around no one else seemed fazed by this situation, even the poor women played their role in the whole cycle of maintaining the status quo of this economic and social divide.

My uncles from Purushpal and I grabbed a plate of rice and curry amongst the organised chaos of feeding frenzy that seemed to have engulfed Nana's bari. I was extremely glad to see them and after lunch we headed out towards the steps of the pond and sat underneath the shade of the two coconut palms. Aman and Iqbal relayed stories of what was going on back in Purushpal. They asked me when I was returning, I told them that I wasn't sure and that it was up to Mum. Later that afternoon they left with Boro Dada and again another opportunity for me to leave vanished in front of my eyes.

One evening I sat with my brother and sister on one of the wooden beds in the main room next to the kitchen. I was holding Gulz to prevent him falling off the three foot high bed, whilst Sheli played with a rudimentary Bengali doll, surrounded by pillows for her protection. Mum sat by the kitchen door on a mura with an ever watchful eye on all three of us, with Nani and Elder Mami in the kitchen with her two children. I turned to mum and asked, "Mum, when are we going back to London?"

"Well, no date has been set and your father didn't specify when," she replied.

"When are we going back to Purushpal then?" I continued.

Mum looked towards Nani before answering, who wanted Mum to give a response that would indicate a lengthy stay at Sreedhara.

"I'm going to stay for at least forty days to give your Nani some help," she said, confirming my worst fears.

I dropped my head towards the bed and a knot developed in my stomach as I felt my freedom and life ebbing away. Mum must have noticed my anxiety to which she said, "Sabu, you can go in a few days if you want? I think your Bibi would need help in Shupatola."

"Really?" I piped up.

"Yes, if someone comes from Purushpal or if your Uncle Babul goes over to Beani Bazaar, he can take you."

"Where's Uncle Babul now, then?" I asked impatiently, wanting to go and see him myself to find out when he was going to go to Beani Bazaar.

"Hey, don't be in such a rush like your dad," Nani said jokingly.

"No Nani, I just want to know where Uncle is."

"He doesn't like us that much nor staying with us, that's why he's in such a state to go back to Purushpal," Mami said in a semi-serious kind of way.

I knew it was the truth so I didn't reply and shied away from facing Mum. Mum, however, didn't say anything further and I carried on playing with my siblings. The next few days seemed to drag and I couldn't get a concrete answer from Uncle Babul as to when he would make a trip to Beani Bazaar and no one seemed to be arriving from Purushpal. It felt as if I had been abandoned at an unknown port and no ship was travelling my way, with the only boat moored at the docks indefinitely. Whilst my mum and her family went about the daily rituals of prayer, reading the Koran and conducting activities of daily life, I was getting more and more fidgety and restless, with no means of venting my frustration and boredom.

One afternoon I was in Nana's courtyard playing with a football, just kicking it about without any purpose or reason; I was on my own so I couldn't even play competitively. I noticed from the corner of my eye that someone was walking up the path from the main road. I turned to see who it was and I was surprised to see Boro Dada walking towards the courtyard. Upon seeing him I picked up the ball, clutching it under my arms I ran towards him.

"Salaam alaikum Dada, are you well?" I shouted before reaching him.

"Alaikum salaam Grandson," he smiled ear to ear.

"What's your news?" he asked me.

"Not much, Dada," I replied. "What are you doing here?" I continued.

"Well, I have some news for your mum that is quite important," he said with a serious tone.

I didn't probe any further as I escorted him into the house announcing, "Boro Dada has arrived."

With my announcement Mum emerged with Nani, as Dada took a seat on the edge of the bed in the room next to the kitchen. Both Mum and Nani said there salutations to Dada, to which he replied and made himself more comfortable by lifting his feet and putting them in a lotus position on the bed.

"Abba, would you like something to eat?" Mum asked Dada, referring to him as father, which was a loving form of addressing a father-in-law.

"No, nothing my dear, some tea will do," he requested.

"No Abba. I will get you something more substantial," Mum countered.

Even though Dada protested, Mum asked Mami to prepare a snack for Dada. This offering of food and protestation by the guest was a ritual performed throughout the whole of Bangladesh, whenever someone visits a relative or friend. One thing about the Bangladeshi people which became very obvious to me during my stay was the emphasis on feeding guests. No matter whether the guest was expected or not there was always room for one more person at the table. The hospitality and generosity was such that the guest would have food piled on their plate by the hosts, regardless of their appetite.

So, Elder Mami brought out small plates of sweet milky vermicelli and gave one to Dada, me and Mum. Nani did not want any and my siblings were too young to manage a plate on their own, so Mum gave them a spoonful here and there.

"Dear daughter," Dada began. "I have here a telegram from Sabu's father which I must read to you."

At this my mum's eyes widened in fear and wonder as to what the seriousness behind the telegram could be, and why Dad was sending a telegram so soon after she had left England. With the rustle of the piece of paper unfolding Dada prepared to read to the telegram. The paper looked more like a scrap torn from the edge of a paper pad rather than an official telegram.

...Can you come back to London as soon as possible... it is of grave importance that you return immediately... and bring Sabu back with you.

Dada read the telegram in a serious tone, after which he

handed it to mum. The telegram was in Bengali so mum read and re-read it and I could see her world was shattering away before her. It was only a fortnight since Nana had passed away and here she was being asked to return to London immediately. Tears started to roll down her face which she dabbed with the end of her sari.

"He doesn't understand anything about my loss and pain," Mum mumbled through her tears, referring to Dad. "I've only just arrived, my father's gone and he wants me to go back."

"Look Mina, he must have a good reason to want you to go back," Nani comforted Mum.

"When did this come?" Mum asked Dada.

"Yesterday. I was in Beani Bazaar and someone handed it to me having picked it up from the post office."

"Look daughter, what can we do, my nephew is a bit rash like that, maybe something is up, hence he has asked you to return," Dada continued.

There was a pause when everyone seemed to be hanging onto Mum, waiting for her to make the next move.

"Well, at least I saw my father alive and was here for his burial," she seemed to say it more to herself as a way of self-comfort. "Abba, can you get our return flights confirmed and I will return to Purushpal within a couple days," she told Dada.

"Okay, my dear. I will do that, do you want me to send a telegram to Sabu's dad telling him that you are returning?" Dada enquired.

"No, he's asked for us to return so he'll know when we get there," she replied with a hint of anger in her voice.

Nani noticed this and shied her head away and looked towards the kitchen. She did so because it was frowned upon for wives to question the decisions of their husbands, and for Mum to do so in front of Dada was tantamount to a marital delinquency. However, Dada was such a nice man and he loved

Dad, Mum and us to bits so he would never take offence or relay what was discussed back to Dad.

I was both happy and sad about realising that my stay in Bangladesh was coming to an end. On the one hand it would be great to go back home and be with my family as a whole, yet deep within me I was scared of the possible reprimand from my parents over my behaviour during my stay. I was also fearful of leaving my carefree lifestyle here with Bibi. I did not say anything to Mum and accepted that my tour of duty in Bangladesh was coming to an end. My heart was getting heavy and butterflies of anxiety were doing their dance in my stomach.

With Mum's decision made, Dada stayed a short while longer before leaving then excused himself for having many things to do for our departure. Uncle Babul was pretty much out of the bari most of the day and even though Nana's land was managed and cultivated by other farmers I never knew what he did when he was out of the bari. Anyway, when he returned home that evening, Mum and Nani discussed with him about the telegram and Mum's imminent departure back to London. Uncle Babul wasn't too happy and he got a bit angry with Dad, saying that Dad didn't understand anything about protocol. He did calm down eventually and Mum asked him to take her back to Purushpal in a couple of days' time, to which he agreed.

The next two days were a complete blur and the same was to come in Purushpal. I accompanied my mum to her numerous family and friends in Sreedhara before we left. I hated the whirlwind visits as they ensured us Londoner's were treated even more specially as guests, with a variety of sweet and savoury dishes thrust into our faces to eat. Some dishes I would take a spoonful into my mouth and then have to hold my breath as I chewed minimally before swallowing. I was glad when our departure from Sreedhara arrived, but there were tears all around as Mum and Nani and Elder Mami cried. Mum promised Nani that on the day we left for the airport she would make a detour via Sreedhara and say goodbye.

We left late morning and reached Purushpal mid-afternoon. Our bari was awash with people, somehow they had heard that we were arriving from Nana's place and that we were leaving soon. Some even seemed to know the date that we were leaving. So, we landed from one fraught and chaotic situation of burying and mourning Nana's death and the subsequent farewell to another maelstrom of visitors and people wanting to send stuff with us to their loved ones in London.

The autumnal day started off cool but had turned very hot by the time we had reached Purushpal. Sheli and Gulz were uncomfortable and they were desperately seeking Mum's attention. Luckily, Bibi and the aunts of the bari were at hand to ease Mum's burden. Boro Dada came into our house and told Mum that he had booked a flight in a week's time, departing Sylhet during the weekend.

I did not hang around for long to hear any of the other details of our departure as I rushed out to the pond to catch up with Iqbal, Aman and Amad and relay the news that I was leaving. As ever, not being one to do things by halves I over compensated for those days of being cooped up at Nana's bari and swam and played water games like there was no tomorrow. I swallowed so much water that any hunger I had before dissipated. To top it all, I belly-flopped into the pond from the tops of trees so much that the skin on my stomach was red raw. But as I walked away from the pond with my uncles I was the happiest child on earth at that moment in time.

Back at the house it seemed that the people we had seen upon our arrival had somehow vanished. I dried off and put on a pair of dry shorts and a short-sleeve shirt. I applied mustard oil on my skin for moisturising and then went off into the kitchen to look for some food to eat. Dada and Uncle Babul were there already so I took a seat next to Dada. Mum was feeding sago to my siblings and Bibi was at hand with Boro Dadi, getting the lunchtime meal ready for all. One by one the male members of the two families arrived in to eat.

"So Grandson, you're not going to stay with us?" Dada asked, knowing what the answer would be.

"No Dada, I guess I have to go back now."

"Stay Uncle, you can re-join school again," piped in Aman.

I cringed at that suggestion and stole a glance towards Mum's direction, hoping she didn't catch the gist of what Aman had said. Luckily, a bowl of rice and dishes of lentils, fish and potatoes were laid on the bamboo mat for us so my departure was quickly forgotten. Uncle Babul left after lunch, saying that he would be back tomorrow.

As in Sreedhara the last five days were anything but normal. Mum was overwhelmed by visitors all wanting to send letters to their loved ones in London and beyond, others wanted to send gifts of fruit, vegetables and delicacies. In the late seventies and early eighties very few exotic fruit, vegetables and delicacies were available in the shops in London, so a lot of people would take them back in their suitcases, especially dried products which would last for months. Mum, as diplomatically as possible, refused many of the visitors and Bibi backed her up. Especially with two young kids and a ten-year old in tow she had enough on her plate, let alone cram her luggage with people's gifts.

Mum also made visits to several baris to take messages back to people in London. One of the first questions visitors in London would ask was, "Did you see my so and so?"

So Mum, forever being compassionate and caring, tried to visit as many people as she could. I, on the other hand, avoided being dragged along and would disappear off before being collared. On the odd occasion I did get cornered and was unable to escape, reluctantly I would be the good eldest son and accompany Mum to the various baris. Purushpal, being one of the smallest villages in the Beani Bazaar district, had the highest number of émigrés in London. Possibly eighty per cent of the village had someone in the United Kingdom.

That evening whilst Mum cradled Gulz to sleep under the lights of the oil lantern, Old Auntie said her prayers and Bibi, after her prayers, came and sat next to me as I lay on the bed. Sheli was already fast asleep amongst us.

"Amma, do you know what this telegram is all about? Why is Sabu's father asking me to go back in such a hurry?" Mum questioned of Bibi.

"I don't know my dear, I really don't know what could be up," she answered.

"What I can't understand is that he didn't say anything about how long I should stay and he didn't even confirm the return flight so that I could properly mourn if my father passed away, which he has," Mum continued. I could hear a slight anger in her voice.

Old Auntie realised Mum was very upset and the situation could get out of hand, so she tried to placate her. "My dear sister, what can we say? Sabu's dad is a force unto himself, he does things without consulting anyone or hardly talks to anyone and once he's made his mind up he never changes it."

By now Gulz had fallen asleep in Mum's lap, who was teary eyed, trying to contain her emotions and not to breakdown in front of Bibi and Old Auntie. Both of them comforted Mum as best as they could, asking her not to cry. Mum laid Gulz on a pillow next to Sheli and got the mosquito net out to cover their bed. I slowly dozed off to the whispers of the elderly matriarchs of the family and Mum shuffling about with the net.

The next few mornings I spent my time with Boro Dada out in the fields, watching the cattle as they grazed now that the fields were dry again. In the afternoons once Aman and his brothers returned from school I would be out on my adventures with them. Uncle Babul visited pretty much every day and Mum, with the help of Bibi and Uncle Babul, packed two suitcases with some clothing items, some dried and some fresh fruits and vegetables, as well as letters and small gifts from a select group of individuals.

I mentioned to Bibi about going to Shupatola but she said that there was no time for us to go and return. She said that once we had gone she would go back to Shupatola and watch over the construction work that was due to start imminently on the new house. I was saddened that I would not be able to see my bari in its original form one final time before the work began, as well as saying a final goodbye to Bolai. The next time I visited, the bari would be totally unrecognisable with a seven foot high perimeter wall around it and two new houses built on it. I would not see Bolai again until my 1987 visit. By then she was married and I accidently saw her because she made a day trip to her parent's bari. She briefly said hello before disappearing into her bari and I never saw her again after that.

Our day of departure came round so quickly that one minute it was six in the morning and the next thing we were boarding rickshaws to take us to Eid Ghah Bazaar, where we would board the Toyota Liteaces. Uncles Babul, Naz and Boro Dada would escort us to Sylhet Airport. Even during the few days in Purushpal I didn't get a chance to see Uncle Naz, and I was glad to see him with us. His wife's application for settlement to the United Kingdom was due soon and once it arrived he would go back to London with her. As we left the bari, I was back in the suit and tie that I came in and within seconds was sweating buckets.

There were tears all round with Bibi crying, Mum crying and my siblings crying because of all the commotion. The two Dadis and their daughters were shedding tears. Old Auntie hobbled out onto the porch and her wrinkled face made a slow descent of the tears that she let roll. I paid my respect to Bibi, Old Auntie and Boro Dada by touching their feet and then touching my head. Mum asked all to forgive her for being a trouble during her short visit. The whole courtyard thronged with people from half the village by the looks of it.

As the rickshaws pulled away I wiped a few tears that were rolling down my face, I looked longingly at Bibi and Old Auntie. This would be the last time I would see Old Auntie, as in a couple of years she would pass away.

As the morning sun was warming the countryside, from the path leading out of the village, I took one last glance towards the corner of the village that was the pond of our bari and I could see a group of people watching, I guessed them to be Bibi and all my other relatives. By the time the rickshaw turned onto the Mathiura road I was feeling a bit more comfortable and thinking more about the journey ahead.

As promised, Mum had the Liteace driver detour via Nana's bari to say farewell to Nani. Even though Mum cried along with Nani, I did not feel much emotion or sense of loss, not because I did not love Nani but I just never had the strong bond with her that I had with Bibi. The stopover was brief and soon enough we were on our way towards the airport. Again the journey was treacherous and slow as the driver tried to navigate the potholed roads.

We made a stop during the journey at one of the many bazaars dotting the route to Sylhet town, where Uncle Naz bought us Fanta to drink and Nabisco biscuits to eat. We arrived at the airport mid-afternoon and the scene had not changed since I had arrived eleven months earlier. We fought our way through the beggars, touts and vendors into the hot interior of the terminal building. The check-in procedure was a nightmare as the airline officials were known to take bribes or your passport would disappear if you didn't keep an eye on it. So, Uncle Naz and Babul argued and cajoled the airline men and airport officials to expedite our check-in. This bartering was being done by every family that was travelling.

Whilst in the queue for the check-in Uncle Naz spoke to another man who was going to London with his family and asked if he would keep an eye on Mum and lend a helping hand during our journey. The man agreed and even though he was overwhelmed with his own family he helped us all the way. Our flight to Dhaka was about half an hour and once there we were ferried to the Hotel Zakaria for an overnight stay, with our flight to London being early the following morning. We were fed and watered at the hotel before we grabbed a brief nap. We left the hotel before sunrise and all of us were groggy. I held Sheli's hand and a shoulder bag with the other as mum carried Gulz on her hip along with a bag containing her bits and bobs. We boarded the bus for the airport under the cover of darkness, like refugees fleeing a doomed banana republic.

Once on board our Boeing 707, Mum let out a sigh of relief as the traumatic part of the journey was over and we were now on the home stretch of it. Our plane made a stopover in Dubai for an hour, during which we stayed on board before continuing onto London's Heathrow Airport.

On the plane Mum asked me to hold on to our passports. I decided to have a browse through our travel documents in the navy blue cover with the embossed royal insignia on the front. I looked at my black and white picture before reading my personal details. The details highlighted my black hair and brown eyes and my height. My eyes then caught the date of birth recorded beneath my name. I realised that my eleventh birthday had come to pass about four weeks ago. I had not realised that it had come and gone without me remembering it. Well, my eleven months were totally devoid of any time or date keeping. The passing of my birthday was not something notable, for birthdays were not celebrated back in those days in Bangladesh. Even in England I never celebrated any of my birthdays, it was just another date on the calendar. I did not feel any emotion about being another year older and it did not bother me at all, as I couldn't miss something that I had never experienced. So I flicked through the other passports in my possession and put them away in my jacket pocket, as soft drinks were being served by the air hostesses.

We landed under a grey November sky where the pilot announced the temperature outside was an autumnal ten Celsius. Once we had cleared through customs and after having picked up our luggage, we went out into the arrivals hall where there was no Dad to pick us up. The man who helped us during the journey put us in a black cab before making his own way home with his relatives who had come to collect him from the airport.

The biggest shock I got was how cold it was, as I had forgotten about such cold weather during my eleven months away. Our journey to the East End of London took just over an hour and as the taxi ride came to an end my sense of longing for Bibi and Bangladesh kicked in, as images of Shupatola and the fun times I had flashed across my mind's eye.

Once the taxi pulled up outside our house we unloaded ourselves and Mum asked me to knock on the door and get some money from Dad to pay the taxi driver. I knocked on the door which Dad opened, and upon seeing us rushed out and grabbed my brother Gulz, as I saw Alom racing up the stairs from the basement. I grabbed my brother in a bear hug as we all made our way down the staircase to the basement, after Dad had paid the taxi driver. In the warm confines of the basement I took off my jacket and shoes and stood next to the paraffin heater. Dad with Gulz on his lap turned to Mum and asked, "What are you doing here?"

"What do you mean, you sent a telegram asking for me to return immediately," Mum replied with a quizzical look.

"What telegram?" Dad replied.

"I never sent any telegram, you and the kids being here is a surprise, let me see the telegram."

Mum rifled through her handbag to retrieve the telegram and gave it to Dad. He examined the piece of paper carefully and said, "It looks like there are people in Bangladesh who don't want us to be a happy family."

"What do you mean?" Mum asked.

"Well, this telegram is a fake," Dad replied and swore at unnamed people in general.

Mum asked Dad not to swear, saying that there's nothing to be gained by doing so, and those who tried to harm us will never win. To this day nobody ever admitted to concocting the telegram and my parents never found out why it was done or who did it.

My unfounded fear of chastisement from my parents never materialised and soon enough I was back at school for my last year at Harry Gosling Junior School before heading off to Morpeth Comprehensive. I never talked to anyone at school about the eleven months I spent out in Bangladesh, and no one asked me about my time out there. It was as if it never had happened, but deep within me the experiences I had during those eleven months are as vivid today as the day they occurred, and will be with me for the rest of my life.